LEADING SCHOOLS
TO SUCCESS

LEADING SCHOOLS
TO SUCCESS

Constructing and Sustaining
High-Performing Learning Cultures

JAMES W. GUTHRIE

*Professor of Education Policy and Leadership, Southern Methodist University
& Senior Fellow, George W. Bush Institute*

PATRICK J. SCHUERMANN

*Research Assistant Professor of Education Leadership and
Public Policy, Peabody College of Vanderbilt University
& Senior Consultant, George W. Bush Institute*

Los Angeles | London | New Delhi
Singapore | Washington DC

For information:

 SAGE Publications, Inc.
2455 Teller Road
Thousand Oaks, California 91320
E-mail: order@sagepub.com

SAGE Publications India Pvt. Ltd.
B 1/I 1 Mohan Cooperative Industrial Area
Mathura Road, New Delhi 110 044
India

SAGE Publications Ltd.
1 Oliver's Yard
55 City Road
London EC1Y 1SP
United Kingdom

SAGE Publications Asia-Pacific Pte. Ltd.
33 Pekin Street #02-01
Far East Square
Singapore 048763

Printed in the United States of America

Library of Congress Cataloging-in-Publication Data

Guthrie, James W.
Leading schools to success : constructing and sustaining high-performing learning cultures / James W. Guthrie, Patrick Schuermann.
    p. cm.
Includes bibliographical references and index.
ISBN 978-1-4129-7901-6 (pbk.)
    1. Educational change—United States—Case studies. 2. Academic achievement—United States—Case studies. 3. Learning—Case studies. I. Schuermann, Patrick Jude. II. Title.

LA217.2.G785 2011
371.2′07—dc22   2010039708

This book is printed on acid-free paper.

10   11   12   13   14   10   9   8   7   6   5   4   3   2   1

Executive Editor:	Diane McDaniel
Assistant Editor:	Ashley Conlon
Production Editor:	Eric Garner
Copy Editor:	Mark Bast
Typesetter:	C&M Digitals (P) Ltd.
Proofreader:	Susan Schon
Indexer:	Jean Casalegno
Cover Designer:	Gail Buschman
Marketing Manager:	Erica DeLuca
Permissions Editor:	Adele Hutchinson

Brief Contents

Detailed Contents

Preface

*L*eading Schools to Success: Constructing and Sustaining High-Performing *Learning Cultures* draws upon modern leadership concepts, rigorous research results, and carefully examined professional experiences to assist education leaders and their colleagues in shaping and sustaining a high-performing learning culture in a school. The book is aimed at all school leaders, but it pays particular attention to challenges facing school leaders responsible for turning a low-achieving or stagnant school into a high-performing learning organization.

The book consciously concentrates on school leadership. In the time since the issues of the disquieting 1983 report *A Nation at Risk,* the United States has evolved a set of education reform components that appear to make a great deal of sense. These include high learning standards for students, aligned and engaging curricula, sophisticated tests, educator performance incentives, modern performance management data systems, a modicum of private-sector market-oriented solutions in the form of performance incentives and charter schools, and accountability.

Alarmingly, even when woven together into a coherent operational tapestry, these reform components seldom seem to produce desired elevations in students' academic achievement. What is missing?

This book contends that the frequently missing education reform element is leadership and, specifically, the ability of district and school leaders to construct and continually nurture a culture of sustained high performance.

We have designed this book to be useful for those aspiring to, in training for, or already serving in education leadership positions. This includes principals, assistant principals, charter and independent school heads, teacher leaders, central-office administrators, and superintendents. It also provides new conceptual, research, and practical insights for state- and federal-level educational administrators, government and elected officials in related spheres, scholars, and others engaged at the intersection of instructional leadership and school culture.

Comparable student demographic profiles, rigorous learning expectations, adequate physical facilities, extensive curricular offerings, and amenable governance and financial arrangements characterize many schools and school districts. Nevertheless, somehow, only a select few of these schools consistently display high levels of student achievement. This condition is particularly true when value-added measures of student performance are taken into account, not simply measures of academic attainment or achievement gain.

Many schools, even those with adequate financial resources, exhibit either low or inconsistent academic performance. Research published by Tom Loveless of the Brookings Institution reveals that schools characterized as low-achieving at one point are almost invariably going to be low ranked when examined later. The challenge to "turn around" low-performing schools seems daunting. How can this be? What explains such differences and difficulties?

One critical factor in the answer to these questions is effective school leadership. Successful principals, often assisted by their own staff and school district central-office colleagues, contribute to the formation of a shared vision of school success and then consistently motivate existing and new faculty, support staff, parents, students, and community members to contribute to high levels of student performance.

However, this response provokes even more questions, such as the following:

- What vision of schooling do successful school leaders construct?
- In what ways and through what means do effective principals shape successful school cultures?
- What day-to-day practical actions do they take to enhance school culture and improve student performance?
- What personnel policies do highly effective principals pursue?
- Upon what incentives and support structures do they rely, and in what ways do they infuse incentives and support structures successfully into the culture?
- What are the material and actionable organizational dimensions upon which they rely to contribute to a culture of consistent high performance?
- How portable are highly effective school cultures, and upon what key constituent groups are they dependent?
- Will a school leader from a high-performing school be able to replicate prior success when transferred to a new school setting?
- What might best define a modern secondary school, one that replaces the existing model, the nineteenth-century curricular amalgam known as the "Comprehensive High School"?

Answers to the foregoing questions comprise the content and conditions important for school leaders, particularly those leaders attempting to turn around a presently low-performing school, to understand in order to craft a successful school culture, a culture oriented toward and consistently displaying high levels of student academic performance. This book provides ideas and strategies that address these questions and provides principals and others with operational knowledge they can employ to construct and sustain a highly effective school culture focused on enhanced student performance.

WHY IS AN EMPHASIS ON SCHOOL CULTURE IMPERATIVE FOR SUCCESSFUL SCHOOL LEADERSHIP?

Creating cultural dynamics contributing to sustained organizational success is highly promoted in sectors outside of schooling. Private-sector analysts have consistently recognized the power of a productive organizational culture. Scholars such as Jim Collins, author of *Good to Great* and *Built to Last*, and Tom Peters and R. H. Waterman, authors of *In Pursuit of Excellence*, have relied upon systematic research and insightful organizational probing to identify unusually successful companies and then distill their management practices and unlock their organizational secrets of success.

Highly visible business CEOs such as the iconic General Electric leader Jack Welch have written and spoken extensively regarding practices upon which they relied to build an unusually profitable and consistently high-performing organization. Remarkably dynamic government leaders such as former New York City mayor and 9/11 recovery leader Rudolph Giuliani have written regarding the management techniques they have employed to render general government effective. Famous management gurus such as Peter Senge and Edward Demming have routinely extolled the notion of organizational culture as a major variable contributing significantly to the late-twentieth-century rebuilding of American industry's globally competitive condition.

However, as insightful as many such business sector analysts and authors have been, it is sometimes difficult to translate their principles and successful practices immediately into the operation of success-challenged schools. For example, Jack Welch's seemingly harsh, but perhaps effective, mandate of annually replacing the 10 percent of employees judged to be low performing, however much a good idea, would not be easily swallowed in America's highly legalistic and egalitarian model of educational management.

Something more than private-sector examples and authoritative admonitions is needed to enable school leaders to construct, turn around, and sustain a productive school culture. While this book draws upon a substantial body of successful research and proven practical knowledge from many sectors, both public and private, it also takes the next step of blending such knowledge constructively into a useful amalgam of principles and practices that school leaders can use to create a sustained culture of success within an education setting. Moreover, this book provides a fresh look at these important issues from within the current educational landscape, thus providing current and aspiring principals with contextually appropriate understanding.

WHY THIS BOOK IS USEFUL NOW

Intensified instructional emphases, elevated expectations for teachers and administrators, concerns for school organization, reexamination of education management, constant revisions to education policy, and education governance intensely reflect the significant transformation through which American schooling is now evolving. The 2001 No Child Left Behind Act and the Obama administration's proposed alterations symbolize this transformation.

America's policy system is seeking means for aligning education's massive material resources with vastly elevated and expanded societal expectations for student achievement. The standards and accountability movement, market and competition strategies, and policy system admonitions for added productivity and heightened student achievement frequently place finance, resource allocation, legal, and accountability issues at the heart of education leadership, policy, and school management considerations.

However, after more than a quarter century of attempting to enhance American education through policy changes, a condition that began as a response to the publication of *A Nation at Risk* in 1983, a parallel set of ideas regarding the significance of school culture is also strongly emerging. Assuredly, having state and district learning standards, adequate resources, well-trained teachers, and appropriate accountability measures matters.

However, even in their totality, these policy levers do not by themselves magically transform a failing or once mediocre school into a thriving and performance-oriented organization capable of enabling all children to achieve academically at higher levels.

A body of knowledge is evolving that suggests means by which schools more effectively can meet many of these heightened expectations for student performance and added organizational and economic efficiency. This knowledge comprises a *strategic* education organizational culture and practice paradigm.

This book embodies this *strategic* outlook and explains the significant role that school culture plays within it and how school leaders can harness these ideas.

The following illustration (Figure 0.1) captures the idea of school reform leader as cultural catalyst.

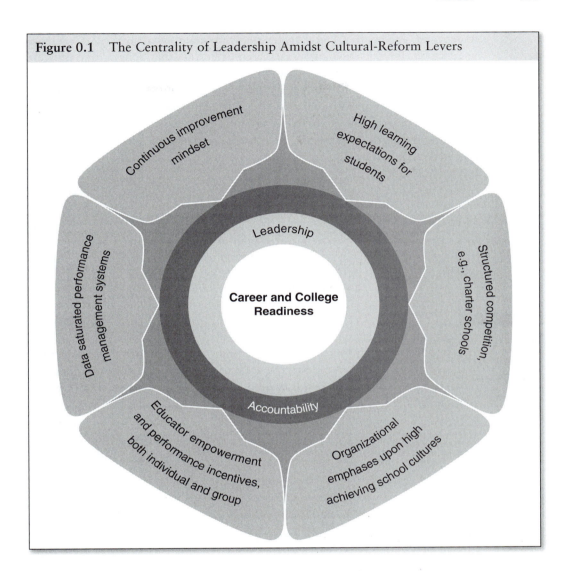

Figure 0.1   The Centrality of Leadership Amidst Cultural-Reform Levers

A CAVEAT REGARDING REALITY

It is currently fashionable to advocate constructing a learning-oriented school culture and a set of high-performance expectations for educators and students. Such an end is unquestionably admirable, and this book is committed to providing research-based practical advice for achieving this objective.

However, creating a learning-oriented school culture is a far more difficult goal to achieve in reality than many policy advocates and public school critics may fully understand. As Figure 2.1 in Chapter 2 portrays, and virtually all of Chapter 8 underscores, there is much about American education that upholds and protects the status quo, abhors fundamental changes, and reinforces business as usual.

Among these conservative conditions are federal and state laws specifying teacher certification requirements, employee bargaining arrangements, self-interested political action groups benefiting from the status quo, state regulations specifying the minimum and maximum length of the school day and hours of instruction, state-provided textbooks, the single salary schedule for teachers, and on and on.

The point here is not to be discouraging of creating learning-oriented school cultures. It is possible to succeed in constructing such environments, and examples abound of dynamic leaders who have led such a charge. Children, their parents, and the larger society likely benefit as a result. However, to be useful, a book on shaping school culture must be realistic and provide a reader with a full understanding of both challenges to be overcome and resources to which one can turn to succeed.

AUDIENCES

This book is aimed at a wide range of informed and able individuals concerned with elevating America's education systems. Particularly, this book should serve well in graduate courses directed at aspiring principals, advanced graduate courses for presently serving school leaders, as material for discussion in professional development institutes for school leaders, and as a supplement for active professional and school district workshops for school leaders. The book should also be useful in general courses in education policy and public policy.

ORGANIZATION

Each chapter is preceded by a case study that illustrates practical day-to-day student, school performance, and culture-constructing challenges faced by current education leaders such as principals, superintendents, and teacher leaders.

Chapter 1 traces the meaning of "culture," applying the concept to schools, reviewing pertinent research results regarding effective school culture traits, and explaining why the concept of "school culture" is increasingly crucial for constructing an organization that effectively elevates student performance.

Chapter 2 argues that an effective school culture is characterized by an empirically validated set of core components regarding learning standards, instructional strategies, individualization, parent and community engagement, and learning-centered leadership.

Chapter 3 explores leadership in two ways. The first is the actions leaders can and should take to construct and sustain an effective school culture. The second is the means for determining one's personal leadership style and effectiveness.

Chapter 4 describes processes for recruiting and retaining an effective faculty, encouraging their understanding of a high-performance culture, gaining commitment to school goals, evaluating teacher performance, and rewarding success.

Chapter 5 examines means for maximizing returns on financial resources and offers illustrations of the manner in which resources can be marshaled and deployed to elevate achievement.

Chapter 6 describes means by which data pertaining to school, community, and student performance indicators can be continually gathered and used to guide decisions and manage school personnel performance.

Chapter 7 explains the significance of and practical avenues for undertaking performance evaluation, the means by which performance responsibility can be assigned, and how excellent performance is appropriately rewarded.

Chapter 8 provides conceptual and contextual understandings regarding American education generally and external opposing forces and internal impediments to constructing a productive and high-performing school culture.

UNIQUE BOOK COMPONENTS

Several innovative components are included in this book, in addition to the following eight chapters of text and graphics.

School Culture Checklist. This is unique to this book. It is not intended as a stand-alone "silver bullet" document. It is best used in conjunction with an instructor or mentor who can then relate checklist items and ideas to the book's eight chapters of explanatory texts.

ELCC Standards. At the outset of each section of text, short contextual statements explain the relationship of chapter content to ELCC standards, which are provided in detail on page xxxix. Within each chapter, a reader will find a wealth of information that is pertinent to the knowledge and skills encompassed by the ELCC standards. Discussion questions reference pertinent ELCC standards and encourage readers to consider how chapter content is applicable to successful leadership performance in the domains contained in the standards.

School Culture Challenge Case Studies

The case studies presented prior to each chapter of this book illustrate practical day-to-day student, school performance, and culture-constructing challenges faced by current education leaders such as principals, superintendents, and teacher leaders. Several of these cases illustrate processes by which a cooperative and productive culture can be constructed. Selected other cases present a less favorable image, providing information regarding the intense challenges that a principal and others face in overcoming a negative school culture. These cases serve as a frequent subject of subsequent chapter reference as a reader is led to see the relevance of the book's content, concepts, research findings, and analytic approaches to solving problems raised in operational settings.

Each case study is about an actual school, actual people, and actual conditions. Nothing is fabricated. All cases are about situations school leaders routinely encounter. However, in each instance, names of people, schools, and locations have been altered to ensure confidentiality.

Technical Accuracy

This book provides greater technical knowledge on important dimensions than is typical in education graduate texts. For example, sections on testing and value-added testing are not easily found in any other place. Similarly, the information regarding educator performance pay is not included in other books of this nature.

Conceptual Clarity: Leading With PRIDE

The book relies upon a mnemonic, *PRIDE*, to convey to a reader the major levers available to a leader for constructing an effective school culture. These levers include policy and personnel, resource deployment, incentives and accountability, data and assessment, and empowerment and energy. It is important for a leader to have a vision of the desired culture. The book's first two chapters articulate components of a high-performing school culture. After that, however, it is equally important for a leader to know how to bring a vision to reality. PRIDE suggests levers that can be used for this purpose. Both of these dimensions, the essential components of a high-performing culture and the implementation levers, are pictured in Figure 0.2.

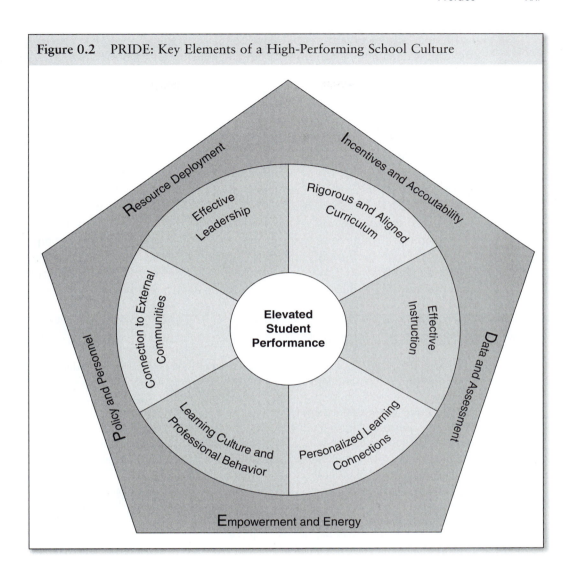

Figure 0.2   PRIDE: Key Elements of a High-Performing School Culture

AUTHORS' CREDENTIALS

The authors combine 70 years as classroom and university teachers and school administrators; are currently engaged in teacher and leadership training for school and district-based teams in 20 states; are consistently involved in significant empirical research regarding teaching and school effectiveness; and are highly knowledgeable regarding modern theories of human learning, effective instruction, school organizational development, personnel incentive systems, application of technology to instruction, and education as a profession.

The authors are engaged in ongoing consulting work for school, district, and state level education organizations and regularly make conference presentations, keynote addresses, and provide expert legal testimony on a variety of educational issues. For 10 years, James Guthrie served as department chair of the Department of Leadership, Policy, and Organizations at Peabody College. This department routinely is rated as the nation's top-ranked program in educational leadership. He now serves as senior fellow and director of education policy studies at the George W. Bush Institute and professor of education at Southern Methodist University, in Dallas, Texas. The Institute's principal education initiative is to elevate further the quality of school leadership in the United States. Patrick Schuermann is a research assistant professor in the Department of Leadership, Policy, and Organizations at Vanderbilt University's Peabody College, serves as a chair for the Peabody Leadership Institutes, and works at the intersection of education research and leadership practice at the district and school levels.

REFERENCES AND SUGGESTED READINGS

Bolman, L. G., & Deal, T. E. (2003). *Reframing organizations: Artistry, choice, and leadership*. San Francisco: Jossey-Bass.

Collins, J. (1994). *Built to last: Successful habits of visionary companies*. New York: HarperBusiness.

Collins, J. (2001). *Good to great: Why some companies make the leap . . . and others don't*. New York: HarperBusiness.

Deal, T. E., & Peterson, K. D. (1999). *Shaping school culture*. San Francisco: Jossey-Bass.

Giancola, J. M., Hutchson, J. K., & Hawthorne, R. (2005). *Transforming the culture of school leadership: Humanizing our practice*. Thousand Oaks, CA: Sage.

Institute for Education Sciences (2008). *Turning around chronically low performing schools*. IES practice guide, What Works Clearinghouse, NCER, United States Department of Education.

Loveless, T. (2010). *How well are American students learning?* Washington, DC: Brown Center, Brookings Institution.

National Commission on Excellence in Education. (1983). *A nation at risk: The imperative for educational reform*. Washington, DC: U.S. Government Printing Office.

Peters, T. J., & Waterman, R. H. (2004). *In search of excellence: Lessons from America's best-run companies*. New York: Harper Collins.

Sarason, S. B. (1996). *Revisiting "the culture of the school and the problem of change."* New York: Teachers College Press.

Senge, P. H. (2006). *Fifth discipline: The art and practice of the learning organization* (5th ed.). New York: Doubleday.

Shafritz, J. M., & Ott, J. S. (2001). *Classics of organization theory* (5th ed.). Belmont, CA: Wadsworth Group/Thompson Learning.

Zmuda, A., Kuklis, R., & Kline, E. (2004). *Transforming schools: Creating a culture of continuous improvement*. Portland, OR: Book News.

Acknowledgments

The first author of this volume is James W. Guthrie, senior fellow and director of education policy studies at the George W. Bush Institute and professor of education at Southern Methodist University. He was previously professor of public policy and education at Peabody College, chair of the Leadership, Policy, and Organizations Department, director of the Peabody Center for Education Policy, director of the National Center on Performance Incentives, and policy director for the Center on Educator Compensation Reform.

The second author of this volume is Patrick J. Schuermann, a research assistant professor at Peabody College, policy director and director of technical assistance for the Center on Educator Compensation Reform, and chair of the Independent School Leadership Institute, a joint venture between the National Research and Development Center on School Choice and the Peabody Professional Institutes. Peabody's Department of Leadership, Policy, and Organizations is among the most highly rated academic units in the nation concerned with the preparation of education leaders and offers advanced degree programs for both researchers and professional practitioners.

Much of the underlying knowledge of education leadership and successful school operation upon which this volume rests was pioneered through decades of research and design efforts undertaken at Peabody College with the financial support of the Institute of Education Sciences of the United States Department of Education, the Office of Elementary and Secondary Education within the United States Department of Education, the Tennessee State Education Department, the Tennessee Department of Human Services, the Texas Education Agency, Metropolitan Nashville Public Schools, and national philanthropic foundations, prominent among which have been the AT&T Foundation, Bill and Melinda Gates Foundation, the Ball Foundation, Kauffman Foundation, Kern Family Foundation, the Stewart Foundation, the William and Flora Hewlett Foundation, the Wallace Foundation, W. T. Grant Foundation, and the Public Education Foundation of Nashville. While deeply appreciative of the resources and opportunities all of these agencies have contributed, these authors are responsible for the content and recommendations contained in this volume.

We wish to express our appreciation to Peabody College's Dean Camilla P. Benbow. Further, we are thankful to Diane McDaniel and Ashley Conlon, of Sage Publications, and Joyce Hilley, who managed the Peabody Center for Education Policy for 15 years, now is an education policy assistant at the George W. Bush Institute, and has kept the writing and production processes connected with this book on track and on time.

The authors are especially appreciative of the contributions of Peabody College and Vanderbilt University faculty colleagues Jason S. Adair, Kathryn H. Anderson, R. Dale Ballou, Steven R. Baum, Leonard Bickman, Leonard K. Bradley, Timothy C. Caboni, Robert L. Crowson, Mark D. Cannon, Janet S. Eyler, John G. Geer, Ellen B. Goldring, Ted Hasselbring, Stephen P. Heyneman, Eric K. Hilgendorf, Michael K. McLendon, Joseph F. Murphy, Bruce I. Oppenheimer, Cynthia D. Prince, Daniel J. Reschly, Pearl G. Sims, Matthew G. Springer, and Thomas T. Ward. Additionally, the authors are grateful to Michael Christian, Robert Meyer, Chris Thorn, and Peter Witham for their contributions to the text.

As well, the authors have benefited from the advice and friendship of a number of professional colleagues, among whom are Jake P. Abbott, California independent education executive search consultant; Jacob E. Adams, Claremont Graduate University; Jane R. Best, Mid-continent Research for Education and Learning; Gina E. Burkhardt, Learning Point Associates; Sir Clive Booth, Oxford Brookes College; Devin Brown, Asbury University; Sharon Brown, Transylvania University; Charles W. Cagle, Lewis, King, Krieg & Waldrop, P.C.; David Chard, Southern Methodist University; Stacy Cinatl, George W. Bush Institute; Geraldine J. Clifford, University of California, Berkeley; Robert M. Costrell, University of Arkansas; Dennis Collins, SUNY-Fredonia; Ruth Collins, Berklee College; Ross A. Danis, Drew University; Ric Dressen, Edina Public Schools, Minnesota; Christopher T. Cross, Cross & Joftus, LLC; Vincent Durnan, University School of Nashville; John W. Evans, Educational Testing Service; Kenneth Fenoglio, AT&T University; Pedro E. Garcia, University of Southern California; Jason Glass, Eagle County Schools; Ambassador James K. Glassman, George W. Bush Institute, Jay P. Greene, University of Arkansas; William Green, Minneapolis Public Schools; Daniel Goldhaber, University of Washington; Marilyn Peters Guske, Fresno; Babette Gutmann, Westat; Eric A. Hanushek, Hoover Institution of Stanford University; Janet S. Hansen, Committee for Economic Development; Gerald C. Hayward, California Community College System; Allison Henderson, Westat; Michael Hinojosa, Dallas Independent School District; Carolyn D. Herrington, Florida State University; Frederick M. Hess, American Enterprise Institute;

Paul T. Hill, University of Washington; Eric A. Houck, University of Georgia; Joseph Jaconette, Orinda, California; Sally B. Kilgore, Modern Red School House; Michael W. Kirst, Stanford University; Julia E. Koppich, J. Koppich & Associates; Richard Laine, Wallace Foundation; Sabrina Laine, Learning Point Associates; Charlene Lake, AT&T; April Lee, United States Department of Education; Alfred A. Lindseth, Sutherland, Asbill & Brennan, LLP; Goodwin Liu, University of California, Boalt Hall School of Law; Susanna Loeb, Stanford University; Theodore Lobman, Chicago; Robert H. Meyer, University of Wisconsin-Madison; David H. Monk, Pennsylvania State University; Martha McCarthy, University of Indiana; Ambassador Mark Langdale, George W. Bush Institute; J. Dennis O'Brien, Office of the Governor, Minnesota; Allan R. Odden, University of Wisconsin-Madison; Ryan Olson, Kern Family Foundation; Jennifer L. Osterhage, Hanover College; Miguel Quinones, Cox School of Business, Southern Methodist University; Rosemary Perlmeter, Uplift Education; Paul Peterson, Harvard University; Darcy Pietryka, Westat; Marjorie Plecki, University of Washington; Michael J. Podgursky, University of Missouri-Columbia; James Rahn, Kern Family Foundation; R. Anthony Rolle, University of South Florida; Kevin M. Ross, Lynn University; Richard Rothstein, Economic Policy Institute; Roger Sampson, Education Commission of the States; Kevin Skelly, Palo Alto, California; Neil Slotnick, State of Alaska Office of the Attorney General; James R. Smith, Management Analysis and Planning, Inc.; Sandra Smyser, Eagle County Schools; Robert E. Stepp, Sowell, Gray, Stepp & Laffitte, LLC; Rocco E. Testani, Sutherland, Asbill & Brennan, LLC; Christopher A. Thorn, University of Wisconsin-Madison; Marina Walne, Arnold Family Foundation; Timothy Waters, Mid-continent Research for Education and Learning; Jason L. Walton, Lynn University; Jerry D. Weast, Montgomery County, Maryland; Peter Witham, University of Wisconsin, Madison; Elizabeth Witt, United States Department of Education; Patrick J. Wolf, University of Arkansas; and Ellen Wood, Teaching Trust.

James Guthrie and Patrick Schuermann would like to thank their immediate families, extended families, and school families from whom they have learned much by example about leadership and the importance of integrity in action.

This volume was initiated while E. Gordon Gee was the chancellor of Vanderbilt University. Seldom have the authors witnessed an individual who so fully and genuinely pursued and exemplified the strategic leadership principles and practices described and espoused in this book. Few leaders think as globally and act as personally as Gordon Gee. We were fortunate to have had him as an exemplar from which we could learn so much and employ as a favorable model so often. We hold Ambassador James K. Glassman, executive director of the George W. Bush Institute, in similar high regard. Seldom have we encountered such an encompassing intellect harnessed with such sustained concern for human welfare, organizational effectiveness, and personal relations. Finally, the mentorship and wisdom of H. Thomas James, Stanford University, is evident throughout this book.

We also want to thank the following reviewers who provided feedback on the prospectus and the draft reviews:

Matthew Boggan, Mississippi State University at Meridian

Darlene Bruner, University of South Florida

Sister Patricia Helene Earl, Marymount University

Virginia Phillips Foley, East Tennessee State University

Doreen Gosmire, University of South Dakota

Russ Higham, Tarleton State University

Patricia Hoehner, University of Nebraska at Kearney

Sherryl A. Houdek, University of North Dakota

James W. Koschoreck, University of Cincinnati

Clyde Winters, Governors State University

Velda Wright, Lewis University

As authors, we are flattered by reader interest in this volume and welcome suggestions for improving its accuracy and utility. As should be obvious in such ventures, errors and omissions are the responsibility of the authors alone.

James W. Guthrie
George W. Bush Institute, and
Annette Caldwell Simmons School of Education, Southern Methodist University
Dallas, Texas

Patrick J. Schuermann
Peabody College
Vanderbilt University
Nashville, Tennessee

School Culture Checklist

The following is not a checklist such as airline pilots use in preparing for takeoff. In their instance, every item on the list is a critical "must do" action: an individual item's omission may render a plane incompletely prepared for flight and perhaps put passengers at risk. Knowledge regarding the specific components of "school effectiveness" is, regrettably, nowhere near as scientifically sound or technically prescriptive as an airplane's flight.[1]

Rather, the following is an illustrative list of school actions and attributes to which a reader, perhaps a decision maker for a school or schools, or even a parent, can turn to assess if a school culture component is sensible and likely to enhance learning in a specific organizational setting. In more simple terms, one can use this checklist to see if there are conditions or actions the appropriate implementation or alteration of which might possibly enhance a school's effectiveness. If nothing else, a reader's attention to each of the following operational items may prove provocative. For historical or contextual reasons, one may have a good reason for omitting or avoiding some item on the list, but the act of thinking about it may prove beneficial by itself.

---

[1]A word regarding evidence is in order. There is little by way of valid research regarding the relationship of any particular school activity or condition to elevated student achievement. Even the Institute for Education Sciences' (IES) practitioner-oriented pamphlet on school effectiveness acknowledges that the evidentiary base in support of its four general school effectiveness recommendations is low. This is in contrast to the effectiveness claims frequently made by advocates, true-believer zealots, and some self-serving consultants. However, the absence of scientific validation does not mean that nothing is known or that education leaders and reformers should be paralyzed, sitting idle awaiting more definitive and empirically proved change prescriptions. There is much than can be done to render schools more effective that stems from the craft knowledge of successful professional educators, reflections of thoughtful reformers, leaders' carefully considered alternatives to present-day practice, and logic. Such common-sense sources form the foundation of this book.

The list is segmented into logical and actionable categories, components of which, if appropriately tailored, can likely contribute to a productive school culture. The list is not intended to be exhaustive. Nor is the sequence of these categories necessarily intended to convey their individual significance. However, attention has been given to Maslow's proposed hierarchy of human needs in the sequencing of the presentation that follows.[2] The assumption here is that fundamental conditions such as safety and personal well-being likely influence human readiness to learn.

This is not intended as a school operations checklist. Such a list would be much longer. Nor is it an accreditation survey checklist. Only items are included here that logically bear some relationship to the formation and reinforcement of a productive school culture. Greater explanations of each of the following items are included in the eight substantive chapters that follow. One way to approach each of these ideas is to regard it as a hypothesis. Consider whether or not the addition or adoption of such an idea, in the context of an existing, turnaround, or new school, would likely enhance school culture and contribute to elevated student performance.

The development and implementation of a high-performing school culture is a complex endeavor, involving many moving parts and relying upon the expertise of individuals from across the full spectrum of organizational departments in a school or district. While visible and consistent leadership is a critical factor to successful planning and implementation efforts, no individual can realistically have the resources or capacity to complete each activity on this checklist. In order for each item on the checklist to be marked in the affirmative, some action must be taken—action that sometimes is not under the direct guidance of, or undertaken by, the school or district leader. Therefore, the authors would encourage school and district leaders to assemble teams of experts with specialized skills across the spectrum of the following topics to share responsibility for actively considering and acting on each checklist item. A distributed leadership model and team-oriented approach will facilitate stakeholder engagement, reinforce a culture of shared responsibility, and increase the likelihood that all of the diverse domains of activity articulated on the checklist are adequately addressed.

---

[2]Abraham Maslow, *Motivation and Personality*. (New York: Harper, 1954).

SCHOOL CULTURE CHECKLIST

Safety	Yes	No
A school official is designated as a comprehensive campus safety officer and, where appropriate, transportation coordinator.	[ ]	[ ]
Physical condition of buildings and surrounding school areas are routinely appraised for safety and known to meet specified safety codes.	[ ]	[ ]
A schoolwide safety and building evacuation plan is well publicized, known to all school personnel, regularly updated, and routinely conveyed to parents.	[ ]	[ ]
Reasonable procedures are in place to ensure that school outside visitors are cordially guided to a central point in the building at which their purpose, needs, and identity are appropriately assessed.	[ ]	[ ]
School staff, a safety officer (if such exists), and teachers are routinely briefed regarding school safety, fire, terrorist, gunman, sniper, and hazardous spill or toxic materials procedures and regulations.	[ ]	[ ]
Consideration is given to elementary-grade parental contact and afterschool pupil pickup and transport.	[ ]	[ ]
Parents are routinely briefed on school safety and student health matters and their respective roles regarding issues such as children's vaccination, contagious diseases, bullying, child molestation, and illness.	[ ]	[ ]
Clearly communicated procedures exist for parents to express safety and health concerns to school officials.	[ ]	[ ]
Guidelines specify conditions under which the school communicates with children's services, police, or criminal justice officials when an abnormal or threatening situation appears in a student's life or in the context of school operation.	[ ]	[ ]
Students' Personal Well-Being	Yes	No
Any individual student's exceptional medical conditions or specialized health, mental health, or nutritional needs are known, confidentially communicated to those in the school affected, and appropriate records are on file at the school.	[ ]	[ ]

(Continued)

(Continued)

Students' Personal Well-Being	Yes	No
School officials are alert to or know of students' home or parental conditions sufficiently debilitating so as possibly or likely to impair student learning or immediate safety.	[ ]	[ ]
School officials are knowledgeable regarding community support activities available to students in need of health, mental health, nutritional, or financial assistance.	[ ]	[ ]
Students' free and reduced meal eligibility information is obtained, recorded as specified by federal and state regulation, and monitored in the least personally intrusive manner.	[ ]	[ ]
Arrangements exist for providing impoverished students with clothing, eyeglasses, or other critical personal or health-related items if evidence suggests such is otherwise not routinely available to a student.	[ ]	[ ]
Leadership Style	**Yes**	**No**
School leaders, administrators, teachers, or classified staff are motivated consciously and continually to appraise, seek feedback about, and determine means for improving individual and team leadership style and effectiveness.	[ ]	[ ]
Leader(s) exhibit openness to and reward productive suggestions for their own professional or the school's improvement.	[ ]	[ ]
Clear lines of administrative accountability exist.	[ ]	[ ]
Continual consideration for improvement of both internal organizational dynamics and external relationships is a priority.	[ ]	[ ]
Leaders are continually conscious of school mission and learning objectives and tailor their time and efforts to further these goals.	[ ]	[ ]
School Mission	**Yes**	**No**
Consciously constructed	[ ]	[ ]
Comprehensive of purposes	[ ]	[ ]
Understandably worded	[ ]	[ ]
Prominently displayed	[ ]	[ ]
Referenced regularly and routinely reexamined	[ ]	[ ]
Relevant to school clientele and context	[ ]	[ ]
Capable of guiding action and shaping resource allocation	[ ]	[ ]
Worthy and amenable of accomplishment	[ ]	[ ]

Student Learning Objectives	Yes	No
Consistent with school's mission	[ ]	[ ]
In their totality, capture and specify schools' multiple purposes	[ ]	[ ]
Directed at student knowledge and performance outcomes	[ ]	[ ]
Specified sufficiently to establish instructional expectations	[ ]	[ ]
Capable of guiding formative and summative assessments	[ ]	[ ]
Encouraging of pedagogical creativity	[ ]	[ ]
Integrated across all subject content and scaffolded sequentially from grade to grade	[ ]	[ ]
Useful for communicating school purposes to parents and other publics	[ ]	[ ]
Consistent with external, district, state, and federal formal expectations	[ ]	[ ]
Financial Resources	**Yes**	**No**
Aligned with organizational purposes (e.g., mission and learning objectives)	[ ]	[ ]
Allocated to enhance instruction	[ ]	[ ]
Distributed equitably, where such is appropriate, and efficiently	[ ]	[ ]
Subject to routine procedures for fiscal and performance accountability	[ ]	[ ]
Linked to performance data so as to be amenable to midcourse distributional alterations when evidence warrants	[ ]	[ ]
Subjected to and linked to incentives to ensure efficient use	[ ]	[ ]
Allocated with longevity in mind (regular, not episodic, maintenance of building features, operational items, and technology)	[ ]	[ ]
Organizational Climate	**Yes**	**No**
Dominance of Learning: Virtually every communication, visible symbol, reasonable incentive, and organizational dynamic is directed at establishing and reinforcing the school's role in enhancing students' intellectual, physical, and personal development.	[ ]	[ ]
Civility: Leadership, examples, formal communication, and regulations model and reinforce civility and professionalism in exchanges between all individuals, adults, and students comprising and engaging with the school community.	[ ]	[ ]
Risk Encouragement: All adults, and students where appropriate, are encouraged to take responsible risks where an innovative action has the potential of enhancing learning, student well-being, or organizational resources.	[ ]	[ ]

(Continued)

(Continued)

Aesthetic Environment	Yes	No
Facility repair and cleanliness, including surrounding school grounds, is undertaken to maintain attractive learning environment.	[ ]	[ ]
Plentiful art, including student art, and other symbolic displays enhance aesthetic environment and reinforce school's academic purpose.	[ ]	[ ]
Visual and performing arts are provided equal time to athletic events in school activities.	[ ]	[ ]
Intellectual Environment	Yes	No
School mascot, visual symbols, student rallies and assemblies, honor roll and honor society memberships, highly visible performance charts and data displays (e.g., school test scores, college admissions, afterschool program participation, and parental engagement)	[ ]	[ ]
Visiting scholars, school guests, and classroom lecturers often representing community residents with unusual prominence in a field or high recognition as a craftsperson, scholar, public official, business leader, musician, or artist	[ ]	[ ]
School communiqués, be they intended for internal or external audiences, always undertaken to a high literary standard and carefully proofread	[ ]	[ ]
Sanctity of Instructional Time	Yes	No
School day, week, and year extended to maximum allowable under statute	[ ]	[ ]
Strong and uniform enforcement of student compulsory attendance	[ ]	[ ]
Electronic student roll taking	[ ]	[ ]
Digitized records to minimize teacher paperwork	[ ]	[ ]
Schoolwide public address used only in emergencies, not for routine communication.	[ ]	[ ]
Primary-grade students move efficiently from one classroom and school activity to the next.	[ ]	[ ]
Passing times between classes, lunch periods, and recesses minimized	[ ]	[ ]
No classroom dismissals into halls by any teacher until scheduled time	[ ]	[ ]
Students excused from classes minimized	[ ]	[ ]
External noise and interruptions minimized (e.g., except in emergencies, major facility repairs undertaken during weekends, evenings, or summers)	[ ]	[ ]
Limited reliance upon state-authorized "minimum days" and restricted number of "snow days" where weather is a factor	[ ]	[ ]

Sanctity of Instructional Time	Yes	No
Teacher professional development takes place after school, on weekends, and during summers, not during valuable instructional time.	[ ]	[ ]
Year-round school schedules minimize summer and holiday student learning extinction and regression.	[ ]	[ ]
Balanced reliance upon homework (suitable to students' age level)	[ ]	[ ]
Reasonable efforts made to use to-and-from school transport time for learning where bus routes are extended	[ ]	[ ]
Ways identified to render conventional "dead" time (e.g., end-of-semester and end-of-school-year textbook turn in and library book collections, locker inspections, and ceremonial activities) productive	[ ]	[ ]
Wherever resources permit, instruction extended into afterschool hours, weekends, and summers	[ ]	[ ]
Adult/Student Interaction	Yes	No
Students are routinely and pleasantly greeted by name by principal or teacher upon entry to school and passing between classrooms.	[ ]	[ ]
Elementary grade teachers eat lunch with their students.	[ ]	[ ]
Students respectfully address teachers (e.g., Ms., Mrs., or Mr.).	[ ]	[ ]
Teachers, administrators, and staff know and respectfully use proper names when addressing students.	[ ]	[ ]
Playground rules are well publicized and routinely enforced by all classroom teachers and staff.	[ ]	[ ]
Parents routinely receive clear and understandable notification of student progress and performance.	[ ]	[ ]
Student Conduct	Yes	No
Students are required to wear simple, tasteful, clean, and inexpensive uniforms to school.	[ ]	[ ]
Student conduct, grooming, and dress code is explicit, succinct, understandable, widely publicized, and uniformly enforced.	[ ]	[ ]
Student conduct code is annually reviewed and approved by parents and community representatives.	[ ]	[ ]
Enforcement of student conduct, dress codes, and discipline is viewed as the individual responsibility of every faculty and staff member and administrator.	[ ]	[ ]
Student bullying, extortion, or intimidation is consistently monitored and consciously discouraged.	[ ]	[ ]

(Continued)

(Continued)

Student Culture	Yes	No
Student honor society is reverentially treated by educators in school, lauded publicly, and provided with a significant role in school operation.	[ ]	[ ]
Students' informal time, outside of class, is organized so as to reinforce formal school learning objectives (e.g., student government, cross-age tutoring, afterschool subject matter clubs, field trips, and afterschool employment).	[ ]	[ ]
Peer group influence is harnessed to reinforce learning objectives through activities such as spelling bees, scholastic and interscholastic academic olympics, debate competition, science fairs, and community displays of student learning and skills.	[ ]	[ ]
Provision of wide variety of afterschool program options exists so as to keep students engaged with school culture for an extended day, beyond formal instruction.	[ ]	[ ]
Afterschool and weekend paid employment is discouraged for adolescent students (because it detracts from time devoted to and commitment to school-valued activities).	[ ]	[ ]
Instructional Arrangements	Yes	No
School and all individual classes always begin on scheduled time.	[ ]	[ ]
Class enrollment size is a function of instructional effectiveness, necessity of instructor feedback to students, and student safety issues. (For example, some P.E. or selected mathematics classes can be larger than English or literature classes, courses conventionally relying upon substantial written assignments deserving of instructor feedback to students.)	[ ]	[ ]
Most fundamental courses or subjects are taught in the morning when student attention and engagement are likely to be highest.	[ ]	[ ]
Scheduling is sufficiently flexible to permit added time allotted to classes routinely relying upon laboratory assignments.	[ ]	[ ]
Attention is given to determining which subjects need be taught daily and which can be taught on alternate schedules.	[ ]	[ ]
Personnel Arrangements	Yes	No
New teacher selection is undertaken with unusual care and is not subject to centralized intradistrict seniority-based transfer privileges and contract dictates.	[ ]	[ ]
New teacher selection is a cooperative function involving administrators and experienced teachers.	[ ]	[ ]

Personnel Arrangements	Yes	No
Teachers are grouped in and students are assigned to teacher teams.	[ ]	[ ]
Elementary students remain with the same teaching team for primary school years.	[ ]	[ ]
Secondary teachers are teamed by subject area.	[ ]	[ ]
Language arts and social studies classes are taught in tandem by the same teachers so as to reduce the absolute number of students for whom individual teachers are responsible during a day or week.	[ ]	[ ]
Teachers of conventionally untested subjects (e.g., P.E., drama, art, and electives) are paired with tested teachers so as to form instructional teams wherein all are capable of reinforcing what is tested and thus eligible for team-based performance awards.	[ ]	[ ]
Teachers are carefully inducted over a one- or two-year period as an "Apprentice." Thereafter, upon meeting professional requirements and satisfying performance appraisals, they are promoted to "Instructor" and then "Master Teacher" or some other appropriate professional-determined hierarchy.	[ ]	[ ]
Teacher remuneration is linked to the just-mentioned hierarchy and performance, not chronological experience or unrelated academic credits.	[ ]	[ ]
Professional development of teachers is highly personalized and linked to results of formative assessments of student performance.	[ ]	[ ]
Incentives/Bonuses	Yes	No
To attract teachers of hard-to-staff subjects	[ ]	[ ]
To attract effective teachers to students most in need	[ ]	[ ]
For minimizing teacher absence and inappropriate reliance upon substitute teachers	[ ]	[ ]
To reward unusually effective teachers and teaching teams	[ ]	[ ]
For teachers and others who assume added professional responsibilities and who achieve professional milestones	[ ]	[ ]
Unexpended allocated amounts able to be carried over to next activity cycle	[ ]	[ ]
Savings from activities such as utility efficiencies or maintenance cost reductions shared with those creating the efficiency	[ ]	[ ]

(Continued)

(Continued)

Assessments, Data, and Feedback Systems	Yes	No
Formative assessments are routinely used in subjects to determine pupil progress and instructional effectiveness.	[ ]	[ ]
Data systems are designed to track students and their academic performance over time and to be able to link students to teachers and teaching teams over time.	[ ]	[ ]
Data system captures measures of parent and, for secondary schools, student satisfaction.	[ ]	[ ]
Data system captures performance of students at next levels, schools to which they matriculate, college, military, employment, etc.	[ ]	[ ]
Students are linked through the data system to all of their individual instructors, enabling the accountability and research systems to undertake retrospective analyses of teacher or teacher team effectiveness.	[ ]	[ ]
Teacher professional development is personalized and linked to results from student performance data and formative assessments.	[ ]	[ ]
Group or grade performance results are displayed prominently throughout school, both in public and in teacher spaces, in understandable forms such as bar charts.	[ ]	[ ]
Symbols and Ceremonies	Yes	No
Highly visible reminders of significant features of the school's mission, not used for trivial or off-message purposes	[ ]	[ ]
Routinely used to celebrate individual or team student, teacher, or other school community member triumphs	[ ]	[ ]
Altered with sufficient frequency so as not to become stale	[ ]	[ ]
Encompassing of performance across the spectrum of school purposes and programs	[ ]	[ ]
Aesthetically pleasing, not disruptive	[ ]	[ ]
Pedagogy	Yes	No
Teachers are expected to have a thoughtful and consistent approach to instruction that they can describe to supervisors, parents, and professional peers.	[ ]	[ ]
Teachers have a syllabus for their class specifying course purposes, course materials, and class schedule for the semester. Syllabi are consistent with and keyed to school learning objectives.	[ ]	[ ]
At least annually, individual teachers are assembled to provide a report to immediate professional peers regarding their instructional style and their professional accomplishments with students.	[ ]	[ ]
Teachers are encouraged to seek mentoring assistance from their professional peers.	[ ]	[ ]

Parental and Community Relations	Yes	No
Written "contracts" between parents, student, and teacher regarding learning objectives for the semester and the responsibility of each party	[ ]	[ ]
Sustained and informative communication with parents regarding their children's academic progress and the overall performance of the school	[ ]	[ ]
Existence, at secondary schools, of alumni society that sustains adult contact with and allegiance to school	[ ]	[ ]
Successful alumni called upon routinely for informational and inspirational presentations at the school or in classes	[ ]	[ ]
Parents attend, engage with, and support school activities such as drama and musical productions.	[ ]	[ ]
Parents serve as tutors, team coaches, club sponsors, and organizers of academic and athletic competitions.	[ ]	[ ]
Parents are routinely informed of their child's learning goals and how they can contribute at home and through family activities (vacations, museum visits, travel, or religious preparation) to progress toward these goals.	[ ]	[ ]
Public officials are routinely informed regarding progress of school and invited to visit the school, view individual classes, observe student recitals and other performances, participate in assemblies and other public activities, and sponsor events.	[ ]	[ ]
Media attention is deliberately sought for purposes of promoting school and student accomplishments.	[ ]	[ ]
High School Particulars	Yes	No
Attention is given to specific purposes to be served by school, whether they are college preparatory, vocational, etc.	[ ]	[ ]
If college preparatory, course offerings are aligned with a spectrum of college admission requirements.	[ ]	[ ]
If vocational, curriculum is aligned with employer expectations.	[ ]	[ ]
If a theme school, assurance is given that curriculum is consistent with theme and there is parent demand.	[ ]	[ ]
If a career academy, assurance is given that community groups and employers are engaged with the establishment of internship experiences.	[ ]	[ ]
If deciding to maintain a conventional comprehensive high school, attention is given to track or not to track students and the means provided for doing the former.	[ ]	[ ]
Attention is given to the enrollment size of the school. If large, consideration is given to considering schools within schools.	[ ]	[ ]

ELCC Standards

Purposefully, this book draws parallels between content covered in each chapter and the Educational Leadership Constituent Council (ELCC) standards. The ELCC standards are research-based, widely used standards for advanced programs in educational leadership for principals, superintendents, curriculum directors, and supervisors. Each chapter seeks to illustrate how book content is aligned to the core domains of leadership practice. The ELCC standards are defined here.

Standard 1.0: Candidates who complete the program are educational leaders who have the knowledge and ability to promote the success of all students by facilitating the development, articulation, implementation, and stewardship of a school or district vision of learning supported by the school community.

- Develop a vision
- Articulate a vision
- Implement a vision
- Steward a vision
- Promote community involvement in the vision

Standard 2.0: Candidates who complete the program are educational leaders who have the knowledge and ability to promote the success of all students by promoting a positive school culture, providing an effective instructional program, applying best practices to student learning, and designing comprehensive professional growth plans for staff.

- Promote a positive school culture
- Provide an effective instructional program
- Apply best practices to student learning
- Design comprehensive professional growth plans

Standard 3.0: Candidates who complete the program are educational leaders who have the knowledge and ability to promote the success of all students by managing the organization, operations, and resources in a way that promotes a safe, efficient, and effective learning environment.

- Manage the organization
- Manage operations
- Manage resources

Standard 4.0: Candidates who complete the program are educational leaders who have the knowledge and ability to promote the success of all students by collaborating with families and other community members, responding to diverse community interests and needs, and mobilizing community resources.

- Collaborate with families and other community members
- Respond to community interests and needs
- Mobilize community resources

Standard 5.0: Candidates who complete the program are educational leaders who have the knowledge and ability to promote the success of all students by acting with integrity, fairly, and in an ethical manner.

- Act with integrity
- Act fairly
- Act ethically

Standard 6.0: Candidates who complete the program are educational leaders who have the knowledge and ability to promote the success of all students by understanding, responding to, and influencing the larger political, social, economic, legal, and cultural context.

- Understand the larger context
- Respond to the larger context
- Influence the larger context

Standard 7.0: Internship. The internship provides significant opportunities for candidates to synthesize and apply the knowledge and to practice and develop the skills identified in Standards 1–6 through substantial, sustained, standards-based work in real settings, planned and guided cooperatively by the institution and school district personnel for graduate credit.

- Substantial
- Sustained
- Standards-based
- Real settings
- Planned and guided cooperatively
- Credit

To read the full standards go to http://www.npbea.org/ELCC/ELCCStandards %20_5-02.pdf

Source: National Council for Accreditation for Teacher Education Unit Standards.

Case Study 1: Buchanan Middle School

Can School Culture Get Better Than This?

In Either Case, What Do You Do Next?

Buchanan Middle School is located in a transition area. It was once in the center of a rich agricultural region, a community with a proud pioneer history and rich rural flavor. More recently, rapid population growth in a nearby city of one million had turned Buchanan's attendance area into a suburban school. Where once there was productive farmland, there were now expansive single-family homes, leafy green subdivisions, luxury townhouses, gated communities, and even a senior retirement complex. Where once there was a general store with dry goods, grocery staples, hardware, and farm supplies, there were now big-box discount stores, boutique specialty shops, fashionable restaurants, and hair salons and day spas. Where once there was a Grange Hall, barbershop, and blacksmith, there was now an eight-screen Cineplex. Where once there was a modest county fairground, there was now a modern auto mall. There was a new and expansive town hall and a huge new regional high school in the planning stage.

"Doc" Lamonica had grown up in the old community. He still owned a sizeable parcel of valuable farmland on the periphery of town that he had inherited from his father. However, he never acted like he was wealthy, and he certainly was not pretentious. He had been a town hero, starring in football and baseball in high school and at the local college, and then a nationally known quarterback on a championship NFL team. Now in his late 50s, everyone knew Doc. He had served a term on the City Council. He was still active in the Rotary Club. He had frequently been discussed as a candidate for mayor or even a member of the state legislature. He had moved back to this community, after his active NFL playing days, become a high school coach, obtained an administrative credential, enrolled in an executive-style EdD program, been mentored by the popular former school district superintendent, and assumed the principalship of Buchanan Middle School about 10 years ago.

Buchanan Middle School was relatively new physically, having been totally reconstructed four year ago. The school board had torn down the old school and constructed a new one in a more central location that naturally integrated students from the shiny new subdivisions

---

Note: This case study, as with others associated with other chapters, is about an actual school, actual people, and actual conditions. Nothing is fabricated. All cases are about situations school leaders routinely encounter. However, in each instance, names of people, schools, and locations have been altered to ensure confidentiality.

with those from the traditional farm worker housing developments and nearby trailer parks. Consequently, Buchanan had about half of its students from financially comfortable middle-class families and another large portion from Hispanic and Hmong families who performed the manual labor in the remaining strawberry fields, truck farms, and vineyards.

The school board did not destroy all of the old Buchanan School. Great care was taken to ensure the preservation and reinstallation of major symbols from the old building. These included the school bell, the Spartan mascot, the Depression era Diego Rivera wall murals, the trophy cases recounting the old school's past athletic and academic glories, the disciplinary bench from outside the principal's office, and even the goalposts from the football field. The symbolic essence of the old Buchanan School had thoughtfully been preserved and integrated into its new physical successor.

The new Buchanan building was classical in is external appearance but state-of-the-art inside with a great deal of instructional space, many specialty rooms, and loaded with up-to-date technology. It had substantial surrounding acreage for playfields, faculty and visitor parking, and future expansion, if needed. It was well maintained and nicely landscaped.

What took place inside of Buchanan Middle School was just as impressive as its tasteful exterior. Doc was clearly the "Boss." He continued to be proud of his having become the principal of the high school that he had attended and his father before him. However, he knew his strengths and limitations. He handled parental and community relations. He was the link to the superintendent and school board. He attended the weekly Rotary meetings and made sure the mayor, city counsel, and other public officials were well informed, and he handled relationships with the press and electronic media.

Doc enjoyed the partnership of Sandy Quentin, the assistant principal for curriculum and instruction. It was a good team. Doc thought it was "Dream Team." He admired Sandy greatly. He personally made no claims regarding instructional expertise, and Sandy had little taste for either the public or publicity.

Doc did have, even if limited in scope and perhaps motivated by matters somewhat superficial, several curricular concerns. He focused like a laser on a very few things. He insisted that youngsters at Buchanan knew how to read and do math, and their scores on annual state tests *had* to be high. This for him was nonnegotiable. In addition, he made sure that there was always a good school band that could perform at public events. He was obsessed with the necessity of having one school drama event each year to which the public and local dignitaries were always invited, and he required that afterschool sports teams were well coached and well equipped (the latter being the annual project of the Rotary Club). If these criteria were met, then Doc was satisfied, and all else was within Sandy's domain.

Sandy was happy with Doc's public relations priorities, but she had other goals too. She wanted to ensure that all Buchanan students, upon graduation, were well prepared for college and career success. She knew the high school faculty well, having once taught there herself. She knew that simply being rated "proficient" on state standardized tests, and meeting all benchmarks imposed by No Child Left Behind and other legislation, would not suffice to meet the rigorous college expectations they would encounter later. She knew that just reading for acceptable state test scores would not enable her school's graduates to attend college, a goal she held for all Buchanan students. There was hardly a subject about which she was not enthusiastic. History—local, state, national, and world—was important to her. She lived and breathed classical literature and thought her teachers ensured students felt the same way. She believed poetry was glorious and spontaneously recited it to students and colleagues. Buchanan's field trips were to museums, ballet performances, and art galleries, not to bottling plants, auto dealerships, and livestock shows.

Buchanan Middle School had little need for new teachers and no shortage of applicants when there was a rare opening. Partly, this condition was a result of the school's quite favorable pay scale. Buchanan operated larger-than-average class sizes, a tradeoff imposed to ensure that teachers were well paid, better by far than in surrounding districts.

The Buchanan base schedule for salaries was augmented by a performance pay plan. This was an artful blend of individual teacher and instructional team awards. Performance targets were set so as to avoid individual teacher competition. The bonuses were for reaching predetermined and measurable goals. The amounts of money at stake were not trivial. A highly successful teacher on a successful grade level or subject matter team could enhance her annual salary by up to 25 percent by successfully meeting goals. Teachers in untested subject areas (e.g., art, music, and drama) were creatively blended into teams so that they too could contribute to school goals.

Another part of the teacher recruitment and retention mosaic was that Buchanan's veteran teachers were well treated, felt privileged, and quickly proselytized their able colleagues from other schools when a Buchanan position opening was on the horizon.

Sandy interviewed all prospective new teachers. She was remarkably careful in her review of applicants. Also, others from among the school's Master Teachers always participated in these hiring endeavors. Doc had the final say, and he was the last to interview all finalists that Sandy recommended. He had veto power, but Sandy knew he would not overturn her. What was important is that in his interview, Doc reinforced the notion of how fortunate one was to be selected as a Buchanan teacher and how high the expectations were for those who taught there.

Candidates were almost always anxious about this final interview. Sandy had told them that impressing Doc was a crucial component of being hired. For his part, Doc told them the school's history, emphasized its commitment to the Greek ideal of a sound mind and strong body, explained the school's Spartan mascot, and made clear that candidates understood the school's exalted place in the community. When the interview was completed, however, finalist candidates were thrilled and felt as though some deity had anointed them.

Teachers were accorded status as "Apprentice," "Instructor," and "Master Teacher." The Buchanan salary plan did not reward years of service or college credits in pedagogy courses. Rather, it rewarded mastery of instructional skills, added evidence of subject matter prowess, and the assumption of added responsibility. Master Teachers were not given a lifetime title. It had to be renewed, through rigorous appraisals, every four years. Buchanan teachers routinely chose not to unionize.

Teachers were not the only individuals to be given careful attention. Students too came in for close scrutiny and plentiful personal attention. Buchanan Middle School had a student (as well as teacher) dress and behavior code. Students were required to wear the simplest of uniforms, and a discretionary fund existed to assist families who had financial difficulty purchasing the required white shirts and blouses and khaki or black long pants. Shirts were always to be tucked in, and pants were to be worn at the standard position on one's hips. Shoes were oxfords or loafers for both boys and girls. Girls could wear colorful scarves around their necks, if they chose. Most did. Boys were required to have their hair cut so that it was above the collar of their shirts and did not cover their ears. (The American Civil Liberties Union had sued the school a few years back in behalf of a plaintiff family whose son had wanted to wear long hair or a ponytail. After Doc appeared in court and explained the school's philosophy and the fact that the community and parents convened annually and reaffirmed its support for the dress code, the judge threw the case out of court and suggested that the plaintiffs had engaged in a trivial suit.)

The school had many internal student competitions involving spelling, mathematics, science, intramural athletics, geography, and on and on. Almost always these were team efforts and grade level or classroom competitions. Trophies, awards, plaques, outstanding performer lists, team photographs, and gold stars were to be found in large measure in every hall and every public space in the school. To walk through Buchanan Middle School was to witness a celebration about seemingly every significant human activity that could take place in a school.

There were disabled students enrolled at Buchanan, and even two self-contained classes. However, steps were always taken to ensure that these students were also included on the various teams that competed unendingly throughout the school year.

The time came, perhaps inevitably, when Doc would leave to become the district superintendent. It was expected, and he thought it a good thing to do. He had assumed that Sandy Quentin would be his successor as principal. To his, and many others', surprise, however, Sandy declined the offer.

This led to a dilemma in the community. No other successor had been groomed or even contemplated. What was to be done? No one wanted to place Buchanan at risk. It was decided that the popular school board president would head the effort to identify a successor. Everyone knew that this would not be an easy assignment.

FOR DISCUSSION

1. What components of the Buchanan school culture do you identify as contributing to its longtime academic success and community popularity?

2. Did Buchanan Middle School seem to do some things to excess?

3. Was Doc Lamonica crucial to the school? Might an argument be made that Sandy Quentin was the secret to the school's success?

4. Why do you suppose Sandy did not want to be principal? Was she to be faulted for lacking professional ambition?

5. What, if anything, would you want to do differently if you were to become the principal at Buchanan Middle School?

6. What counsel would you give the school board president as she set about identifying a principal as successor to Doc?

CHAPTER 1

Defining and Specifying the Significance of School Culture

In this chapter a reader will learn about the following:

- Defining culture, the concept's contemporary significance for education reform, and its productive application to schools
- Research validated traits of a productive school culture
- Operational levers for constructing an effective school culture

ELCC STANDARDS

ELCC standards addressed in this chapter include the following:

- 1.1—Develop a vision of learning
- 1.2—Articulate a vision
- 2.1—Promote a positive school culture
- 3.1—Manage the organization
- 6.1—Understand the larger context

INTRODUCTION

The thesis of this book is that for a school to be maximally effective, individual components of an education reform effort must be woven together into a coherent, consciously constructed, and purposeful tapestry. It is insufficient and possibly counterproductive to graft incremental change after incremental change onto the side of an ongoing school. A tiny speck of teacher performance pay here, a dab of curriculum alignment there, a tiny piece of teacher professional development over there, block scheduling and a day or two of leadership training here, and a friendly nod to parent engagement somewhere for good measure is no way to systematically enhance the performance of a learning organization. However, these individual, ad hoc, and sometimes shortsighted and superficial school improvement components will have much more meaning, and are likely to have a substantially greater cumulative and lasting impact on student achievement, if woven into an organizational substrate where they are consciously considered, crafted to be internally consistent, examined for empirical validity, and rendered mutually reinforcing. That internal substrate, the purposeful organizational tapestry of shared values, beliefs, and expectations into which individual education reform threads should be sewn, is what is meant in this book by the label "school culture."

This book will describe means by which this coherent tapestry can be envisioned, then woven together, and then sustained. However, it is first useful to gain an understanding of several crucial component concepts, beginning with the notion of "culture," and then "school culture." This chapter will begin by discussing what is meant by "culture" generally and move on to discuss what is meant by "school culture" particularly.

THE LARGER CONCEPT OF "CULTURE"

"Culture" is a theoretically encompassing, analytically significant, and practically useful concept. However, it is elusive. While the concept is amenable to definition, description, illustration, and intuitive understanding, it is not easily measured. Nevertheless, once comprehending the essential components of the concept, its analytic application to schools and its practical perspective for enabling schools to become effective emerges more clearly.

Defining and Describing the Concept of "Culture"

In social science, *culture* is a theoretical and analytic concept employed by anthropologists and sociologists to capture the totality of a people's way of life, both material and immaterial. All tribes and clans, many nations, and most any other coherent collectivity of humans (and even animals) have a culture. A culture does not dictate precisely what individual members of a collectivity believe, think, or do. Rather, culture is an amalgam of individuals' modal actions, articles, and attitudes that have evolved over time. These various dimensional components are known as "traits." Traits are present everywhere and shape, but do not necessarily dictate in detail, virtually every object and action in the day-to-day lives and environment of a collectivity's members.

Culture shapes what one eats and wears (even *how* one eats and *how* one wears one's clothes), how one earns a living, the language or dialect one speaks, the formal title or titles one holds, times and terms under which one communicates with others, and how one finds a mate or interacts with siblings, parents, relatives, and others within the collectivity. Culture shapes the status hierarchy and social networks among a people and how the collectivity is governed or ruled. Some of a culture's rules may be formally and explicitly specified (e.g., constitutions and laws). However, most of a culture's mutually shared beliefs and traditions are unwritten, informal, and conveyed through casual and continuous contact and socialization, rather than through direct indoctrination or formal education. When direct and formal efforts exist to socialize the young or new members of the society, such efforts may take place in schools. However, there are other venues as well, for example, coming-of-age religious ceremonies such as confirmation for Christians and bar mitzvahs for Jews or the instruction that characterizes organizations such as Girl Scouts and Boy Scouts, Indian Guides, and Explorers.

These many shared traits serve as the behavioral and perceptual substrate into which one is born and into which individuals as children, youth, adolescents, and adults continually are socialized. Of great importance, culture shapes how one views the actions of others and how a member of a collectivity believes others will perceive and react to him. Culture shapes roles. A "role" is the bundle of expectations held for the behavior of an individual in a specified position interacting with others (e.g., the role of a father, mother, brother, uncle, boss, elected official, teacher, or principal) or undertaking a task or engaging in an endeavor (e.g., being an attorney, pipefitter, farmer, mayor, editor, or a school leader).

Culture is a comprehensive collection of a people's actions and beliefs that enables a collectivity to adjust to its physical environment, continually renew itself, and sustain its gene pool. Hence, culture has many self-reinforcing features, reciprocal activities and beliefs, and sanctions that guide individuals' and institutions' immediate and long-range action and thought and, thus, assist in sustaining a collectivity and its individual members over time.

Culture, climate, and physical environment have an impact upon one another. It is a people's culture, be it Etruscan or Eskimo, Kwakiutl or Kurd, Sioux or Siberian, Balinese or Bedouin, that enables the group to take advantage of and survive in their particular physical world and where necessary to cope with the adversity of cold, heat, drought, flood, fire, or other threatening environmental conditions. However, there is reciprocity. A culture can shape climate and other parts of the physical environment; witness the likely impact of contemporary carbon emissions upon the atmosphere, the mass cutting of tropical rain forests, or the construction of mammoth dams that tame wild rivers and possibly alter weather patterns.

Cultures are not immutably molded; the shared behaviors and beliefs of a people are not forever fixed in time or space. Cultures, to survive, must continually adapt to the environmental, economic, technological, and demographic changes that impinge upon them. Not to evolve jeopardizes the ability of a people, and their culture, to survive. The historical and archeological record is replete with the remnants of once-vital cultures that did not adapt sufficiently or could not defend themselves from the incursions of other cultures (e.g., Huns, Vikings, Visigoths, and Aztecs).

Whereas each culture is a unique blend of a spectrum of shared beliefs and actions, there exist a few universal traits that appear to occur in all cultures. For example, all cultures have some kind of creation story, means for ensuring that children are raised, expectations about adult sexual conduct, and rules regarding property.

Creation

A creation story captures how the earth came into being and how humans appeared on earth. There are plentiful versions of creation, some scientific, some quite primitive in terms of modern cosmology. However, fact or fiction in this instance matters less than the apparent universal desire to have a justification or rationale for human existence.

There are other universal cultural elements, including several that, as later will be explained, can carry over particularly to schools. One is a story regarding the particular culture's beginning and its idealized purposes. This frequently involves a set of historical explanations for the culture's formation, usually a story based upon one or multiple heroes. These heroes usually embody ideals, values, sometimes superhuman abilities, characteristics, preferred behaviors, and outlooks that the culture promulgates across generations.

Values

A second universal cultural element is a set of core beliefs, those parts of its idea system and ideology that enable culture participants to make sense of life and to live in harmony with themselves and peers. This often appears as "religion." It also can be a common code of conduct such as that adhered to by Spartan or Samurai warriors or Christian knights of the Crusades. The Judeo-Christian ethic, a blend of religious and secular actions and personal values, perfuses much of Western culture. There also can exist a pervasive and toxic set of beliefs such as that found at the common core of Hitler's Nazi philosophy of Aryan racial supremacy or jihadist imperatives regarding the avowed elimination of "corrupt Western culture."

In summary, culture is a collectivity's historically rooted, but continually evolving, set of shared beliefs and preferred behaviors. These common beliefs and preferred action patterns form an encompassing mental matrix that envelopes and shapes the active lives and conscious actions of those who are part of the collectivity sharing the culture. Culture is a people's way of life and their way of interpreting life and all that they see around them. This common outlook is inculcated into children and other new members of the culture.

Culture shapes what behavior one can expect of others and what one believes others will expect in return. This common outlook influences the rewards and status that individuals strive to achieve and that are accorded by others in the culture. Culture enables a people to adapt to their physical environment, and it shapes their social interactions among themselves and outsiders.

A tribe, clan, society, or people without culture would be like an individual never having had a memory. There would be no knowledge of who one was, from where one came, where one lived, what one was named or even what a name was, to whom to relate, how one acquired food, what one did day to day, or even how to dress, drive, drink, talk, or live. In such circumstances, instinct might prevail, and primitive survival of a sort might be possible. However, the spectrum of material and perceived risks would be bewildering and the level of physical and personal comfort at its most minimal.

Culture is not a circumstantial or casual correlate of contemporary living. It is a critical condition of human survival. In the abstract, this concept can be applied to schools. Every school has a culture. It is impossible for such not to exist. However, the thesis of this book is that simply having school culture is insufficient. Rather, *what is desired is a consciously constructed school culture, one that consistently aspires to and that can contribute to high levels of student academic performance.*

APPLYING THE CONCEPT OF CULTURE TO SCHOOLS: WHAT IS SCHOOL CULTURE?

Similar to change efforts in other sectors, organizational growth in education does not occur in an isolated environment. Rather, it occurs within institutions that have norms and values, assumptions and expectations. While often used interchangeably, several authors distinguish the constructs of school climate and school culture on the basis of organizational climate being the descriptive beliefs and perceptions individuals hold of the organization, where culture is the shared values, beliefs, and expectations that develop from social interactions within the organization (Rousseau, 1990; Schein, 1992). School culture is "the way we do things around here" (Bolman & Deal, 1993, p. 6)—those tangible and intangible norms and values shared by members of a school that help shape the behaviors of teachers and school leaders.

Certainly, a school's culture is but a microscopically narrow swath of what comprises an entire culture of a people. Whereas even elementary schools certainly are complicated institutions, no school encompasses even a small percentage of all the traits that a complete culture, particularly a modern postindustrial or information-oriented culture, contains. However, schools, even if encompassing only selected components of a culture, are an integral part of an entire culture. In contemporary times, schools are a major societal instrument for formalizing and reinforcing a body of shared beliefs, for transmitting culture from generation to generation, and for enabling a people to ensure that their civilization is capable of renewal and adapting to new conditions.

However, it is not the utility of schools for sustaining culture that is of significance here. Rather, it is the converse. This section explores the significance of culture for sustaining the successful operation of schools. Before doing so in detail, however, it is useful to explain why a concern for school culture is now particularly timely and significant.

Failure of Contemporary Education Reforms and the Regrettable Absence of a Concern for a Coherent and Productive School "Culture"

The United States currently continues with a several-decades-long effort to render its schools more effective. The inception of this reform epoch can be traced most specifically to the Reagan presidency's publication and distribution of a highly visible public report, *A Nation at Risk* (National Commission on Excellence in Education, 1983). This document dominated media headlines and policy deliberations literally for years following its 1983 release. It continues to be a historical major reference point today. It triggered a rash of legislative and administrative efforts to render schools more rigorous and to elevate student academic achievement.

A Nation at Risk was filled with hyperbole and implied the imminent implosion of American world dominance. It proclaimed that the root causes of this endangerment were to be found in the low academic expectations for pupils held by what were trumpeted as America's all too flabby and anti-intellectual public schools.

A Nation at Risk was inaccurate in its caustic criticisms of American schooling. There was no evidence provided at the time that schools were performing for their students in any way worse than had historically been the case. However, aside from its inflammatory and imaginative rhetoric, there was a more fundamental dynamic undergirding the issuance of *A Nation at Risk*. The report was emblematic of the United States' transition from a domestic-oriented to a global economy.

This transition signaled the end of a manufacturing-dominated era, comfortably devoid of intense worldwide market competition, wherein a youngster could do poorly in school, fail to graduate, drop out, obtain well-paying employment, marry a high school sweetheart, raise a family, and enjoy the material part of a middle-class dream of a nice home and new automobile. Henceforth, in the new postindustrial or information age society, the path to material, and perhaps spiritual, success was to run through a far more extended and thorough education. Whereas the nation once was well served by educating a mere 10 percent of the total population to high standards, an elite that could command the world's most powerful economy, university systems, government, industry, and military, such days were over.

A student in Iowa was now competing for a good job with a counterpart in India. A student in Boise had continually to look over his shoulder at the academic performance of youthful economic competitors in Beijing. As a consequence of the new worldwide economy, now virtually the entire population had to be educated to high standards, something that no large industrialized nation had ever striven to accomplish.

But, how does one convert a previously serviceable but nevertheless mediocre public school system into an engine of mass high academic performance? The question is not rhetorical but neither is it easily answerable. *A Nation at Risk* triggered multiple reform proposals and for more than a quarter of a century, the United States has experienced wave after wave of trial-and-error reform strategies. These have ranged from relatively inexpensive and politically palatable programs and proposals such as reduced high school electives and more extensive high school graduation requirements to the enormously costly (tens of billions of dollars) program of reducing average class size from 28 to 15.

Figure 1.1 contains a list illustrating the strategies that have been tried throughout the nation beginning in 1983. Figure 1.2 depicts the most encompassing and most costly reform of all, the employment of thousands of additional certificated professionals in the American education system.

Figure 1.1   U.S. Education Reform Strategies Following *A Nation at Risk*

Post *A Nation at Risk* Education Reform Strategies

- **Intensification of academic requirements** (high school graduation and college admission)
- **Education finance** (intrastate and intradistrict equal spending, smaller classes)
- **Governance changes** (mayoral takeover or administrative decentralization)
- **Curricular and instructional alignment** (goals, textbooks, curriculum, and tests synched)
- **"Professionalization" of teachers** (more preservice preparation, career ladders)
- **Accountability** (sanctions related to student achievement results)
- **Market solutions** (vouchers, charter schools, performance incentives, outsourcing of services)
- **School-based solutions** (small learning communities, schools within schools)
- **Out-of-school aid to students** (health, housing, nutrition, supplemental services)
- **Technology** (laptop programs, online materials, distance learning)

Source: Compiled by the authors

Figure 1.2   Number of School Employees in the U.S. From 1972 to 2008

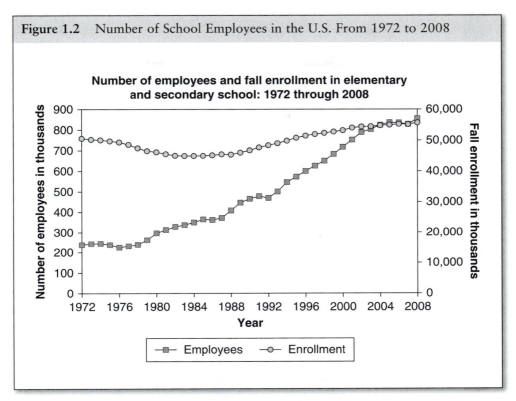

Source: National Center for Education Statistics, 2008

Of course, given the crazy-quilt decentralized governance of American education, 50 state-based systems relying upon more than 13,000 historically autonomous local school districts, there has seldom been a coherent effort to weave these reforms into a pattern. Their full implementation, with consideration of fidelity to the theories of action or logic patterns behind them, or even leaving any one of them in place for a sufficient time to see what it might contribute by way of elevated student achievement, was never a high priority.

The closest effort to having a coherent national policy was the 2001 enactment and 2002 initial implementation of the No Child Left Behind Act (NCLB). Even this highly proclaimed and costly piece of legislation, out of deference to historic state autonomy over education issues, contained no detailed comprehensive reform strategy embedded within it. Its principal contribution was to alter the criteria by which schools' success was to be perceived. No longer would levels of resources schools received be taken as measures of success. Rather, after NCLB, it was to be the level of academic performance achieved.

There is nothing inherently wrong with the reform ideas identified in Figure 1.1. Many individual items on it continue to make a great deal of sense. However, the cumulative consequence of this massive effort has been maximally costly and minimally effective, as evidenced in nearby Figures 1.3 through 1.6. Here can be seen the ever upward historic trajectory of U.S. school spending, its costly nature relative to other developed nations, and the regrettable flat lines of achievement results and high school graduation rates.

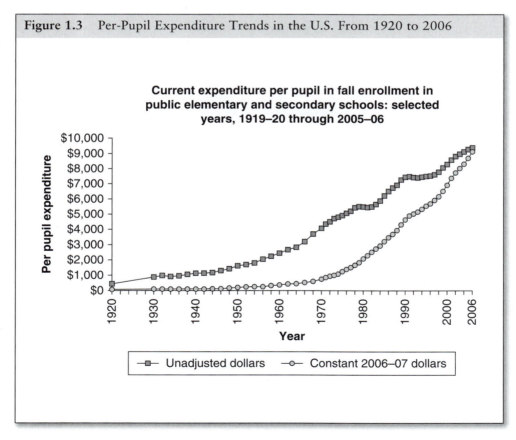

Figure 1.3   Per-Pupil Expenditure Trends in the U.S. From 1920 to 2006

Source: National Center for Education Statistics, 2006

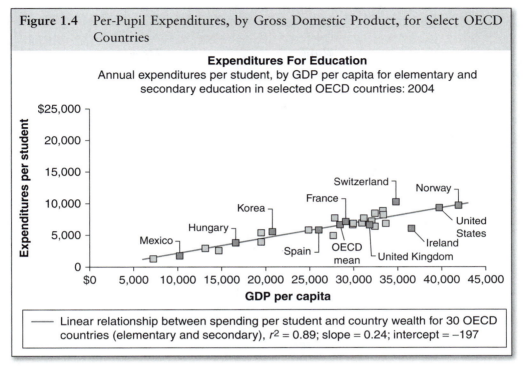

Figure 1.4 Per-Pupil Expenditures, by Gross Domestic Product, for Select OECD Countries

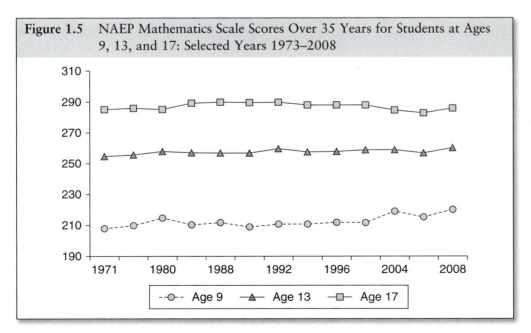

Figure 1.5 NAEP Mathematics Scale Scores Over 35 Years for Students at Ages 9, 13, and 17: Selected Years 1973–2008

Source: The Condition of Education 2008 (NCES 2008-031). National Center for Education Statistics, Institute of Education Sciences, U.S. Department of Education. Washington, DC

Source: National Assessment of Educational Progress, 2009

[18   LEADING SCHOOLS TO SUCCESS]

Figure 1.6   High School Completion Rates 1968 to 2006

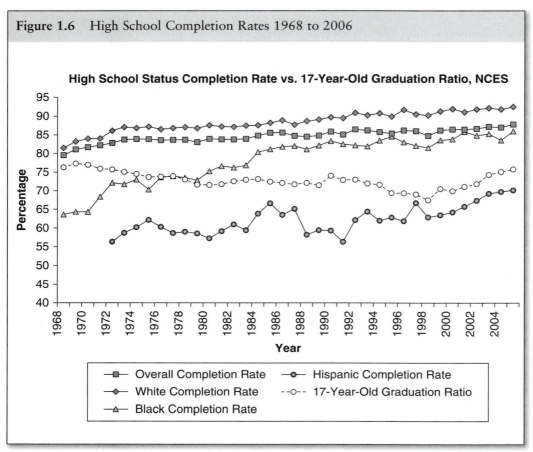

Source: Reproduced from NCES publication "Dropout Rates in the United States: 2005" (Laird et al., June 2007). Rates prior to 1972 are based on authors' calculations using CPS data. The status completion rate is the percentage of 18- through 24-years-olds not enrolled in secondary school who have a high school credential. High school credentials include regular diplomas and alternative credentials such as GED certificates. Hispanic ethnicity is not available before 1972. The 17-year-old graduation ratio is from the Digest of Education Statistics. HS graduates for the graduation ratio include both public and private school diplomas and exclude GED recipients and other certificates. October 17-year-old population estimates are obtained from Census Bureau P-20 reports

Why Have Reform Efforts Proved to Be Unproductive?

There is no absolutely conclusive answer to this question. Explanations range from assertions of lazy teachers and administrators to macro sociological theories claiming that the alleged fundamental anti-intellectual nature of American life eviscerates virtually every effort to render schools effective for all but the most gifted students. Other explanations claim that the nation has failed to make a sufficient financial commitment to public education, trains teachers insufficiently, is unable to create sufficiently powerful teacher performance incentives, or is lacking the fundamental dynamic of institutional competition that characterizes many successful achievement efforts in sectors of society other than education.

The explanation that seems most plausible, and the rationale that provokes and pervades this book, is that individual reforms, regardless of how sensible each is in the abstract, are insufficient by themselves and sum to less than the total value of their individual parts because of the frequent absence of a consistent culture into which they can fit, a culture that is not simply coherent but also one that visibly and intentionally proclaims the centrality of academic achievement and reinforces this message at every reasonable turn.

The Special Case of High Schools

One certainly might wish that all elementary and middle schools were more effective. However, the larger challenge is high schools. The United States settled upon its current comprehensive high school model a century ago. The Progressive Era marked the transition of secondary schooling from an elite to a mass enrollment institution, an institution featuring a curriculum rooted in the classics to one equally concerned with vocational training. Whereas the comprehensive high school may well have suited the nation at the height of its manufacturing hegemony, it is not clear that the model is suited to the still-emerging information age and global economy. However, knowing with certainty with what it should be replaced is not now possible. What is possible is to construct of a variety of high school models worthy of experimentation and to tailor the precepts of productive cultures to each of them.

Concern for Context

An effective public school seldom has the luxury of operating in a contextual vacuum. Rather, there are federal, state, and local school district regulations and expectations with which a school must comply. If these contextual conditions are at odds with what it takes for a school to be effective, then the principal and teachers are swimming upstream against difficult odds. The following are elements of a contextual minimum. These are the elements for which the larger community is responsible. Their presence does not guarantee an effective school. However, their absence renders an effective school improbable.

Prototypical effective school cultures operate within the context of an effective state and school district environment where the following are true:

- The larger community, particularly the business sector, district school board, and central-office leadership are organized around, forcefully and consistently supportive of, and publicly committed to the pursuit of high academic achievement.
- Financial resources are adequate.
- Student academic learning goals are specified and highly visible.
- A structure of routine testing or achievement assessment exists.
- An alignment of goals, tests, administrator selection, teacher recruitment induction, professional development, textbook acquisition, and school supports (e.g., counseling) is in place.
- Financially related resources and student assignments or attendance boundaries are arranged in a rational and equitable manner.
- Day-to-day operational infrastructure matters (e.g., transportation, attendance enforcement, food delivery, supply ordering, and payroll distributions) are undertaken in an effective manner.
- Concern for student and staff safety and well-being is sufficient.

MAKING THE TRANSITION TO A HIGH-PERFORMING SCHOOL CULTURE

A supportive school district and community and the presence of effective federal and state policies do not guarantee a school's culture will be productive. There is much that is determined internally, rather than contextually. This section reviews what is known from research regarding crucial internal components of an effective school culture.

Exploring What Is Known Empirically About "Turnarounds"

When first entering a school one almost instantly notices whether the setting is loud or quiet, orderly or messy, bright or dim, relaxed or frantic, whether students are well behaved or disorderly, and on and on. All of these conditions and components, and much more, are manifestations of a school's culture.

Deal and Peterson defined school culture in 1990 as "deep patterns of values, beliefs, and traditions that have formed over the course of [the school's] history."

School culture is "a group's shared beliefs, customs, and behavior . . . culture includes the obvious elements of schedules, curriculum, student demographics, grading and attendance policies, as well as the social interactions that occur within those structures and give a school its look and feel."

For the purposes of this book, school culture is conceived as the way that inhabitants of and others connected with a school act, interact, think, and feel; specifically, the nature of relationships and tone of conversation between individuals, the appearance of a school and the manner in which it is presented, and the social norms, values, expectations, and attitudes that its adults, students, and other constituents hold and act upon.

Some make a distinction between the climate and culture of a school, but, for the purposes of this book, the two concepts are considered together because they are closely intertwined. It is interesting to note that, historically, climate has always affected culture (e.g., the arctic climate led Eskimos to build igloos, hunt whales, etc.), but, in schools, the opposite can be true. The cultural values espoused by the faculty, staff, and students greatly affect the climate, or atmosphere, that is present within the building.

School culture is important, both conceptually and concretely, because it can influence student academic achievement, employee satisfaction and productivity, parent engagement and commitment, and the support of the larger community.

The following section of this chapter illustrates selected conditions and characteristics of successful schools and schools that, while once failing their students and communities, turned themselves around and became effective. The research is slender and, in part, stems from sectors other than education (e.g., business and the police). However, it is worthy of attention.

Empirical Findings on Effective School Culture Components

Hassel and Hassel (2009a) posit that if we could bring schools from the brink of doom to stellar success, thousands of students would permanently benefit but that education typically has failed to recognize turnarounds as a means of school improvement, primarily because they have been tried rarely in education and studied even less. Those that have analyzed case studies of turnarounds of all types and sectors, including schools, find great similarities in leadership characteristics and practices. Hassel and Hassel note that

> bad-to-great transformations require a point-guard leader who both drives key changes and deftly influences stakeholders to support and engage in

dramatic transformation. To be sure, staff help effect a turnaround, but the leader is the unapologetic driver of change in successful turnarounds. Effective turnaround leaders follow a formula of common actions that spur dramatic improvement. The actions interact to move the organization rapidly toward impressive, mission-determined results that influence stakeholders to support additional change. (Hassel & Hassel, 2009a, p. 23)

Although Hassel and Hassel (2009a) draw their lessons from cross-sectional studies of the Continental Airlines turnaround and the New York City Police Department success against crime, they suggest how school leaders might use similar techniques. One is to choose a few high-priority wins with visible payoffs and success to build momentum. In an elementary school, they suggest as a quick win that a principal might aim to raise reading scores to within one grade level of year-end goals for 90 percent of fifth graders by the end of the first semester, something they argue that high-poverty start-up schools have achieved. "Imagine the impact when teachers realize that the school need never again graduate a class of non-readers," Hassel and Hassel speculate (2009a). They also suggest "norm-busting," perhaps by bending school time-use norms. A principal might also replace some key leaders to help organize and drive change, transforming the culture by having staff capable of leading instructional change identified by student progress data, providing the principal with greater clarity regarding needed staff changes.

Successful turnaround leaders are focused, fearless "data hounds." They choose their initial goals based on rigorous analysis. They report key staff results visibly and often. All staff who participate in decision making are required to share periodic results in open-air sessions, shifting discussions from excuse making and blaming to problem solving (Hassel & Hassel, 2009b, p. 26).

LINK TO CASE STUDY 1

Case Study 1 describes the culture of Buchanan Middle School—a school with many rich traditions and strong historical roots, yet having recently undergone a relocation and currently facing the reality of a leadership change. Reflecting on your current school, in what ways does the school culture shape an individual's actions? In what ways is the established culture facilitating or impeding individual and collective progress?

Earlier, Duke (2005) studied 15 case studies of elementary school turn-arounds and found that in 10 of the 15 cases, the principal was replaced, and in all cases, the manner in which leadership was exercised was changed:

Among the facets of leadership style that changed as part of the turn-around process in the case study elementary schools were the following:
- Principal spending a great deal of time in classroom (4)
- Principal closely monitoring teachers to make certain new practices are implemented (3)
- Principal modeling good teaching practice and coaching teachers (3)
- Principal makes a point of being visible in school (3)
- Principal makes a point of being accessible (2)
- Principal is highly directive (1)
- Principal handles most disciplinary cases (1) (Duke, 2005, p. 8)

Duke also found that although there was no one particular principal leadership style, principals, after providing teaching staff additional training, took action to remove staff members who lacked the skills or desire to raise low-achieving student performance, transferring them, counseling them out of teaching, or encouraging retirement. This permitted new positions for highly specialized teachers.

Kowal and Hassel (2005) conducted a thorough literature review at the time about turning around low-performing schools with new leaders and staff, reviewing both cross-industry research compared to incremental-change research and school, noneducation, and change leadership. They also interviewed national experts on school turnarounds. They suggest that turnarounds may be even more challenging in schools than in other social institutions:

While a school's failure has serious consequences for it students, only rarely does chronic failure have similar existence-threatening consequences for the school and its staff (Walshe, Harvey, Hyde, & Pandit, 2004). . . . "Failure" has historically had a much more complex definition in public schools than in business. . . . Practical and political challenges to turnarounds are more likely in public schools than in the private sector. Public school turnarounds are generally externally motivated while most for-profit turnarounds initiate somewhere within the organization. The external impetus in a school turnaround may affect school stakeholders' commitment to the change. (Walshe et al., 2004, pp. 3–4)

They also find the existing knowledge of turnaround research limited:

The evidence is strong that a school's leader makes a big difference in student learning in all school settings. However, understanding of the characteristics that distinguish high-performing school leaders from the rest is very limited. In addition, no research yet describes how the characteristics of high-performing leaders differ in emerging school contexts such as start-up and turnaround schools. A large body of research and theoretical writing explores school leadership in general, and some of this may apply to aspects of turnaround school leadership. However, no school leader research yet provides a model of school leadership that is

- validated, or has been proved to accurately describe what distinguishes high performers from the rest, eliminating items that are appealing but inconsequential and including items that may not be intuitive from limited observations;
- limited to characteristics that describe the person not the job; and
- detailed enough on those characteristics that districts may use it for accurate selection of high-performing leaders.

To the extent that the existing school leader research is useful for understanding high-performing school leaders in general, it lacks any studies that describe the distinguishing characteristics of school leaders who are very successful in a *turnaround* situation specifically. . . . No high-quality research has been conducted to clarify the competencies that distinguish successful school turnaround leaders from those who are moderately successful or unsuccessful. (Kowal & Hassel, 2005, pp. 17–18)

In "What Does It Take to Transform a School?," a report prepared for the Wallace Foundation by Public Agenda, Johnson (2007) surveyed turnaround principals to discover what successful "turnaround" principals actually do and what skills they need. She discovered that principals who are "transformers" have a clear vision for their schools and a can-do attitude that enables them to get past obstacles versus "copers" who seem overwhelmed by the challenges and have difficulty prioritizing teaching and learning. The transformers, who were often formerly vice principals, created a culture in which each child could learn: devoting the majority of their efforts to evaluating, coaching, and supporting their teachers; walking the halls to stay in touch with what was going on in the classrooms; reviewing data on student performance to set goals, analyze problems, and reallocate resources; becoming "a turnaround specialist" who seizes control of an underperforming school, often replacing staff and establishing new rules with a firm hand. Johnson also found that money, in the form of higher salaries and signing bonuses, would help attract and retain transforming principals.

Brinson, Kowal, and Hassel (2008) found that the research on turnarounds was sparse, particularly beyond merely replacing the school principal. They asked what must happen in a turnaround situation for it to succeed, what actions the new principal must take, and what the linkage between those actions and improved student learning might be. They found 14 leader actions that were associated with successful school turnarounds:

1. Collect and analyze data

2. Make action plan based on data

3. Concentrate on big, fast payoffs in year one

4. Implement practices even if requiring deviation from norms or rules

5. Require all staff to change ineffective practices

6. Implement necessary staff changes

7. Concentrate on successful tactics; discard the ineffective

8. Report progress but focus on high goals

9. Communicate a positive vision

10. Help staff personally feel problems

11. Gain support of key influencers

12. Silence critics with quick success

13. Measure and report progress often

14. Require all decision makers to share data and participate in problem solving

The Institute of Education Sciences' *Turning Around Chronically Low-Performing Schools: A Practice Guide* (Herman et al., 2008) defines turnaround schools as meeting two criteria:

First, they began

- as chronically poor performers—with a high proportion of their students (generally 20 percent or more) failing to meet state standards of proficiency in mathematics or reading as defined under No Child Left Behind over two or more consecutive years.

Second,

- they showed substantial gains in student achievement in a short time (no more than three years). Examples of substantial gains in achievement are reducing by at least 10 percentage points the proportion of students failing to meet state standards for proficiency in mathematics or reading, showing similarly large improvements in other measures of academic performance (such as lowering the dropout rate by 10 percentage points or more), or improving overall performance on standardized mathematics or reading tests by an average of 10 percentage points (or about 0.25 standard deviations). (Herman et al., 2008, pp. 4–5)

In addition, the IES practice guide only included case study research for those turnaround schools that performed better than expected from their demographics, which are "beating the odds" schools, 10 case studies that looked at turnaround practices at 35 schools, 21 at the elementary level (Herman et al., 2008, pp. 4–5).

The guide identifies four practices unique to "beating the odds" schools, followed by selected recommendations for school principals:

Recommendation 1: Signal the need for dramatic change with strong leadership.

A change in leadership practices in the school is essential. Because the current school leader may be enmeshed in past strategies, installing a new principal can signal change. The case studies on school turnarounds have numerous instances of new principals being catalysts for change. Teachers often cited the new principal as the motivating force.

Recommendation 2: Maintain a consistent focus on improving instruction.

Turnaround schools need to examine student achievement data to identify gaps and weaknesses in student learning. Principals can establish a data leader or data teams to organize and lead the effort. They can examine student learning through standards-based assessments and classroom assessments. Using the state assessments or other measures aligned with the state standards helps ensure that the progress in learning will result in higher achievement on high-stakes tests. School personnel can also look at data on factors that contribute to or impede student learning, such as attendance, discipline, and fiscal expenditures.

The school leader should become the instructional leader and be highly visible in classrooms. Strong instructional leadership shows the importance of strengthening instruction that is aligned to standards, curricula, and assessments and guided by ongoing data analysis of both achievement and nonachievement outcomes. The principal needs to set an example, lead the effort, and maintain vigilance toward the targeted, measurable goals.

Professional development should be based on analyses of achievement and instruction and differentiated for teacher needs and the subject areas targeted for instructional improvement.

Recommendation 3: Make visible improvements early in the school turnaround process (quick wins).

Having set goals for the turnaround, school leaders should identify one or two that build on the school's needs and strengths, are important to staff, and can be achieved quickly.

School leaders should consider strategies that minimize dependence on others for decisions or financial support.

One goal that a school may set for a quick win is to change the way it uses time—change that can be pursued quickly, with immediate effects on instruction.

Establishing a safe and orderly school environment is another quick win.

Recommendation 4: Build a committed staff.

The school leader should assess the strengths and weaknesses of the staff and identify staff members who are not fully committed to the turnaround efforts.

The school leader should redeploy staff members who offer valuable skills but are not effective in their current role and bring in new staff with specialized skills and competencies for specific positions, such as intervention or reading specialists.

The school leader should replace staff members who resist the school turnaround efforts. (Herman et al., 2008, pp. 8–9)

Goldring, Huff, May, and Camburn (2008) also found that rather than individual attributes distinguishing principals, only contextual conditions predicted how principals allocated their attention across their major realms of responsibility, although the study did not examine how leaders and principal practices related to school outcomes. Marks and Nance (2007) also found that different accountability contexts differentially affected principals' influence and that the principals' influence in both the supervisory and instructional domains is strongly related to that of teachers' active participation in decision making.

Distilling What Matters Operationally

Research results, logic, craft knowledge, and examined professional experience suggest that effective school culture is characterized by six crucial learning conditions. These are conditions that by themselves may be insufficient to guarantee elevated student achievement, but they appear to comprise a set of necessary instructionally related components.

Figure 1.7 displays these crucial cultural components and aligns them with operational levers upon which a leader can rely for implementation.

Figure 1.7   Operational Levers and Key Components of an Effective School Culture

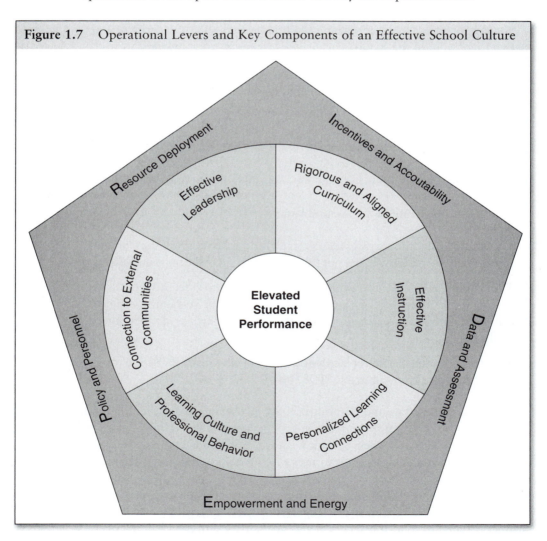

One way to view this figure is to see the circularly displayed six desired components as a portion of the "vision" that should characterize an effective school. The next chapter describes and analyzes these components. Then, remaining chapters explain each of the five operational levers in detail.

Figure 1.8 provides a contrasting illustration of selected characteristics that distinguish effective from ineffective schools and school culture.

Figure 1.8	Comparison of School Characteristics in Effective and Ineffective Schools	
Characteristic	*Effective Schools*	*Ineffective Schools*
Teacher professional development	Opportunity to advance classroom practice	No impact on teaching and learning
Student discipline	Students know of, but do not feel the need to test or violate, school rules	System overwhelmed with discipline problems
Human expressions	Smiles, hugs, laughter	Sighs of frustration
Teacher attitude toward job	Want to be the best in their field	Want to clock in, clock out, and receive a paycheck
School appearance	Welcoming, bright, cheerful, well organized, reflects attitudes and achievements	Unwelcoming, sloppy, dirty, decrepit, reflects attitudes
Adult and adult-student relationships	Collaborative, friendly	Tense, antagonistic
Performance expectations	High for everybody	Don't want to get hopes up
Feelings about learning	Enjoyable and important activity	Tedious and useless; chore
Self-confidence	Failure is not an option	I/We can't do anything right
Self-efficacy	Any facet of the school can be changed	No matter what is done, things will never change
Day-to-day social environment	Friendly, calm, people work together	Tense, chaotic, everything is a battle
Leadership	Leads by example and exhortation	Demands that everybody follows
Collaboration	Two heads are better than one	Everyone for him or herself
New ideas	There's always room for improvement	Not worth the effort; the current system is fine

Source: Compiled by the authors

PULLING IT ALL TOGETHER FOR DISCUSSION

The following cultural prototypes are provided for illustrative purposes to demonstrate to a reader that there is more than one way a school can be organized in order to implement what is known to be effective. These three prototypes embody the previously reviewed visionary elements or threshold conditions that, as best they can presently be identified or deduced, are crucial to the operation of an effective school. The following three prototypical schools are not ideologically or empirically pure. Their distinguishing characteristics and components can be mixed and matched to form hybrids.

"Modern management schools" are characterized by conditions such as the following:

- High-performance orientation visible in symbols and adult language
- Emphasis given to continuous improvement
- Formal curriculum and curriculum structure and sequence emphasized
- Routine reliance by teachers and administrators upon student achievement data as a formative tool for guiding and individualizing instruction
- Formal curriculum focused and interpreted narrowly
- Student performance data relied upon by management for the supervision and evaluation of teachers
- Heavy reliance upon scripting and relative lack of teacher instructional discretion
- Reliance upon technology (computer-assisted instruction)
- Time orientation heavy in the present and accomplishment seen as urgent priority and attention given to efficient use of student and teacher time
- Professional development tightly tied to teachers' perceived instructional deficiencies
- Performance incentives in place, both collective and individual
- Evidence of competitive orientation (e.g., rankings, ratings, comparisons)

"Achievement schools" are characterized by conditions such as the following:

- "Charter" from community or from history to pursue high achievement
- Organized around and frequent visible reference to a unifying theme (e.g., science or occupational training) or mission (e.g., International Baccalaureate)
- Attention and visibility given to symbols of school purpose and achievement (e.g., award ceremonies, kudos, attention to exemplary performers)

- Processes, as opposed to immediate outcomes, and traditions seen as important
- High integration of formal and informal curriculum
- Broad interpretation given to purposes of schooling
- Informal curriculum given great weight
- High future orientation and time seen as a continuum; persistence valued
- Intentional fostering of sense of elitism or separatism
- Minimal hierarchy in administration
- Attention to fostering and sustaining a sense of community
- Likely formal links to alumni or networks of similar schools

"Leadership-dependent schools" are characterized by conditions such as the following:

- School autonomy in selection, reward, and assignment of teachers and staff
- Broad discretion at the school level in resource allocation
- Hierarchical administrative structure
- Strong sense of individual school (as opposed to school system)
- Greater attention to outcomes than processes
- Highly visible leadership

CONCLUSION

In this chapter, a reader is introduced to the concepts of culture and school culture: their definitions, descriptors, and traits, the outcomes that often result in successful schools, and steps to take when initiating a change in a school's culture.

It is important to remember that there is no such thing as a perfect school culture, but there are a number of tangible traits that tend to set successful schools apart from less successful schools. Positive relationships, individual and collective confidence, a sense of efficacy, high performance expectations, and continuous learning lead to a positive community in which students learn more, and innovative strategies may lead students to love learning. By thoroughly describing how they want a school to think, act, behave, and feel and informing staff members that they play a crucial role in the process, it is possible for a school leader to gain the commitment necessary to transform the culture in a school.

QUESTIONS FOR DISCUSSION

1. When somebody refers to the culture of a school, to what types of things are they referring?

2. What are some characteristics that differentiate the culture of a successful school from the culture of a less successful school?

3. Have you ever been in a school that you felt was very successful? What types of things did you notice while you were there?

4. Have you ever been in a school that you felt was quite unsuccessful? What types of things did you notice while you were there?

5. If you became the principal of a school, what facet of the school's culture would you want to address first? Why?

6. If you should inherit an ineffective school, and desire to alter the culture, what steps might research results suggest you take?

7. If you were successful in establishing a positive culture in your school, how might you expect the outcomes to differ as a result?

REFERENCES

Bolman, L., & Deal, T. (1993). *The path to school leadership: A portable mentor.* Newbury Park, CA: Corwin.

Brinson, D., Kowal, J., & Hassel, B. C. (2008). *School turnarounds: Actions and results.* Lincoln, IL: Center on Innovation & Improvement. Retrieved from http://www.centerii.org/survey/

Deal, T., & Peterson, K. (1990). *The principal's role in shaping school culture.* Washington, DC: Office of Educational Research and Improvement.

Duke, D. (2005). The turnaround principal: High stakes leadership. *Principal, 84*(1), 12–23.

Goldring, E., Huff, J., May, H., & Camburn, E. (2008). School context and individual characteristics: What influences principal practice? *Journal of Educational Administration, 46*(3), 332–352.

Hassel, E. A., & Hassel, B. C. (2009a). The big U-turn: How to bring schools from the brink of failure to stellar success. *Education Next, 9*(1), 21–27.

Hassel, E. A., & Hassel, B. C. (2009b). Try, try again: How to triple the number of fixed failing schools without getting any better at fixing schools. *Public Impact.* Retrieved from http://www.publicimpact.com/try-try-again/

Herman, R., Dawson, P., Dee, T., Greene, J., Maynard, R., Redding, S., et al. (2008). *Turning around chronically low-performing schools: A practice guide (NCEE #2008–4020).*

Washington, DC: National Center for Education Evaluation and Regional Assistance, Institute of Education Sciences, U.S. Department of Education. Retrieved from http://ies.ed.gov/ncee/wwc/publications/practiceguides

Johnson, J. (2007, March). *A mission of the heart: What does it take to transform a school?* The Wallace Foundation Public Agenda.

Kowal, J. M., & Hassel, E. (2005). *School restructuring options under No Child Left Behind: What works when? Turnarounds with new leaders and staff.* Naperville, IL: Learning Point Associates.

Marks, H. M., & Nance, J. P. (2007). Contexts of accountability under systemic reform: Implications for principal influence on instruction and supervision. *Educational Administration Quarterly, 43*(1), 3–37.

National Commission on Excellence in Education. (1983). *A nation at risk: The imperative for educational reform.* Washington, DC: U.S. Government Printing Office.

No Child Left Behind Act, Public Law 107–110, 115 Statutes 1425. (January 8, 2002).

Rousseau, D. (1990). Quantitative assessment of organizational culture: The case for multiple measures. In B. Schneider (Ed.), *Frontiers in industrial and organizational psychology: Vol. 3* (pp. 153–192). San Francisco: Jossey-Bass.

Schein, E. H. (1992). *Organizational culture and leadership* (2nd ed.). San Francisco: Jossey-Bass.

Walshe, K., Harvey, G., Hyde, P., & Pandit, N. (2004, August). Organizational failure and turnaround: Lessons for public services from the for-profit sector. *Public Money & Management, 24*(4), 201–208.

Case Study 2: Possible Reform at Washington High School

How Far Can a Productive Culture Stretch?

Otto Jungherr had been the leader of Washington High School for 20 years. He had been its founding principal and was now preparing to turn over the leadership reins to one of his hand-picked, highly trusted, experienced-tested assistant principals, Gordon Lal.

Washington was located in a large and sophisticated city, the center for a huge and diverse metropolitan area. It was a large school, both in its geographic footprint and its enrollment. It had three thousand students distributed over three grade levels. The school occupied six acres of prime land in one of the city's most desirable residential areas. The physical facility, even if two decades old, was impressive. The school was perched on the top of a hill and could be seen from a great distance. In addition to its three-story academic buildings, it had a large performance-oriented auditorium, an Olympic swimming pool, a new three-thousand-seat basketball pavilion, and a football stadium seating 15,000. Its architecture was Palladian and imposing. Its white paint made it gleam in the sunlight. Its appearance was inspirational.

Washington had long been known for its students' academic and athletic prowess. Its graduates routinely were accepted at the nation's top-ranked and most selective public and private colleges and universities and the nation's military academies. Moreover, in football and basketball, both men's and women's, it was a powerhouse, favored to be top ranked year after year. Its athletes regularly were sought by colleges, and its coaches were lionized and continually being elevated into the college ranks.

The school's enrollment was large because its attendance area covered a great deal of the city. Consequently, it drew upon middle-class families from virtually every ethnic and cultural segment. Its students came from the homes of professionals, business executives, academics, successful shop owners, and expert artisans and craftsmen. Mean family income was high, but so was the diversity. White, Black, and Asian and Pacific Island students had long attended the school and had long gotten along. Muslim and Hispanic students were relatively new to the school but were increasingly common. Racial tension was seldom seen at Washington High School. However, academic and athletic competition was a long-valued and routine part of the school's culture.

Otto Jungherr started his public school teaching career as a Latin instructor. After 10 years of successful teaching, he began to climb the administrative ladder. He had been

---

Note: This case study, as with others associated with other chapters, is about an actual school, actual people, and actual conditions. Nothing is fabricated. All cases are about situations school leaders routinely encounter. However, in each instance, names of people, schools, and locations have been altered to ensure confidentiality.

Washington's first principal, and his powerful personality had indelibly colored the school. He was the son of a German immigrant. His family had scrimped financially so that he could become well educated. He was proud of his German heritage, well informed regarding the rigor and curriculum of classical European secondary schools, and it was in this image he had created Washington High School. Academic and athletic excellence had enabled him to succeed as an American, and he was intent on creating an environment where these qualities would enable other students to succeed also, regardless of their family background.

Washington High School had acquired a rich set of traditions and a national reputation under Jungherr. Students wore uniforms, even though it was a public school. They were simple uniforms, but they clearly suggested that to attend Washington was to be part of something larger than yourself.

Teachers always dressed professionally. They treated students with great respect and civility. However, teachers were well inducted and thoroughly indoctrinated that they were authority figures, not friends, when it came to students.

The halls during passing periods were lively and full of animated students. However, there was certainly no excessive roughhousing, and violence was just not a factor. Classes were 50 minutes in length, and instruction was expected to begin immediately. No class was released early. Excuses for leaving class during instruction were exceptional.

Friday had a shortened class schedule, only 40 minutes per class. However, the time saved was devoted to an all-school assembly concentrating on either a musical or dramatic performance, an award service, or a lecture about a contemporary topic, be it current events, the economy, culture, or technology.

A student honor society, known as the Eagles, was responsible for student conduct and hall monitoring. Eagles also oversaw all athletic events and assemblies. The Eagles handled student conduct well.

There was a Washington High School Student Honor Code that was highly publicized and heavily reinforced by the school's administration and faculty. Classroom or instructional infractions, such as suspicions of plagiarism or cheating, were handled by a combination of faculty and student Honors Court. Punishment for proven violations was severe, including having to repeat a course and notification on one's transcript.

The Washington High School curriculum featured solid three-year subject requirements for English literature, U.S. history, civics and world history, foreign language, mathematics (through calculus), and science. (Latin was offered, and the classes regularly filled.) Advanced-placement courses were offered throughout all of these areas. In addition, physical education was a constant requirement, and a variety of art, music, and drama courses were all offered as electives. There was a full slate of men's and women's athletic teams and additional activities such as a school marching band, orchestra, drama club, glee club, chess club, and a great deal of community service. All students were expected to partake of the academic curriculum and to engage in an extracurricular afterschool activity. Technology was woven into the instructional program in virtually every course.

Washington was a comprehensive high school. That is, it operated three curricular tracks, one for the college bound, one for vocationally oriented students, and another rather amorphous track known as the "general curriculum." The latter seemed oriented mainly toward a mixture of the liberal arts and business courses.

Washington High School teachers tended to be among the more senior in the district. There was always a waiting list for any subject matter opening. However, principal Jungherr had made a practice of mixing youth with experience in the teacher force he employed. He spent an enormous amount of time selecting and overseeing teachers. He favored subject matter master's degrees and some amount of prior teaching experience elsewhere. Formal credentials, other than for specific subject areas, were minimally important, while Jungherr seemed to specialize in finding an unusual blend of personalities. The school appeared to be a virtual Noah's Ark of personality types. Jungherr wanted it this way. He thought that the adolescents who attended Washington High School would benefit from seeing a variety of adult role models, one or more of whom might well be attractive to a youngster and perhaps provide lifelong inspiration.

Finally, Washington High School had a large and active alumni society. Many of the school's graduates had moved on to become Hollywood celebrities, Olympic participants, professional athletes, prize-winning scientists and researchers, highly visible public officials, business executives, and successful entertainers. The school's Hall of Fame, and the first-floor-corridor gallery of their photographs, was composed of individuals that would have made most any college proud. Moreover, many of these graduates were generous in their financial support of the school, as reflected in a new gym, new music auditorium, new band uniforms, and so on. Other schools in the district were understandably envious. The Friday assemblies, planning for which Jungherr personally oversaw, were regularly populated by one of these successful alumni returning for a personal appearance and an inspirational presentation.

Jungherr had overseen the formation and expansion of Washington High School. He was instrumental in its success. He was widely recognized as one of the most successful school principals in America. He was frequently lauded in person, by the profession, and in the press. He was understandably proud of his accomplishment.

Still, a question remained. Was Jungherr Washington High School? Would it survive his retirement and replacement? Could his successor walk in his shoes, or was Jungherr, or at least his reputation, bigger than life?

Jungherr was imposing, not only by virtue of his towering physical presence but also because of his stunning reputation. To be in his company was to experience a living educational administration icon. Jungherr consciously contributed further to this dominant sense of his presence by furnishing his office in a manner that prominently displayed his many awards, honorary degrees, trappings of authority, and photographs of him in the company of high-level luminaries from all walks of life. Jungherr had accomplished much, and he was not bashful about displaying his success.

Lal was quite a contrast, at least by way of appearance, personality, pedigree, and past experience. He also was far more modest in his demeanor. He is Polynesian. He had migrated to the United States during the 1960s with his parents. He was physically quite fit, had been a college athlete, and worked diligently to retain his athletic demeanor. He had served in the United States Navy.

Jungherr had liked all that he saw in Lal, and he admired his keen, Ivy League–honed intellect, organizational and political savvy, and analytic capacity. He and Lal often engaged with each other after-hours by reading passages from Greek classics and discussing their meaning for modern times. They held each other in reciprocal high regard.

Jungherr was bombastic. Lal, even if forceful, was quiet. Jungherr often had an answer before there was a question or a solution before he knew the problem. Lal was a good listener and almost always succeeded in engaging others in striving to define the problem and searching for a solution. Jungherr micromanaged fiercely. Lal was artful at delegating. Jungherr had a spontaneity about him that was good and bad. He celebrated success quickly and criticized failure just as rapidly. Jungherr was charismatic and magnetic, even if bullying. Lal was calm and poised, even when he was obviously happy. Jungherr praised others lavishly, sometimes too lavishly. Lal was more restrained, but he left no doubt when he was pleased by the performance of another.

Gordon Lal was honored to have been selected to follow Otto Jungherr. He had served a six-year apprentice as assistant principal under Jungherr. He knew Washington High School in and out, its facilities, its personnel, its curriculum, its various parental and public constituencies, and its students. He thought he was ready. He admired and was grateful to his mentor; however, he was not sure that he wanted everything to stay the same.

Lal knew the differences between him and his predecessor. He was comfortable with himself. He was happy to have the baton passed to him. However, he was reasonably sure that some changes were needed.

Here are some of the changes he was contemplating:

- Lal was not persuaded that student uniforms added to the success of the school. He was open to eliminating this policy.
- He thought the curriculum was outmoded. He believed that many of Washington's incoming students would benefit more if the academic requirements were decreased and a greater range of vocational and technical courses were offered.
- The weekly assemblies struck Lal as overkill and undertaken more to satisfy Jungherr's ego than educate students.
- The school's Hall of Fame, in Lal's perception, seemed to celebrate the wrong thing. It made it appear that unless you achieved absolute stardom you were a failure.
- The classic Greek model of excellence in both mind and body seemed somewhat outmoded in the twenty-first century. Lal wondered if less attention should be given to athletics, while still maintaining a concern for physical conditioning and nutrition, and more attention given to modern technological applications.
- Heavy reliance upon the Eagles to maintain order and student discipline struck Lal as placing too great a responsibility upon students to police their peers.

- Lal was fearful that the vaunted Washington High School Honor Code was being honored more in the breach than in reality, and he wanted to examine its continuing relevance and practical utility.
- Jungherr's blend of old and new teachers seemed to Lal to be alienating to students. He wanted to alter the blend to favor a larger infusion of younger teachers.
- The Washington High School Alumni Society seemed too powerful to Lal. Why cede so much influence to a group no longer vested in the outcomes of the school and out of touch with its present-day student body?
- Lal questioned the overwhelming didactic or direct instructional approach and overwhelming use of lectures by teachers at Washington High School. He thought a heavier reliance upon constructivist learning principles, more student engagement in projects, and greater reliance upon experiential learning was probably the way to go.
- Lal thought the school could be improved by relying upon teachers to make more decisions. He had read about distributed leadership, and it had made sense to him. He and his assistant principals could not be expected to be experts about instruction in every content field. Department chairs and teacher leaders could usefully supplement administrators' knowledge, and he was moved to delegate greater authority to the school's teachers.
- Finally, Lal was sure that his office should change and become less of a temple in which others could worship him and more of a place for listening and engaging.

FOR DISCUSSION

1. What do you think about Washington High School? How much is it like your high school? Would you like to have attended Washington in your youth?
2. How would you characterize the culture of Washington High School under principal Jungherr? What is good? What is less than good?
3. Is the Washington High School tripartite curriculum—college, vocational, and general studies—suited for the twenty-first century?
4. Is Washington High School a cult of personality? In your judgment, can its current culture survive after the departure of principal Jungherr?
5. Did Jungherr groom the right successor?
6. What do you think of Lal's possible changes? Is he on the right track, or would you urge him to move slowly?
7. What degree of evidence exists favoring Lal's vision of how Washington High School should operate?
8. Do you think Lal is endangering or improving Washington High School's culture?
9. Should Lal realize that if something is "not broken, then don't fix it"?
10. Is Lal interested in change for change's sake, so that he can put his personal imprimatur on the school, or does he genuinely believe that the school should be changed to be more effective?
11. How far can a school's culture be stretched before it is a different kind of school?

CHAPTER 2

Components of a High-Performing School Culture

In this chapter a reader will learn about the following:

- Forces influencing the construction and enhancement of a high-performing school culture
- Key components of an effective school culture
- How leaders communicate a vision and gain commitment for a successful school culture

ELCC STANDARDS

ELCC standards addressed in this chapter include the following:

- 1.1—Develop a vision of learning
- 1.2—Articulate a vision
- 1.4—Steward a vision
- 2.1—Promote a positive school culture
- 4.1—Collaborate with families and other community members
- 5.2—Act fairly
- 6.1—Understand the larger context

INTRODUCTION

As school leaders set out to establish, or reestablish, a school culture and to render it productive of high student academic achievement, they should be prepared for a complicated challenge. Building, or rebuilding, a productive school culture is certainly possible, and individual leaders and their cooperating colleagues frequently accomplish this goal. Indeed, the purpose of this book is to suggest means by which this end can be reached. However, as described in the case studies introducing each chapter in this book, establishing a high-performing school culture is not an easy goal to achieve, and there are strong resistant forces with which to contend.

This chapter first highlights the major forces that influence schools and that school leaders must contend with when shaping a school culture. With so many forces impacting schools, it is no surprise the prevailing condition is that forces favoring schooling's status quo usually outweigh those favoring different arrangements. Thus, the fundamental challenge for a leader and cooperating colleagues is to overcome inertia and passive opposition and create a critical mass of support for reform. This chapter also describes key components of an effective school culture and suggests how school leaders can articulate a vision and gain commitment for a high-performing school culture.

FORCES INFLUENCING THE CONSTRUCTION AND ENHANCEMENT OF A HIGH-PERFORMING SCHOOL CULTURE

American public education has a proud past and a potentially productive future. However, schools in need of change are presently faced with daunting challenges. As explained in Chapter 1, no nation has ever before been faced, as is the United States now, with determining how to educate a large and unusually diverse population to a high standard. Unfortunately, there is no easy roadmap or set of known silver bullets for those charged with this change. As such, inventive and strategic leadership will be one of the necessary reform tools.

The challenge of school reform and constructing a high-performing school culture is complicated for multiple reasons: (1) the high degree of technical uncertainty that characterizes the core technology of instruction and schooling, (2) the spectrum of proliferating public purposes that continually confound issues, create confusion, and constrain the constructive operation of schools, (3) the plethora of politically protected privileged interests that oppose redeployment of education resources, (4) the formidable force of organizational inertia that schools, and the governmental systems in which they are embedded, regularly confront, and (5) an institutional outlook that has evolved from the public school luxury of a longstanding monopoly. These reform impediments are exacerbated by a sixth impediment, America's unusually high degree of decision-making decentralization. This is a structural condition that is sometimes dysfunctional in its effects on education. Figure 2.1 illustrates several of these forces and depicts their relationships to school culture.

Figure 2.1   Forces Influencing School Culture

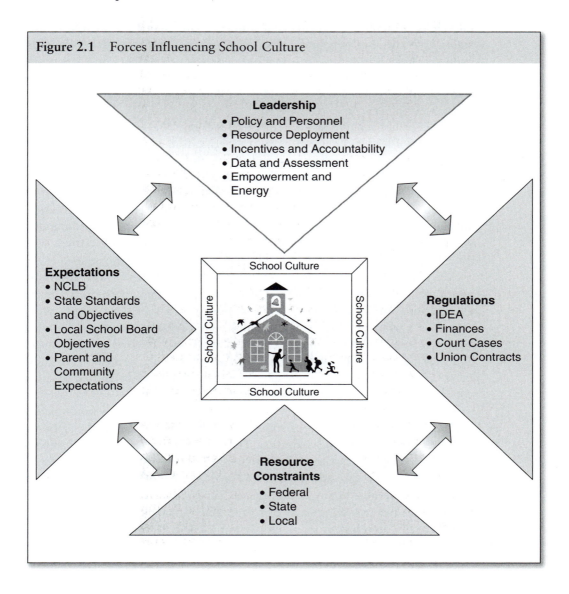

Expectations

Schools and school leaders are confronted with multiple, sometimes-competing expectations. These range from meeting adequate yearly progress targets specified by No Child Left Behind, to accomplishing the objectives outlined in state standards, to ensuring local school board priorities are achieved, all while attending to aspirations expressed by local parents and the surrounding school community. Some of these influences are formal and stem from substantial structural or chartered authority (e.g., superintendents, school boards, state and federal government education departments). Others may have little formal authority but may nevertheless exert substantial influence by virtue of resources they distribute or withhold (e. g, philanthropic foundations) or political capital they carry.

While complicated, these interactions are not necessarily fearsome. An adroit school leader often can harness external forces, shape them toward a collective purpose, and take advantage of their financial capital, organizational energy, and political momentum to gain significant improvements for his or her school, school district, or other agency. Nothing of what follows is intended to derail, dissuade, or discourage a reform-oriented reader. School change is possible. However, it is more probable if one has a realistic understanding of the obstacles a leader likely will have to confront. Armed with understanding, a reform leader can construct countervailing strategies.

America expects a great deal of its schools. Many of these expectations are admirable, yet there is a problem. The problem is that there are so many expectations, and often there are few priorities assigned to them. What counts? To what purposes should schools give the most attention? To what should the most resources be allocated? What should be used as the bases of educator performance reward systems? Can schools accomplish all of these tasks? Should not some of these expectations deliberately be shifted to other societal institutions?

When confronted by overwhelming numbers of impossible or even conflicting goals, institutions retreat to predictable, but ultimately dysfunctional, responses. These responses protect the institution. They do not necessarily accomplish public goals. Among the responses are (1) to become operationally immobilized with the prospect of having to address such an extended array of goals, many of which may be unachievable in any circumstances, (2) dysfunctional conflict, (3) platitudinization and trivialization of purposes, and (4) cannibalization, devouring themselves by devoting resources mostly to the concerns of employees and self-interested constituents.

Immobilization

Often when overburdened with multiple purposes, institutions may in actu-
ality lose all purpose. An institution may be so distracted by all it is expected
to do that it fails to concentrate on what it can do and accomplishes little.
Amidst such booming, buzzing confusion and conflict regarding purpose, the
system simply becomes rigidly immobilized, adhering to dysfunctional internally generated rules, and accomplishes little or nothing.

Dysfunctional Conflict

A condition of overspecified expectations can trigger another kind of dysfunctional dynamic. A swirling vortex of protagonists, each in support of his
or her own self-proclaimed preferred purpose, could trigger waves of conflict
that can engulf a school and distract faculty and staff from fulfilling academic goals.

Platitudinization

One can sometimes read school mottos or even mission statements that are
abstract to the point of being meaningless: "Our school educates the whole
child," "Our school facilitates development of every child to his or her maximum
potential," or "We will do whatever it takes." These statements do not lend
themselves to measurement and perhaps do not even come close to reality.
However, such empty bromides sound good, may placate mindless community
members, and thereby defend the school from constituents, many or at least
some of whom hold conflicting preferences.

Cannibalization

Employees and other immediate beneficiaries of the system can co-opt the
institution for their own self-interests. If there is little agreement upon what
should be accomplished, then any accomplishments, almost no matter how
trivial, can be proclaimed to be successful. This phenomenon is sometimes visible when a school is proposed to be closed for a lack of student academic
progress by its defenders voicing dismay or claiming that a grave injustice is
about to take place, or by enrollees' parents claiming to be satisfied, or by some
other interest group attesting to the school's success.

The lesson for would-be education reformers, those desirous of creating or
re-creating a school culture oriented toward elevated academic achievement,

is that one should be confident in one's purposes and, just as important, be able to explain and justify them to others who hold different views.

Resource Constraints

Figure 2.2 displays a pie chart capturing the portion of total U.S. K–12 spending contributed by each of the three levels of government (federal, state, and local). What is evident is that the federal government is by far the junior revenue-contributing partner when contrasted to state and local governments.

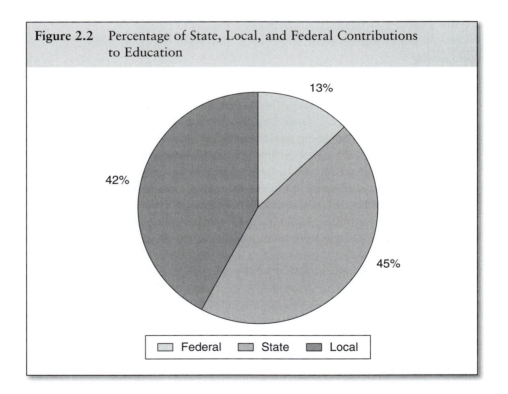

Figure 2.2   Percentage of State, Local, and Federal Contributions to Education

However, these contribution proportions should not easily deceive a reader. Federal regulations for the use of categorical revenues ensure that the practical influence of federal funding far outstrips its actual dollar contributions to operation. One need only be conscious of No Child Left Behind (NCLB) as a dominant influence over the nation's education system, even if providing to local districts but a portion of the resources expended. What revenues it contributes are generated by the federal government, principally through personal and corporate income tax proceeds.

State-contributed revenues to school operation are usually generated through personal income tax receipts, sales taxes, or both. Locally, contributions stem principally from property tax receipts. On all levels, these resources are finite and impose constraints that impact schools.

Regulations

Because so much now is expected of the education system, because the stakes have become so high, because resources invested are now so vast, and because the technology of instruction has become so complicated, the policy and regulatory environment imposed through government, the judicial system, and clients on schools and school leaders has intensified. This regulatory environment stems from actions of both executive and legislative branch officials and the judicial system. It emanates from local, state, and federal governments. An education leader ignores this regulatory mosaic at great peril. It is part of the knowledge base one needs to perform effectively in today's complicated education context.

A critical regulatory influence that school leaders must consider is our nation's system of laws and legal procedures. Legal matters are particularly important in shaping the landscape of school leadership because K–12 education is lawfully compelled everywhere in the United States. Once school compulsion is in play, an imposition upon the freedom of families and their children found in few other instances in American society, then the oversight and intensity of the court's interaction with the activity is elevated substantially.

Timid, or perhaps insufficiently informed, education leaders can mistakenly view the law and courts as constraints, narrowly concentrating only on the limits courts impose upon their authority and viewing laws as impediments to their otherwise legitimate need to change their organizations. Such a negative view is reinforced by the heavy presence of the law when it comes to elementary and secondary education. Because K–12 schooling is compelled by society, courts are quick to ensure that those subjected to this compulsion, namely students and parents, are fairly treated and protected when it comes to their fundamental liberties. A K–12 school administrator is influenced substantially more by an applicable body of law than, for example, is a postsecondary administrator or private-sector manager. However, going to college or working at Wal-Mart is a voluntary act. Going to elementary and secondary school is not an option open to individuals of school age in the United States.

Thus, through one set of lenses, courts and the law can be viewed as a restriction. However, a strategic leader must be confident that he or she is not simply hiding behind the skirts of the court, using the fear of law and litigation as pretexts for passivity. There are multiple conditions in which the law can be seen as a facilitator of, not simply an impediment to, change.

Taken together, elevated expectations, resource limitations, and a host of regulations all impart significant influence on school culture. However, within this context of constraint, leaders are able to exert their influence by drawing upon key levers of change to create and sustain a high-performing school culture. Figure 2.3 provides a model for how leaders affect the core goals of schooling.

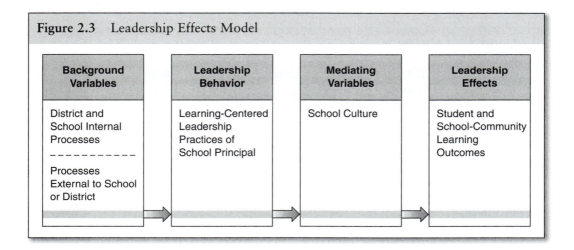

Figure 2.3   Leadership Effects Model

Background Variables	Leadership Behavior	Mediating Variables	Leadership Effects
District and School Internal Processes ---------- Processes External to School or District	Learning-Centered Leadership Practices of School Principal	School Culture	Student and School-Community Learning Outcomes

The model in Figure 2.3 displays the important role that school culture plays in mediating the influence of leaders on desired student and school outcomes. The diagram also highlights how important it is for school leaders to intentionally craft a high-performing school culture, as the school culture is an important vehicle that enables a leader to affect desired outcomes.

> **LINK TO CASE STUDY 2**
>
> Case Study 2 presents two very different administrator personas and leadership styles. How has the school culture mediated the influence of the principal in your current school? How might the future principal in Case Study 2, Lal, need to intentionally reconstruct elements of the culture to facilitate his vision for Washington High?

COMPONENTS OF AN EFFECTIVE SCHOOL CULTURE

Central to a school leader's success is his or her ability to focus on two goals amidst numerous other responsibilities: (a) ensuring high-quality teaching and instruction and (b) creating a culture of learning that both challenges and supports students. This section of the text reviews the primary components that the literature has identified as essential conditions for school leaders to address in pursuing the goals just listed. An effective school culture is characterized by an empirically validated set of core components regarding learning standards, instructional strategies, individualization, professional behavior, accountability, and parent and community engagement.

Schools succeed not because they adopt piecemeal efforts that address all of the just-listed dimensions but because they use coordinated, sustained practices that organize their collective activities around the pursuit of goals. Meaningful reforms are woven into a school's existing organization to create internally consistent and mutually reinforcing practices. As such, their success is explained by more than the simple sum of their parts.

Key elements of a high-performing school culture, aimed at elevating student performance, are described on the following pages. The underlying model, depicted in Figure 2.4, is drawn from essential conditions that research has captured when studying effective schools. However, it is important to emphasize that beyond the components themselves, school leaders must pay particular attention to the relationships between these components and the broader structural supports that facilitate their implementation in schools.

Figure 2.4   Key Elements of a High-Performing School Culture

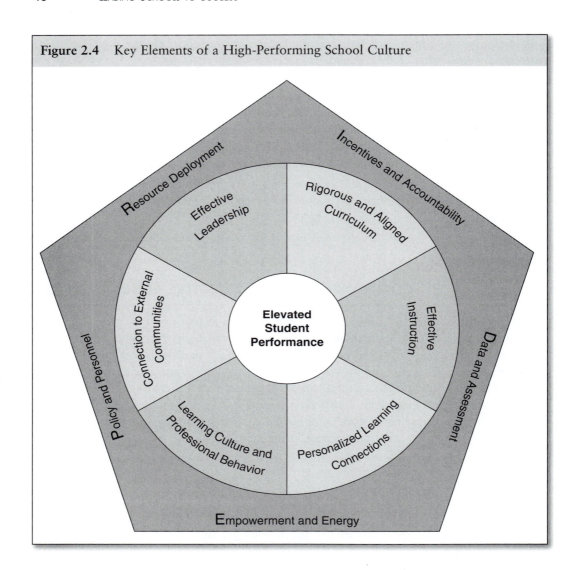

Rigorous and Aligned Curriculum

This component focuses on the content that schools provide in core academic subjects, and it includes both the topics that students cover as well as the cognitive skills they must demonstrate during each course. Effective school leaders ensure that teachers set specific standards and expectations to ensure that their students engage in complex content and demanding activities as they complete each class (Darling-Hammond, Ancess, & Susanna, 2002; Frome, 2001; Kemple, Herlihy, & Smith, 2005). Within the realm of ensuring a rigorous and aligned curriculum, it is important that school leaders ensure the following:

- Alignment of content with high standards for student learning. For example, in Chicago Public Schools, where teachers report purposely aligning their curriculum with state learning standards, researchers have found preliminary evidence that links these conditions to higher student test scores (Newmann, Smith, & Bryk, 2001).
- Coverage of ambitious content. For example, the "High Schools That Work" reform initiative requires that participating schools include college-preparatory math, science, and language courses for all students regardless of their academic plans (Frome, 2001).
- High cognitive demand on students to learn material. Researchers evaluating a Long Island, NY, district's effort to detrack its courses and make International Baccalaureate (IB) classes available to all students found that the number of IB examinations taken by students increased after detracking, and IB test scores remained stable as the program became more inclusive (Burris, Wiley, Welner, & Murphy, 2008).

It only makes sense that the more efficient an organization is, the greater the payoff will be from organizational efforts. In the case of schools, coherence between academic expectations (expressed in the standards and assessments) and educational experiences (expressed in the curriculum and instruction) is a primary mechanism to enhance efficiency. While it is important for a school leader to guide a school in articulating a mission, establishing challenging goals, and setting rigorous standards, these are essentially a proposed destination. Without ensuring that the curriculum and instruction are harnessed in a way to reach this destination, the goals and standards will only serve as a reminder of what might have been. As such, it is important that education leaders facilitate a high degree of alignment among the instructional program, the destination articulated in the standards, and the methods for assessing performance.

Figure 2.5 displays various levels of alignment that call for strategic education leadership. This figure highlights the need for both horizontal alignment, which ensures within-sector integration of activities, and vertical alignment, which ensures state, district, and school level initiatives inform each other.

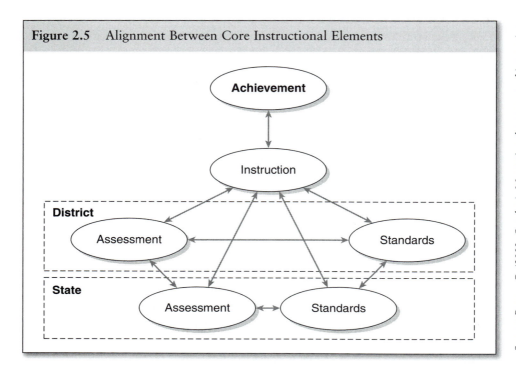

Figure 2.5   Alignment Between Core Instructional Elements

Source: Porter, C. (2002, October). Measuring the content of instruction: Uses in research and practice. *Educational Researcher, 31*(7), 13–14

Figure 2.6 provides another view of the benefit of alignment among key elements of the instructional program. For example, in many education organizations, there is a considerable discrepancy between what the formal curricular guide proposes and what is actually taught in classrooms. Further, it is possible that what is tested does not necessarily align with the curriculum that students are actually engaged in during classroom instruction.

School leaders and teachers are inundated with resources and suggestions regarding what needs to be taught in various subjects and at various grade levels. Yet, many school leaders do not know if teachers are teaching what is described in the content standards, if they are teaching what is in the textbooks, and if they teach in ways aligned with state testing.

When all is said and done, classroom teachers are the ultimate negotiators of what content is covered, how much time is devoted to particular topics, when and in what order material is taught, to what standards of achievement, and to which students. As such, it is imperative that education leaders have accurate information about these important classroom dynamics, including the degree to which there is overlap between what is taught at various grade levels, what is tested, and what the state and local standards require.

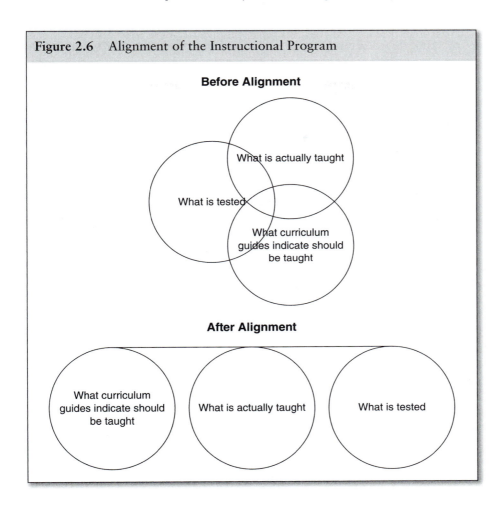

Figure 2.6   Alignment of the Instructional Program

Before Alignment

What is actually taught

What is tested

What curriculum guides indicate should be taught

After Alignment

What curriculum guides indicate should be taught

What is actually taught

What is tested

Effective Instruction

At the core of this component are the teaching strategies and assignments that teachers use to present their curriculum. These strategies are most effective when students use knowledge to solve problems, engage in simulations, or apply knowledge to new contexts (McLaughlin & Talbert, 1993; Wenglinsky, 2002, 2004). The past 30 years of cognitive development, neuroscience, and social psychology have generated a wealth of scientific information about human learning. The research report of the National Academy of Sciences, *How People Learn* (Bransford, Brown, & Cocking, 1999), draws upon this research and discusses the instructional implications of new insights in the realms of memory and the structure of knowledge, problem solving and reasoning, expert performance, met cognitive processes, and community participation. Specifically, these insights are synthesized into the *How People Learn* framework, and they have important implications for the design of learning environments.

Theoretical physics does not prescribe the design of a spacecraft, yet it does constrain the design of a successful interstellar vehicle. Similarly, a synthesis of all available learning theories provides no magic formula for the design of learning environments and experiences, yet it does constrain the design of effective ones. Fundamental tenets of contemporary learning theory assert that different kinds of learning goals require different pedagogical approaches and that the design of learning environments can be enhanced by insights about the processes of learning, transfer, and competent performance. Those processes, and the core competency of schooling, in turn are affected by the degree to which learning environments are student centered, knowledge centered, assessment centered, and community centered. Together, these four components comprise the *How People Learn* framework described in Figure 2.7.

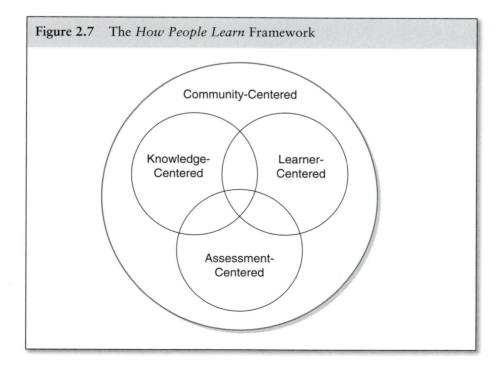

Figure 2.7   The *How People Learn* Framework

Community-Centered

Knowledge-Centered

Learner-Centered

Assessment-Centered

Learner-Centered Environments

Effective instruction begins from the foundation of what learners bring to the setting. This includes cultural practices and beliefs, as well as knowledge of academic content. A focus on the degree to which environments are learner centered is consistent with the evidence showing that learners use their prior knowledge to construct new knowledge and that what they know and believe at the moment affects how they interpret new information. Sometimes learners' current knowledge supports new learning; sometimes it impedes new learning. People may have acquired knowledge yet fail to activate it in a particular setting. This is congruous with a learner having "declarative" or "procedural knowledge," without yet developing "conditional knowledge." Learner-centered environments attempt to help students make connections between their previous knowledge and their current academic tasks. Naturally, parents are especially good at helping their children make connections. Teachers have a harder time because they do not share the life experiences of all of their students. As such, in order to enhance the learner-centeredness of their classrooms, teachers must invest the time and effort required to become familiar with student's special interests and strengths.

Knowledge-Centered Environments

The ability to think and solve problems requires knowledge that is accessible and applied appropriately. An emphasis on knowledge-centered instruction raises a number of questions, such as the degree to which instruction focuses on ways to help students use their current knowledge and skills. New knowledge regarding students' early learning suggests that young people are capable of grasping more complex concepts than was believed previously. However, these concepts must be presented in ways that are developmentally appropriate by linking learning to a student's current state of understanding.

A knowledge-centered perspective on learning environments highlights the importance of thinking about designs for curricula. To what extent do the designs help students learn with understanding versus promote the acquisition of disconnected sets of facts and skills? As discussed earlier, the domain of educational standards plays a role in determining the content, or knowledge-centeredness, of the academic program. Curricula that are a mile wide and an inch deep run the risk of developing disconnected rather than connected knowledge.

Assessment-Centered Environments

Issues of assessment also represent an important perspective for viewing the design of learning environments. Feedback is fundamental to learning, but feedback opportunities are often scarce in classrooms. Imagine you are an archery student seeking to hone your skills with a bow and arrow. Would mere practice help? What if you practiced for an entire day but were blindfolded? Would you improve? Or rather, is it a combination of practice and feedback (seeing your performance relative to the target) that allows you to develop archery skills? Students may receive grades on tests and essays, but these are usually "summative" assessments that occur at the end of projects. What is needed are "formative" assessments that provide students with opportunities to revise and improve the quality of their thinking and understanding. Assessments must reflect the learning goals that define various environments. If the goal is to enhance understanding and applicability of knowledge, it is not sufficient to provide assessments that focus primarily on memory for facts and formulas.

Community-Centered Environments

The fourth important perspective on learning environments is the degree to which they promote a sense of community. Students, teachers, and other interested participants share norms that value learning and high standards. Norms such as these increase people's opportunities and motivation to interact, receive feedback, and learn. Activities in homes, community centers, and after-school clubs can have important effects on students' academic achievement. Virtually everyone can cite examples of the positive impact that being a part of a caring community has had on his or her development. While very challenging, education leaders must ensure that their schools and classrooms provide a caring community of learning to students—to all students.

LINK TO CASE STUDY 2

The changes that Gordon Lal proposes in Case Study 2 will have implications for the learning environment at Washington High. In what ways do the leaders at your school actively shape the school culture to ensure the learning environment has the elements of the *How People Learn* framework discussed earlier?

Personalized Learning Connections

As school leaders and teachers endeavor to help students meet high expectations and performance standards, stronger connections between students and adults allow teachers to provide more individual attention to their students and open dialogue with each regarding his or her circumstances and learning needs (Lee, Bryk, & Smith, 1993; Lee & Smith, 1999; McLaughlin, 1994). Effective schools foster these connections by allowing students to take responsibility for particular activities, practice leadership behaviors, and receive rewards for their achievements (Fredricks, Blumenfield, & Paris, 2004; Newmann, 1981; Wynne, 1980). These personal connections can be incorporated in the following ways:

- Diverse activities for students to become engaged in the life of the school. Multiple studies offer preliminary evidence in support of the important relationship between students' engagement in different activities and grades or standardized test scores. These studies also report that activities requiring greater student initiative such as sports or student government often result in greater student commitment to the life of the school (Finn, 1989; Fredricks et al., 2004).
- Multiple opportunities for students and adults to develop relationships. School programs that provide field trips, parent meetings, and one-on-one mentoring for students by teachers and counselors have been shown to increase students' educational aspirations and persistence in schooling (Gandara, 2002).
- Structures for teachers to monitor and provide academic advice to students. School reform programs such as "First Things First" use smaller, theme-based learning communities in which teachers interact more frequently with a smaller number of students over the four years of their education (Quint, 2006).

Insights gained from years of cognitive science research intersect with several enduring and emerging issues in education. Two of these are discussed here. They include the issue of learning styles and multiple intelligences and an emerging emphasis on tailoring instructional programs to meet needs of learners from diverse socioeconomic backgrounds.

Learning Styles and Multiple Intelligences (MI)

As no two people have the same exact taste in clothes or food, places to travel, and what to do once you get there, so too, few individuals have the same exact learning style or combination of intelligences that are relied on to make sense of the world. Each individual has a host of mental, physical, social, and emotional tools to gain knowledge and interact with other individuals. In the classroom, teachers must be cognizant of the diversity of learning modes that students call upon to understand content and apply it to solving problems. One theory that highlights the diversity of tactics drawn upon in such endeavors is Howard Gardner's theory of multiple intelligences (1983). In this theory, Gardner contends that humans have a host of ways in which to understand, make sense of the world, and make valued contributions to society. The eight dominant intelligences that Gardner has articulated include the following:

- Linguistic intelligence. This is understood to include a host of verbal and "word smart" skills.
- Logical-Mathematical intelligence. This includes number and reasoning skills.
- Spatial intelligence. This is described as picture smart, or seeing patterns and relationships between items in a spatial domain.
- Bodily-Kinesthetic intelligence. This is synonymous with body smarts, coordination, and knowing by doing.
- Musical intelligence. This is understood to be the skills needed to appreciate and create music.
- Interpersonal (or emotional) intelligence. This is known as being people smart, the ability to relate well to others, socially and emotionally.
- Intrapersonal intelligence. This is the skill of introspection and reflection necessary to know oneself.
- Naturalist intelligence. This is understood to be the ability to recognize patterns within one's natural environment and craft products valued by society.

Gardner contends that schools focus primarily on the linguistic and logical-mathematical intelligences. Within America's current policy environment of heightened accountability mandates, one would think that the focus would become, or has become, nearly exclusive. Yet, this theory proposes a transformation in the ways that school environments are constructed and learning experiences are created. In order to present material that is equally accessible to students across a broader spectrum of learning styles, or intelligences, school leaders and teachers must expand their pedagogical toolbox.

The Intersection of Instruction and Socioeconomic Conditions

As students have preferred learning styles that impact how they understand and assimilate information, so too are children influenced by a host of socioeconomic conditions. The reality of children growing up in poverty conditions is not a phenomenon relegated to elementary- and secondary-aged students in other countries. Ruby Payne has articulated one framework for understanding the implications of poverty for educating students in America's schools. Similar to Gardner's MI theory, Payne draws attention to the varying perspectives that teachers must consider when constructing students' learning experiences. The vast majority of schoolteachers and education leaders are situated comfortably in the middle and upper-middle class. As such, educators sometimes find it difficult to relate to the rules, values, and essential survival knowledge that comprise the cultural landscape of those living in poverty.

There is often a significant disconnect between the cultural life experiences of educators and their socioeconomically disadvantaged students. As such, extra effort must be taken to ensure these disparities do not persist between school expectations and students needs. While some educators do this instinctively, others do not. Therefore, it is imperative that successful school leaders are continually appraising the school community, analyzing the needs of all constituents, and then harnessing the collective energy of the community toward productive action. Such a strategic approach to education leadership can ensure that the needs of all students are considered in the construction of learning experiences.

Professional Behavior

This element includes both relationships between all members of a faculty and staff as well as their shared focus on students' academic needs. Highly effective schools' faculty members collaborate to learn from one another and support each other's teaching, and they focus their time together on (a) examining student work, (b) targeting specific, practical strategies to address student needs, and (c) locating relevant resources and training for teachers to implement new programs (Little, 1982). School leaders can play a critical role in facilitating professional behavior by providing time for regular instructional collaboration among teachers, encouraging a shared focus by teachers on students' academic needs, and by ensuring high-quality school-embedded professional development for teachers. These practices pay significant dividends, as teachers who meet regularly to discuss their pedagogy have been shown to have positive impacts on student achievement (Quint, 2006).

Connections to External Communities

Solid evidence confirms the utility of active family and community involvement as a contributor to student and school success. Provisions of the 2001 No

Child Left Behind Act particularly reinforce this desired condition. However, while practical experience, craft knowledge, policy mandates, and educational research combine to endorse the advantages of collaboration among schools, families, and communities, effectively coordinating among these agencies is challenging. However, while successful school leaders recognize the unique difficulties of connecting with parents (Catsambis, 2001; Sheldon & Epstein, 2002), they make these partnerships a central priority in their ongoing operations (Sanders & Lewis, 2005).

Joyce Epstein provides a theoretical framework that usefully guides thinking and action in the realm of community involvement (1995, 2001). She proposes a *theory of overlapping spheres* where home, school, and community environments are "spheres of influence" that shape student growth and achievement. A greater degree of alignment among the three spheres results in supporting endeavors acting synergistically to enhance student development. Conversely, the spheres can be pushed, separated, and dysfunctionally distant when a gap exists between institutional policies and individual beliefs and practices. Ideally, there is a level of dynamic communication and collaboration among each of the three spheres that results in enhanced student achievement. Striving to achieve this alignment, as depicted in Figure 2.8, is one of the many challenging tasks facing educational leaders.

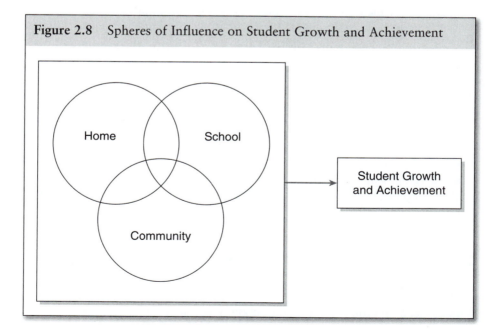

Figure 2.8   Spheres of Influence on Student Growth and Achievement

Home

School

Community

Student Growth and Achievement

Epstein's "spheres of influence" are drawn closer together as interactions among schools, families, and the community become more frequent. However, it is important for leaders to maintain an appropriate balance among spheres so that they align to maximize student achievement. Students receiving consistent reinforcement from respective spheres are more inclined to grasp the importance of education and develop a strong commitment to their schooling.

The model of overlapping segments acknowledges that the individual zones operate independently of one another, yet most school initiatives can become more productive when the spheres collaborate. Schools, families, and communities are influential entities; yet they cannot guarantee successful students. While these spheres play a pivotal role in being able to encourage, direct, and stimulate a student's interest and desire to become successful, student initiative continues to be of crucial importance.

Students are an integral part of a school, family, and community partnership. They have a direct effect on the alignment of the spheres by serving as an intermediary between the school and their family. Students serve in this capacity as teachers frequently depend on them effectively to transmit important messages to their families. Students are more likely to cooperate in these situations if they are motivated and engaged in their education. A heightened level of commitment to educational excellence can occur when students believe that their school, family, and community genuinely care about their personal and academic well-being.

Henderson and Mapp (2002) reviewed 50 empirical studies of the impact of community involvement on student achievement and found the following benefits to be associated with community involvement in schools:

- Elevated grade point averages and scores on standardized tests or rating scales
- Enrollment in more challenging academic programs
- More classes passed and credits earned
- Better attendance
- Improved behavior at school and at home
- Better social skills and adaptation to school
- Higher rates of graduation and postsecondary education

In addition to these benefits, individual research teams have uncovered specific benefits of community involvement within specialized domains of schooling. For example, Arriaza (2004) found that school reform initiatives have greater chances of persisting when the community actively participates as an empowered change agent. In a longitudinal study on school attendance, several family-school-community partnership practices were associated with increases in daily attendance and decreases in chronic absenteeism (Epstein & Sheldon, 2002).

In a study of school engagement among Latino youth in urban schools, the following were found to enhance school engagement: teacher support, friend support, parent support, neighborhood youth behavior, and neighborhood safety (Garcia-Reid, Reid, & Peterson, 2005). Data from 82 elementary schools in an urban area indicate that, after controlling for school characteristics, the degree to which schools were working to overcome challenges to family and community involvement predicted higher percentages of students scoring at or above satisfactory on state achievement tests.

These findings should encourage school leaders to address obstacles to family and community involvement in order to realize the benefits of community partnerships for student academic performance (Sheldon, 2003). Additionally, findings suggest that subject-specific practices of school, family, and community partnerships may help educators improve students' mathematics achievement. For example, when controlling for prior levels of mathematics achievement, longitudinal analyses of elementary and secondary school data indicate that effective implementation of practices that encourage families to support their children's mathematics learning at home was associated with higher percentages of students who scored at or above proficiency on standardized mathematics achievement tests (Sheldon & Epstein, 2002).

Learning-Centered Leadership

At the helm of a high-performing school culture that is operating to elevate student performance, one will find a learning-centered leader. These school leaders prioritize student learning through the multiple responsibilities and decisions they face. They possess a complex vision of what learning is, and they engage both school-level factors (such as the school mission or faculty governance structure) and classroom-level conditions (such as student grouping and instructional practices) to focus staff and resources on strategies that improve students' academic and social learning (Murphy, Goldring, Cravens, & Elliott, 2007).

Learning-centered leaders exhibit commitment to continuous school improvement by cooperating with staff to craft and operate according to an explicit school vision, by building consensus for change, and by focusing their school cultures on supporting new initiatives (Hallinger & Heck, 2002; Leithwood, Leonard, & Sharratt, 1998). Additionally, they demonstrate sustained support for improvement of the instructional program by securing and organizing resources, such as teaching materials (Murphy, Elliott, Goldring, &

Porter, 2006) and new instructional training and professional development (Cawelti, 1997; Newmann, 1997), to promote student learning. They ensure that the school culture is infused with a commitment to the following:

- High standards for student performance. There are individual, team, and school goals for rigorous student academic and social learning.
- Rigorous curriculum (content). There is ambitious academic content provided to all students in core academic subjects.
- High-quality instruction (pedagogy). There are effective instructional practices that maximize student academic and social learning.
- Culture of learning and professional behavior. There are integrated communities of professional practice in the service of student academic and social learning. There is a healthy school environment in which student learning is the central focus.
- Connections to external communities. There are linkages to people and institutions in the community that advance academic and social learning.
- Systemic performance accountability. Leadership holds itself and others responsible for realizing high standards of performance for student academic and social learning. There is individual and collective responsibility among the professional staff and students.

ARTICULATING A VISION AND GAINING SUPPORT FOR A SUCCESSFUL SCHOOL CULTURE

The remainder of this chapter concentrates on means by which school leaders can create a successful culture within their school. There are two important steps in this process: (1) articulating a vision for what an effective school culture will look like and (2) gaining commitment to this vision from others.

Creating a Vision of a Successful School Culture

A first step in creating a successful school culture is to define what the end result should look like. A school leader must be able to articulate this vision before he or she can gain commitment to it from other parties. In order to do this effectively, a school leader must be able to describe with some precision how he or she wants a school to act, think, and feel. This is particularly important if the leader is new to the school or planning substantial changes. The leader should be able to describe how the building will look, what the tenor of conversations will be, and how people in the building will feel and why.

The following is a brief example of a vision statement that an incoming principal might present to members of a school community.

Members of the school community:

Hello, my name is Ruth Barlow, and I will be the new principal of Sunnybrook Elementary. As the new principal, my goal is to help make Sunnybrook the best school possible, and I would like to take a moment to share with you my vision for how Sunnybrook will think, act, and feel when we accomplish this.

I envision a school where relationships are positive, expectations are high, people believe they can accomplish what they value as important, and every single person is constantly learning.

During my years in education I have been inside many schools and have noticed a number of traits that I think we would all want our school to possess (and others that we would not want our school to exhibit).

In some schools, relationships are bitter and tense; students and staff battle each other all day long and leave school stressed. I believe a visitor to Sunnybrook should see people smiling, staff working together, people who care for one another, and people who trust and respect each other.

In some schools, the status quo is accepted. I believe that Sunnybrook has a number of excellent things taking place right now, but I also believe that we should never stop trying to make the school better. I have witnessed open hostility to change, no matter what that change may be, in far too many schools, and my hope is that Sunnybrook staff members continually will, instead, cooperate to create new ideas that will further enhance the quality of our school. I think new ideas should be encouraged and rewarded rather than resisted.

All members of the Sunnybrook community should hold each other in high esteem. That means that we should only expect the best from each other. If we challenge everybody in the community to do more than they thought possible and expect them to succeed, it is my belief that this will occur.

Last, I envision a school free from doubt. Students should not doubt that they can learn. Teachers should not doubt the abilities of their students. Administrators should not doubt the abilities of their teachers. Everybody should feel that they are able to accomplish whatever goals they have set. The only doubt to be encouraged is the feeling that everything we do now is right and cannot be improved.

I know nothing is easy, but I hope everybody will join me in striving to create a school culture of success at Sunnybrook. Together we can make Sunnybrook a positive place where all parties work together to achieve success.

In the coming weeks, I will be in touch with each of you in order to discuss what we all need to do in order to make this vision a reality.

Before members of a community can accept such a vision or plan, they must understand exactly to what they are agreeing. Beyond a general vision for the school, participants must also understand what their role in the change will be. A goal can seldom be accomplished if all parties do not understand what they need to do in order to accomplish the goal.

There are numerous ways in which one could communicate to the various groups what their role in creating a successful school would be. Whether by letter, individual face-to-face meeting, meeting in groups, or some other method, every person in the school must be informed of what is to be expected of him or her individually. This section describes the roles of various participants. What follows is an illustrative list of what is needed from each group in order to construct a positive school culture. New school leaders may wish to start a discussion surrounding a similar list of duties and responsibilities.

Administrators

Administrators should seek to efficiently undertake managerial duties, set an example for others to follow, seek counsel from other community members when making decisions, inform other community members of decisions, assist community members who request assistance, ensure that professional development is helpful to teachers, nurture new ideas, and maintain positive relationships with others.

Teachers

Teachers should seek to instruct to the best of their ability, set a positive example for students, collaborate with other staff members, constantly strive to better their practice, expect only the best from students and colleagues, and maintain positive relationships with others.

Students

Students should seek to expect only the best from themselves, put forth their best effort in learning what teachers ask of them, ask questions, treat others with kindness, and follow the example that adults set for them.

Parents

Parents should seek to ensure that students are in school on time and prepared, ask their children what is happening in school, expect only the best from their children, assist children when they have problems, inform staff members of problems or possible solutions, offer assistance in school projects, attend school events, and maintain positive relationships with others.

Once it is clear to everybody what a leader envisions for the school and the role that each participant plays in this vision, the leader can begin to solicit commitment from various groups.

Gaining Commitment

Getting everybody to agree is often the hardest part, especially for a new administrator. There are right ways and wrong ways to ensure that other members of the school community assist in making the vision a reality. Consider the following scenarios:

Betty Brown has worked with the Central City school district as a regional supervisor for the past five years. When the district asks her to take the principal's job at struggling Frank Smith Middle School, however, she decided to take the leap. As one of the schools she had supervised, she fully realized the challenges she faces; many students are disorderly, the staff has a high turnover rate, and test scores are abysmal. To make things worse, the long history of low test scores means the district is considering closing the school in the next year or two.

A week before the end of the school year, it is announced to staff that the current principal is retiring and that Betty will be their new principal. She has previously collaborated with some of the staff members at the school and is confident that her relationships will allow her to succeed in this job. Over the summer, she sends out a welcome letter to all of the staff members informing them that she would like to meet with each and every one of them prior to the start of the school year. Fifty of the 85 teachers do not make an appointment to meet with her prior to preservice training.

By the time teachers report to school to begin preparing their classrooms, she realizes that it is too late, and she is far too short on time to meet with all of them. She decides to scrap the idea and move forward with her agenda. Since she is new to the school she is not planning on making any radical changes to start the school year but, rather, will take a wait-and-see approach.

As the year progresses, she sees many of the same problems that emerged in previous years and decides they need to be addressed. She wants to take a hard line on a number of issues, but operating a school with 1,500 students is demanding and time consuming, and she simply does not have sufficient time to deal with every little issue. When she does decide to take a stand, it never seems to work the way that she expects. There is a commotion in the lunchroom one day when a lunch aide gives a vulgar response to a student that she feels is being rude. Ms. Brown immediately fires the lunch lady and lets it be known that she will not tolerate foul language directed toward children in her school. Some teachers nod approvingly while others wonder why she will not do anything about the foul language many children are using.

As the year passes the midpoint and people begin to feel stressed, a large number of teachers seem to be complaining about discipline problems in their classes. Every week there is another handful who seem unable to deal with a particular student in their class and request intervention. In some cases she intervenes, in others she decides that she needs to monitor that teacher more closely, and in others she decides that the teacher can deal with it for the rest of the year. She decides that a much stronger discipline policy must be enacted at the beginning of the next year but that it is too late for a radical change this year.

In May, she is preparing to receive the results from the statewide tests and attempting to keep students and staff motivated enough to finish out the school year on a strong note when she is given bad news by the district; the lack of improvement in the school has led district administrators to believe it would be better to shut down Frank Smith Middle School now rather than continue forward with potential consequences under NCLB.

Evaluate the job that Ms. Brown did. What did she do well and not so well? What would you have done differently if you were Ms. Brown? What would you have done the same way?

Next, consider Dennis Thomas.

Dennis Thomas is a bright, young assistant principal in Central City working at Cindy Jones Elementary School. He has long admired the work done at Lincoln Elementary across town, and when that school's principal retires, he decides to apply for the job. He is ecstatic when he learns that he will be the new principal. His new school has been featured in the newspapers for the dramatic turnaround that has occurred there. Once one of the worst schools in the city, the staff developed a new plan centered around an innovative teaching technique that focused all classes on reading contemporary materials. Over the course of 10 years, staff members had slowly come together on the idea and refined and developed their new curriculum while their principal had shielded them from a number of rules and regulations passed down from the Central City Curriculum Planning Office. The staff was cohesive, students seemed happy, and test results were impressive.

As soon as Mr. Thomas became principal, he was contacted by the Curriculum Planning Office and was informed that the city had adopted a new literacy program that all schools would be required to follow. He would be evaluated on the success of its implementation at Lincoln. Convinced that the new curriculum was a good idea, and knowing that the staff had adapted well to change before, he set out to make Lincoln the model school for the new curriculum.

On the first day of preservice training, he excitedly announced the changes to his staff and passed out the manuals for the new curriculum, along with a number of monitoring forms he had devised himself and expected teachers to fill out on a weekly basis. This way he could ensure that his school was progressing nicely and that his evaluations would be positive.

The smile soon disappeared from his face when a number of the teachers began to complain about their new curriculum. They had worked hard to create the existing curriculum from scratch and fine-tune it over time, but they had had no say in this new curriculum. Dennis explained that the new curriculum had been mandated by the city and that there was nothing he could do about it and was sure they would like it if they gave it a chance. Numerous teachers told him that their previous principal had fought the city when he was asked to do things that the staff did not believe in. Mr. Thomas, however, was leery of picking a fight with the city on his first day on the job.

As the school year progressed, he was dismayed to see the reaction of the teachers to the new curriculum. Some gave it a chance, others refused to, and some told him they would and then stopped as soon as he left the room. A number of his weekly forms were not being returned, and a number of the ones that were submitted seemed quite sloppy.

Dennis called a staff meeting to address this issue. He stressed that neither the implementation of the curriculum nor the submission of the forms was optional and said that he expected more from the staff given their reputation throughout the city. He was met with fierce resentment by a number of teachers who complained that their students did not like the new curriculum and argued that their old one was far superior.

The following day, regional inspectors from the district came to examine the school and informed Mr. Thomas that progress with the new curriculum was unsatisfactory. The next week one-half of the staff did not return their weekly forms. He wrote negative letters and placed them in their files and informed them that this would continue if they refused to comply.

Things got worse as the school year continued. The lead teacher in the building cried on a local radio show while saying how frustrated she was with her school and her new principal. Numerous teachers were threatening to quit at the end of the year if he did not change course on the issue, and test scores were falling. By the end of the year Dennis had received a negative review from his supervisor and had begun to wish he had never applied for the job at Lincoln.

Evaluate Mr. Thomas's performance. What did he do well and not so well? What would you have done differently if you were Mr. Thomas? What would you have done the same way? How are the situations that Mr. Thomas and Ms. Brown were placed in similar and different? Which mistakes did they make that were similar?

Both of these principals were put in inordinately difficult positions. One waited too long while the other jumped the gun. Both, however, had one fatal flaw: they failed to gain staff buy-in before implementing reforms.

Before school leaders can successfully make changes, they must ensure that those charged with carrying out those changes believe they will be effective. In the case of Ms. Brown, scheduling meetings with staff members was a good idea, but she failed to follow through on them. In the case of Mr. Thomas, he should not have been surprised when teachers reacted negatively to such a major policy change being suddenly thrown at them.

Since school culture is highly dependent on the preconceived attitudes and beliefs of the staff members at a given school, it is critically important that all staff members are cooperating in pursuit of the same goal. In the case of a principal constructing a vision for a high-performing school culture, the only way to accomplish this is to engage all key stakeholder groups in the planning stages in order to ensure a thoughtful implementation of the vision.

How would one go about gaining commitment from all parties? The answer is simultaneously simple and complex.

An initial step is soliciting counsel from all relevant groups. Asking staff members for their ideas accomplishes more than telling them that they are important. Soliciting ideas, of course, will not suffice if that counsel is disregarded. In the case of Mr. Thomas, the first thing he should have done when he found out about the new curriculum is contact teachers in the school and ask them how the new curriculum might be seamlessly integrated. The advice and ideas of others can be solicited via committees, meetings, suggestion boxes, casual conversations, and many other ways.

A second important step to gaining buy-in from various parties is to define the value and importance of each group. Telling individuals that they are important may not say as much as treating them that way, but it is still necessary. In addition to defining the broad roles that each group is envisioned playing, it is also crucial to emphasize the importance of each of these groups and roles.

Last, each group needs to be constantly encouraged and affirmed. In the case of Ms. Brown, she started on a good note by soliciting advice from teachers, but she then let her idea fall by the wayside to focus on other things. Whether she intended it that way or not, the teachers at her school likely perceived that she believed other things were more important than teachers' ideas and feedback. This makes them less likely to cooperate with her when she tries to implement reforms.

In his book *Three Signs of a Miserable Job*, Patrick Lencioni (2007) discusses the three things that lead people to dislike their jobs. The first is anonymity; management seems not to care who they are. The second is irrelevance; the employee feels that his or her job does not matter and nobody cares what he or she does. The third is measurement; the employee has no way to tell if he or she is doing a good job.

In order to ensure that staff members will commit to a plan, it is important to let them know that they are important as individuals, that they play a significant role, and to let them know when they do something well. If school leaders do these three things, it is more likely that members of the school community will commit to helping achieve their vision of a successful school culture.

CONCLUSION

There are many forces that exert influence on schools and school cultures.

Many of these forces challenge progress and contest growth. However, committed school leaders are a school's greatest ally in the battle for continuous improvement and elevated learning outcomes. Learning-centered leaders who are committed to establishing a high-performing school culture work strategically to create an environment of high performance expectations for themselves, the faculty and staff, and all students (Lee, Smith, & Croninger, 1995). On a personal level, they demonstrate a positive outlook regarding the ability of staff and students to accomplish high expectations and inspire the school community to accomplish things that might seem beyond their grasp (Waters & Grubb, 2004). Along the way, they model risk-taking and create an environment of trust in the service of attaining important learning goals (Prestine, 1991). Such leaders work strategically to weave elements of a successful culture into the fabric of their schools to the benefit of students, faculty, staff, and the broader community.

QUESTIONS FOR DISCUSSION

1. Considering your current school circumstances in light of the forces depicted in Figure 2.1, what do you feel are the most challenging impediments to facilitating school change and the construction of a high-performing school culture?

2. What are the greatest assets in your school community upon which you might draw to sustain a high-performing school culture?

3. What components of an effective school culture do you feel your school already possesses to a high degree?

4. What elements of an effective school culture do you need to strategically target?

5. To what extent have you articulated a vision for your school community? To what extent do you have the commitment of key stakeholders to your vision?

REFERENCES

Arriaza, G. (2004). Making changes that stay made: School reform and community involvement. *The High School Journal, 37*(4), 10–24.

Bransford, J. D., Brown, A. L., & Cocking, R. R. (Eds.). (1999). *How people learn: Brain, mind, experience, and school.* National Academy of Sciences, Committee on Developments in the Science of Learning, Commission on Behavioral and Social Sciences and Education, National Research Council. Washington, DC: National Academy Press.

Burris, C. C., Wiley, E. W., Welner, K. G., & Murphy, J. (2008). Accountability, rigor, and detracking: Achievement effects of embracing a challenging curriculum as a universal goal for all students. *Teachers College Record, 110*(3), 571–608.

Catsambis, S. (2001). Expanding knowledge of parental involvement in children's secondary education: Connections with high school seniors' academic success. *Social Psychology of Education, 5*(2), 149–177.

Cawelti, G. (1997). *Effects of high school restructuring: Ten schools at work.* Arlington, VA: Educational Research Service.

Darling-Hammond, L., Ancess, J., Susanna, W. O. (2002). Reinventing high school: Outcomes of the coalition campus schools project. *American Educational Research Journal, 39*(3), 639–673.

Epstein, J. L. (1995). School/family/community partnerships: Caring for the children we share. *Phi Delta Kappan, 76,* 701–712.

Epstein, J. L. (2001). *School, family, and community partnerships: Preparing educators and improving schools.* Boulder, CO: Westview Press.

Epstein, J. L., & Sheldon, S. B. (2002). Present and accounted for: Improving student attendance through family and community involvement. *Journal of Educational Research, 95,* 308–318.

Finn, J. D. (1989). Withdrawing from school. *Review of Educational Research, 59*(2), 117–142.

Fredricks, J. A., Blumenfeld, P. C., & Paris, A. H. (2004). School engagement: Potential of the concept, state of the evidence. *Review of Educational Research, 74*(1), 59–109.

Frome, P. (2001). *High schools that work: Findings from the 1996 and 1998 assessments.* Research Park Triangle, NC: Research

Triangle Institute. Retrieved August 31, 2009, from http://www.sreb.org/page/1078/high_schools_that_work.html

Gandara, P. (2002). A study of high school Puente: What we have learned about preparing Latino youth for postsecondary education. *Educational Policy, 16*(4), 474–495.

Garcia-Reid, P., Reid, R., & Peterson, N. A. (2005, May). School engagement among Latino youth in an urban middle school context: Valuing the role of social support. *Education and Urban Society, 37*(3), 257–275.

Gardner, H. (1983). *Frames of mind: The theory of multiple intelligences.* New York: Basic Books.

Hallinger, P., & Heck, R. H. (2002). What do you call people with visions? The role of vision, mission, and goals in school leadership and improvement. In K. Leithwood & P. Hallinger (Eds.), *Second international handbook of educational leadership and administration* (pp. 9–40). Great Britain: Kluwer Academic.

Henderson, A. T., & Mapp, K. L. (2002). *A new wave of evidence: The impact of school, family, and community connections on student achievement.* Austin, TX: National Center of Family & Community Connections with Schools: Southwest Educational Development Laboratory.

Kemple, J. J., Herlihy, C. M., & Smith, T. J. (2005). *Making progress towards graduation: Evidence from the talent development high school model.* New York: Manpower Demonstration Research Corporation. Retrieved August 31, 2009, from http://eric.ed.gov:80/ERICDocs/data/ericdocs2sql/content_storage_01/0000019b/80/29/d9/8c.pdf

Lee, V. E., Bryk, A. S., & Smith, J. B. (1993). The organization of effective secondary schools. In L. Darling-Hammond (Ed.), *Review of research in education: Vol. 19* (pp. 171–267). Washington, DC.: American Educational Research Association.

Lee, V. E., & Smith, J. B. (1999). Social support and achievement for young adolescents in Chicago: The role of school academic press. *American Educational Research Journal, 36*(4), 907–945.

Lee, V. E., Smith, J. B., & Croninger, R. G. (1995). *Another look at high school restructuring: Issues in restructuring schools.* Madison, WI: Center on Organization and Restructuring of Schools, School of Education, University of Wisconsin-Madison.

Leithwood, K., Leonard, L., & Sharratt, L. (1998). Conditions fostering organizational learning in schools. *Educational Administration Quarterly, 34*(2), 243–276.

Lencioni, P. (2007). *The three signs of a miserable job.* San Francisco: Jossey-Bass.

Little, J. W. (1982). Norms of collegiality and experimentation: Workplace conditions of school sources. *American Educational Research Journal, 19*(1), 325–340.

McLaughlin, M. W. (1994). Somebody knows my name. In *Issues in restructuring schools* (Issue Report No. 7, pp. 9–12). Madison, WI: University of Wisconsin-Madison, School of Education, Center on Organization and Restructuring of Schools. (ERIC Document Reproduction Service No. ED376565)

McLaughlin, M. W., & Talbert, J. E. (1993). *Contexts that matter for teaching and learning: Strategic opportunities for meeting the nation's educational goals.* Stanford, CA: Center for Research on the Context of Secondary School Teaching, Stanford University.

Murphy, J. F., Elliott, S. N., Goldring, E. B., & Porter, A. C. (2006). *Learning-centered leadership: A conceptual foundation.* New York: The Wallace Foundation.

Murphy, J. F., Goldring, E. G., Cravens, X. C., & Elliott, S. N. (2007, August). The Vanderbilt assessment of leadership in education: Measuring learning-centered leadership. *East China Normal University Journal.*

Newmann, F. M. (1981, November). Reducing student alienation in high schools: Implications of theory. *Harvard Educational Review, 51*(4), 546–564.

Newmann, F. M. (1997). How secondary schools contribute to academic success. In K. Borman & B. Schneider (Eds.), *Youth experiences and development: Social influences and educational challenges.* Berkeley, CA: McCutchan.

Newmann, F. M., Smith, B., & Bryk, A. S. (2001). *School instructional program coherence: Benefits and challenges.* Chicago: Consortium on Chicago School Reform.

Prestine, N. A. (1991). Shared decision making in restructuring essential schools: The role of the principal. *Planning and Changing, 22*(3/4), 160–177.

Quint, J. (2006). *Meeting five critical challenges of high school reform: Lessons from research on three reform models.* New York, NY: Manpower Demonstration Research Corporation. Retrieved August 31, 2009, from http://www.mdrc.org/publications/428/full.pdf

Sanders, M. G., & Lewis, K. C. (2005). Building bridges toward excellence: Community involvement in high schools. *The High School Journal, 88*(3), 1–10.

Sheldon, S. B. (2003). Linking school-family-community partnerships in urban elementary schools to student achievement on state tests. *The Urban Review, 35,* 149–165.

Sheldon, S. B., & Epstein, J. L. (2002). Improving student behavior and school discipline with family and community involvement. *Education and Urban Society, 35*(1), 4–26.

Waters, T., & Grubb, S. (2004). *The leadership we need: Using research to strengthen the use of standards for administrator preparation and licensure programs.* Aurora, CO: Mid-continent Research for Education and Learning.

Wenglinsky, H. (2002) The link between teacher classroom practices and student academic performance. *Educational Policy Analysis Archives, 10*(2), 1–30.

Wenglinsky, H. (2004). The link between instructional practice and the racial gap in middle schools. *Research on Middle Level Education, 28*(1), 1–13.

Wynne, E. (1980). *Looking at schools: Good, bad, and indifferent.* Lexington, MA: Lexington Books.

Case Study 3: Walton Charter Prepares to Select a Head

What Kind of Leader Might Best Create a Productive Culture?

A Midwest school district was about to launch its first charter school. The school board president, Peggy Braxton, was eager to select a headmaster or headmistress that could fulfill the substantial spectrum of public and school board expectations that had evolved for the new school. The issue of a charter school had proved to be quite contentious. Proponents touted a need for innovation in the district and argued that a charter school would pioneer new curricular and instructional ideas that might eventually prove advantageous to the entire district. They also asserted that such a school, presumably less bound by district oversight and regulation, would attract a different and more adventuresome faculty with, ultimately, greater excitement and engagement for students.

Opponents, many of whom were to be found among the district's more senior teachers and administrators, voiced a fear that a charter school would siphon badly needed resources from the remainder of the schools in the district, that it was a Trojan horse aimed eventually at undermining the teacher union, and would only serve as a means for the district's social and economic elite to gain a private school for their children without having to pay private-school tuition.

Ms. Braxton was agnostic regarding the supposed charter school advantages and disadvantages. She perceived her role as a neutral party whose responsibility it was to ensure that the charter school students, parents, and staff had the best possible leadership. She was eager that the project get off the ground well and have a fair chance of proving its utility. Toward this end, board president Braxton had arranged several community meetings throughout the district to solicit suggestions for the charter school operation, purpose, focus, and personnel.

The overwhelming proportion of community forum participants leaned toward an academically oriented elementary school with a broad curriculum including the arts and physical education. It was also agreed that the school should grow grade by grade, beginning with a kindergarten. The eventual size was not to exceed three hundred pupils, for

---

Note: This case study, as with others associated with other chapters, is about an actual school, actual people, and actual conditions. Nothing is fabricated. All cases are about situations school leaders routinely encounter. However, in each instance, names of people, schools, and locations have been altered to ensure confidentiality.

fear of forfeiting the intimacy and engagement that proponents hoped would evolve. There was a great deal of enthusiasm for a Montessori school. What emerged was a hope that some of the Montessori principles might be incorporated throughout the school's instruction. Peg Braxton was not sure a school could be "a little bit Montessori" as opposed to consistently Montessori, but she deferred commenting about this matter. When it came to staffing the school, participants thought this was a set of decisions best left to the new school's director.

Peg Braxton also asked about leadership qualities for the director position. She solicited ideas for both actual candidate names and qualities candidates should possess. She had taken notes and later distilled them into the following list of attributes.

- Youthful vs. Experienced

How much experience is needed to launch a new school and establish a rigorous academic culture? Is this an endeavor that more productively could call upon youthful enthusiasm, commitment, energy, and vigor, or is it an undertaking that more likely benefits from multiple experiences and accumulated wisdom? If balance is in order, where should the line be drawn?

- Expertise vs. Generic Skills

Community forum expression regarding Montessori schooling prompted Peggy Braxton to ponder whether or not there was a specific body of expertise and experience that the new charter school director should possess. Or, she wondered, does that matter? Is this a kind of expertise that an intelligent and eager director candidate could quickly acquire through intensive reading and attendance at several specialized workshops? Or is this the kind of expertise that can only be gained through experience?

- Male vs. Female

Peggy Braxton's own experience, mostly in business and politics, suggested that gender was only rarely a real issue. It sometimes was said to be an issue, but in her experience, such claims usually turned out to be prejudices and ill-founded personal perceptions and stereotypes, not facts. She had worked for effective men and effective women leaders. Something other than gender seemed to be important. Still, the new charter school was to concentrate on the younger grades and younger students. Was there some utility to having a more maternal figure in the school? Would students fare better under a woman director? Moreover, most of the teachers would assuredly be women. Thus, she wondered if a woman director would not be a better fit. On the other hand, simply because so many of the teachers would likely be women, she wondered if the head should not be a male. She reasoned that young boys needed role models also.

- Insider vs. Outsider

Peg Braxton was also ambivalent regarding the source of leadership. She could see many advantages from the selection of an individual already in the district, someone who knew all the ups and downs, had a supportive internal network to whom he or she could turn for advice and help, knew the community, knew the contentious issues surrounding the formation of the charter school, and who would not take long to learn his or her way around the district. It seemed to Peg that an experienced person would be able to hit the ground running, and that would save a lot time and perhaps a lot of heartbreak.

On the other hand, Peg could hardly think of an internal candidate who did not carry some kind of political or organizational baggage; virtually all internal candidates had already taken sides during the charter school debate. To select a proponent would possibly alienate opponents and vice versa. So a big part of Peg was waffling: was inside or outside better, she wondered? She also wondered if there was any valid empirical research that bore productively on the issue.

- Educator vs. Other

Peg Braxton had read of the success that several retired military officers and business executives were alleged to be having in operating school districts. They had not come through the "system," had not gone to education schools, and had not been teachers. Perhaps the new charter school deserved a radically different perspective.

On the other hand, it was important to Peg that the new director be perceived by teachers as knowledgeable about their world, about children, and about learning. Would an outsider have the legitimacy that some teachers thought was important? Peg was perplexed.

- Manager vs. Innovator

Peg had once read that managers maintain an organization's status quo and leaders provoke change. She was unsure what the new charter school needed most. On one hand, it was a daring new venture, at least in her district, and it might well take a leader with an innovative frame of mind, an entrepreneurial spirit, and a willingness to take risk.

On the other hand, there was much about the new position that appeared to Peg to require a steady manager. She did not want the school to fail because someone mismanaged the budget or failed to understand school law when it came to evaluating and dismissing poor-performing teachers. Peg had also read that most charter schools fail for mismanagement, not because they lacked innovation. Still, she was caught in between.

- Advanced Degree vs. Bachelor's Degree

Many of the administrators in Peg Braxton's district possessed master's degrees, and some had a doctorate, an EdD, or a PhD. Peg was admiring of those who had possessed sufficient ambition and curiosity to pursue an advanced degree. Yet, she knew from her experience in business and politics that such degrees were not necessarily a proxy for ability. Some of the most able individuals with whom she had worked or cooperated in government had no advanced degrees. She was open as to the nature and academic utility of qualifications, but she needed guidance.

- Technophile vs. Technophobe

Peg Braxton's quarter century of business experience was in banking. In her work life she had seen this field transformed by technology. She started as a bank teller, and now, with the advent of ATMs, such jobs were shrinking. Optical scanners now handled the Federal Reserve check clearing, and they handled hundreds of millions of checks per day with remarkably accuracy. Her husband was a telephone company executive before mobile phones and modern microchip switching equipment. He had seen employment in the telecommunication field plummet. While capital was replacing labor in these endeavors, by many measures the quality of the service was increasing.

All the while, as a school board member and parent, Peg kept wondering when the technological revolution would hit schooling, and, somehow, it never seemed to. She wondered if the new charter school was not a place to break the mold, to see if there were instructional technologies that could enable youngsters to learn more thoroughly, to enable teachers to instruct more effectively, and, perhaps, reduce costs to the public of doing both of these things. All of this caused her to ponder the degree to which the new charter school director might well be knowledgeable regarding technology.

Yet, several of Peg's teacher friends were quick to counsel caution. They claimed that there were not yet any magic technology bullets in schooling. They told her they had yet to see any machine that came close to replacing what good teachers could do by way of diagnosing what a child needed, and few machines could provoke the motivation of a good teacher.

Again, Peg wondered about it all, and it all had implications for the qualifications of the charter school director she was seeking.

- External Headhunter vs. Internal Human Resources Department

When Peg Braxton's school district had sought a new superintendent, they had used the service of an external executive search firm. Peg was favorably impressed with the professional approach of the individuals with whom the board worked in this regard. She also liked the national scope of recruiting that took place, the thoroughness of background checks, and the screening of candidates prior to the board interviewing them. All in all, it was a fulfilling and productive manner in which to seek new personnel.

Now, Peg wondered if the district should make a similar investment in searching for the charter school director. The fee was equivalent to the first three months of the successful candidate's salary in the position. That was about $25,000. Peg wondered if her fellow board members would think this a good investment. The alternative was to rely upon the district's human resources department. Peg knew there were several capable people in this office, but she was worried that the various internal pressures upon these staff would cause them to acquiesce and put forth only internal or, even if external, status quo–oriented individuals. After all, those administrators already in the district were sometimes reluctant to hire someone really good from the outside for fear of being made to look bad by comparison. Thus, Peg was again pondering which fork in the road was best for her district: outside professional search firm or inside managed search?

With the list of attributes and characteristics distilled, the daunting task set before Braxton and the board was to determine which combination of qualities and skills would most benefit the budding Walton Charter School.

FOR DISCUSSION

1. In your opinion, what leadership characteristics are most desirable in creating a productive school culture?

2. Is Peggy Braxton concerned with the correct conditions? Are there more important search-related dimensions that she should have noted?

3. Has Peg accurately portrayed the pros and cons of the dimensions she has noted?

4. Should she and her board and administrative colleagues simply have advertised the position, carefully reviewed the credentials of those who applied from outside or inside, and then selected the best available individual?

5. On each of the 10 dualistic dimensions listed by Peg, in which direction would you counsel her to lean?

6. Are any of Peg's noted dimensions connected with the construction of a dynamic and achievement-oriented school culture? If so, which ones, and why do you think so?

CHAPTER 3

Leadership and Effective School Culture

This chapter explains the relationship of leadership to the achievement of the "vision" of an effective school culture to which the preceding chapter was addressed.

Specifically, in this chapter a reader will learn about the following:

- Consciously crafting a coherent and authentic leadership style
- Identifying one's core values relevant to leadership
- Constructing a professional philosophy of education and management
- Setting priorities for leadership action in constructing an effective culture
- Considerations in deploying people, resources, and time
- Communicating with a spectrum of audiences
- Employing leadership symbols and influencing follower impressions
- Difficult conversations with colleagues, subordinates, and upperlings
- The significance to a leader of personal ethics and consistent behavior

ELCC STANDARDS

ELCC standards addressed in this chapter include the following:

- 1.1—Develop a vision of learning
- 1.2—Articulate a vision
- 1.4—Steward a vision
- 2.1—Promote a positive school culture
- 3.3—Manage resources
- 4.1—Collaborate with families and other community members
- 5.1—Act with integrity
- 5.2—Act fairly
- 5.3—Act ethically
- 6.1—Understand the larger context
- 6.2—Respond to the larger context

INTRODUCTION

This book, consciously, emphasizes the conceptual knowledge, strategic under-standings, and practical insights needed by a leader appropriately to determine and shape organizational direction and an effective school culture. Leaders need to think, and they also need to act. Thus, this book stresses not only the right things to do, but it also emphasizes the crucial importance of doing things right.

It is through reflection, by which is meant the self-conscious and construc-tively critical examination of one's past professional experiences and personal reactions to or as a result of those experiences, that leaders determine what is important and how well they are performing. It is via their actions that lead-ers give vent to their vision of an effective school culture and begin to imple-ment that which they believe is needed for the long-run well-being of their organization and its clients. But what actions should a leader take to build an effective school culture? How does one begin to implement the items on the preceding considerations checklist? What activities and behavior are most important in an effort to guide and change one's school?

This chapter concentrates on answering questions such as these. Here care-fully considered concepts and concrete conditions are conjoined and then insights are offered on how to convert these into conscious plans and construc-tive behaviors. Advice is provided regarding matters such as self-consciously creating a leadership style; formulating thoughts regarding learning and effective schooling; crystallizing views regarding management of a productive school culture; effectively managing one's time, interpersonal and institutional communications, and professional image; and holding difficult conversations with colleagues, subordinates, and even bosses. These are the actions one takes and attributes one develops to lead an effective school and to build a lasting culture of achievement.

SHAPING AND CONTINUALLY RESHAPING ONE'S LEADERSHIP STYLE IN ORDER TO NURTURE AN EFFECTIVE SCHOOL CULTURE

In large measure, more than position, purpose, persona, poise, professionalism, pedagogy, intellect, morality, education level, appearance, manner of communicating, attire, and day-to-day behavior, an individual in a leadership role will be defined, appraised, and known by his or her leadership style.

What Is Leadership Style?

Leadership style refers to the composite of and interactions among all of the just-listed personal and professional traits and components. It is this mosaic of attributes and actions that comprises the stuff of leadership and the reality of a leader. In some instances, an individual's personal and physical facets fit comfortably in a self-reinforcing amalgam of attributes and actions, and successful leadership is the result. Conversely, sometimes leaders display traits and carry out behaviors that are inauthentic. In these falsely constructed, ill-conceived, or flawed efforts at crafting a leadership style, the composite is inconsistent, the sum of individual leadership components is not synergistic, and all the parts do not equal an effective whole. Followers have an ability rather quickly to discern what is real and what is unreal in a leader. Hence, it behooves a reader to pick and choose and to weld together a leadership style that is congruent, fits with what one genuinely believes, and can be consistently adhered to.

However, developing a leadership style is far from a casual or one-time undertaking. It involves a complicated process entailing observation, reflection, practice, trial, and reformulation. In some ways, it is a time-consuming process and a never-ending search. A good leader is a work in progress. Modeling one's self after others, or facets of others, is one useful means to assembling a leadership style. What follows are some illustrative leadership models taken from history.

George S. Patton, a remarkably successful World War II United States general, was flamboyant; goal-oriented; fiercely patriotic; highly religious, believing he was predestined from on high for leadership; possessed of steely discipline; given to quick judgments; steadfastly loyal to subordinates; and demanding of the highest possible performance from those who worked for him. He was at once feared by his World War II Nazi enemies, revered by subordinate officers and troops, and a source of wonderment and dismay by his commanding Allied forces superiors. No other field commander matched his World War II results. Might he be your role model?

Eleanor Roosevelt, a shy, awkward child, seldom receiving adult recognition and peer acceptance, grew into a woman with great sensitivity to the underprivileged of all creeds, races, and nations. When Mrs. Roosevelt came to the White House in 1933, she understood society's broader and worrisome conditions better than any of her first lady predecessors, and she transformed the role of presidential spouse into presidential partner. She never shirked official entertaining and greeted thousands with charming friendliness. She also broke precedent to hold press conferences, travel to all parts of the nation, give lectures and radio broadcasts, and express her opinions candidly in a daily syndicated newspaper column, "My Day." Might she be your role model?

Jack Welch was the CEO of General Electric for 20 years during the latter part of the twentieth century. Under his leadership the value of the corporation soared by billions of dollars. He made many more billions for the owners of GE stocks, and ten thousand GE employees became real live millionaires on his watch. He pioneered new management strategies including intolerance for failure, set production standards with zero-defect acceptance, and imposed a seemingly ruthless requirement that the lowest-rated 10 percent of all managers be released from the company each year. Since his tenure as GE's CEO, literally dozens of high-ranking Welch protégées migrated as CEOs to other private-sector firms where they implemented his management methods to great effect. Welch had an indelible effect upon private-sector management throughout the United States and the world. What part of Jack Welch's style might fit you and your work circumstances?

Harry S. Truman, who unexpectedly inherited the presidency following Franklin Delano Roosevelt's 1943 death, was self-effacing, genuinely humble, raised in a nondescript middle-class home, and had an undistinguished career as a farmer, military officer, businessman, and low-level public official. Yet, despite such an inauspicious background, he gained election to the U.S. Senate and, upon rising from vice president to commander in chief, rendered some of the most important decisions in the history of the United States, including the dropping of the atomic bomb on the Japanese homeland and constructing the principal defense to the aggressive Cold War actions of the former Soviet Union. Does his self-effacing but effective leadership manner fit you?

Mother Teresa, who grew famous for selflessly ministering to lepers, the homeless, and the poorest of the poor in the slums of Calcutta (Mumbai), joined the Sisters of Our Lady of Lareto in 1928. For 17 years, she taught school and performed charity work throughout the nation of India. In 1950, she founded the Missionaries of Charity, a new order devoted to helping the sick and poor. During the next 50 years, the order grew to include branches in more than 100 cities around the world, and Mother Teresa became a worldwide symbol of charity, meeting with England's Princess Diana and many other public figures. In 1979, Mother Teresa was awarded the Nobel Prize for Peace, and in 1985 she was awarded the Medal of Freedom from the United States. Is her lead-by-doing and servantlike leadership approach appealing to you?

William Jefferson Clinton, president of the United States from 1992 to 2000 and husband of New York state's former U.S. senator and current Obama administration secretary of state Hillary Rodham Clinton, was among the nation's most charismatic presidents. His commanding presence, personal bearing, eloquence, engaging personality, spectacular grasp of complexity, and ability to communicate with multiple audiences were highly evident and striking traits. Regrettably, other than balancing the federal budget (no small challenge), he left only a modest legacy as president (North American Free Trade Agreement—NAFTA—and welfare reform). His term as president is characterized and chronicled by historians principally as squandered opportunity. Instead of towering accomplishments, such as those amassed by Washington, Adams, Lincoln, and the Roosevelts, Clinton will likely be remembered for a stream of unfortunate moral lapses and indelicate personal behaviors, activities outside the zone of follower tolerance.

Martin Luther King Jr.'s actions altered the social and legal landscape of America and were admired globally. His ability to communicate and his strategic interventions elevated issues of race relations and civil liberties to the top of the nation's policy agenda. He informed himself regarding and then consciously adapting the nonviolent tenets of Henry Thoreau and Mahatma Gandhi. When Martin Luther King Jr. engaged in civil disobedience, in an effort to secure racial justice and equal rights, it was a conscious action taken in pursuit of a larger goal. Within his civil rights organization, an organization that he personally founded, there were followers who routinely criticized his "turn the other cheek" philosophy. They preferred actions that were bolder, confrontational, and, on occasion, inviting of retaliatory violence. Of course, among those in the larger society who opposed him, his purposes and practices were even more unacceptable. Still, despite having to maintain a middle ground

Actively Searching for Models

It is not only the passive observation of leaders with whom one is in personal contact that can be useful. In addition, one can actively seek other models to observe. This can be done principally through reading biography and watching films or television footage of leaders in action. It is fruitful to engage in an active search for models, expanding the realm of leaders with whom one can engage and with which one can compare, even if vicariously, in order to find leadership components that one would like to weave into the tapestry of one's own leadership style.

Practice

Adolph Hitler would rehearse his speeches tirelessly. He sought and consciously constructed physical and ceremonial circumstances in which his message would be maximally received by followers. He was a master, however evil a master, of communication and persuasion. However, it did not come naturally to an individual whose early life had been filled with mediocrity and failure. By conscious resolve he molded himself into an awesome machine capable of manipulating large-scale public and follower opinion. Whereas one would hope that a leader's ends were moral, Hitler is nevertheless a good example of the self-conscious crafting of individual action, through practice and trial and error, to mold an effective leader. Of course, one should note that as time progressed and the gap between Hitler's rhetoric and his actions, and the gap between his professed purposes and the reality of day-to-day German life, widened, no amount of speechifying and media manipulation could voluntarily persuade followers; and it was only through force, intimidation, and intrigue that he maintained his leadership position.

Outside Objective Criticism

One can shape and reshape leadership style through conscious solicitation of constructive feedback from knowledgeable observers. Such observers may be friends, family members, upperlings, subordinates, etc. They can even be formally arranged. There exist executive coaches, individuals who specialize, usually for money, in helping shape leadership style. The important point is that the observer providing feedback should be in a position to know what you as a leader have actually done, and are striving to accomplish, and not be so subject to intimidation or reprisal that the individual critic involved is unable or unwilling to provide honest feedback.

Reflection

One's most capable critic can be one's self. Continually subjecting one's own actions to constructively critical self-examination can be useful. After a meeting, after a presentation, after a difficult conversation, after having met a superior, one should wonder: "How did I do?" Could I have done something differently that could have been better? Could my ends have been achieved more forcefully had I acted differently?

An individual incapable of honest self-appraisal is unlikely to be an effective leader. A word of caution is in order, however. One can become so self-absorbed in reflecting upon one's own actions as to become paralyzed, resulting in indecision and inactivity for fear of behaving in a less than fully effective manner. Such obsessive behavior is a symptom of self-examination taken to excess.

CONSTRUCTING PROFESSIONAL PHILOSOPHIES

An education leader is often called upon to explain his or her philosophy regarding learning, school culture, management, and the links among the three. This is particularly true in job interviews and public settings. The precise nature of one's philosophy and all of its individual components is seldom as important as having a coherent view of how learning takes place and how schools as organizations should be managed to maximize learning. Of course, whatever one's views about such matters, of central importance is that they are internally consistent and easily capable of being understood by others and that one is prepared as a leader to act upon these views.

While it comes down to the individual involved constructing his or her personal philosophies regarding learning and management, there are dimensions to which one might fruitfully give consideration in the design process. The following questions are illustrative of the kind one can expect in job interviews and in prequalification questionnaires for education leadership positions. These are also the types of questions that one's references will be asked to comment upon in their recommendations regarding you as a position candidate.

Questions Illustrative of One's Philosophy of Education, Views of School Culture and Instruction, and Management

- What is the mix of subjects and skills that you think students need to know at varying age and grade levels?

- How best do you believe students can learn that which you specify as important?
- Through what medium and means is reading best taught?
- Do you have a view regarding the mix of direct instruction versus situated learning?
- What role does technology, such as computer-assisted instruction, have in a school or district in which you would be engaged?
- Are there any particular pedagogical approaches of which you are especially enamored and would recommend be adopted in a district? Can you cite any evidence regarding the effectiveness of those programs?
- Do you have a view regarding the utility of ability grouping of students for instructional purposes?
- What do you contend is the best way to enable non-English-speaking children to learn English quickly?
- For what characteristics or qualifications have you come to look for in hiring or rehiring teachers? Are there any teacher training techniques in which you have particular confidence?
- What is the role, in the school you would create and operate, for professional development of teachers?
- Are there more cost-effective strategies for enhancing student achievement than the costly method of reducing class sizes?
- What do you believe is the optimum enrollment size for an elementary or high school?
- Do you have a philosophy regarding the middle school years? Would you have students in middle schools taught by specialized teachers?
- How much homework should be assigned to students in the elementary and high school years?

A job interview itself is not the place extemporaneously to formulate such an important part of one's leadership knowledge arsenal. Prior consideration and even rehearsed public presentations regarding one's philosophical predispositions are good ideas.

SETTING PRIORITIES

If you do not know where you want to go, any road will take you there. Witness the following vignette regarding a true-to-life educational leader whose name has been disguised.

The Wondrous and Wishful, but Wayward, World of William Winston

Bill Winston was the superintendent of a large southern school district. He had had the typical administrative career, advancing from classroom teacher to counselor, to assistant principal, to principal, to central-office administrator and then moving through a number of superintendencies from smaller to larger districts. He was articulate, gregarious, energetic, and absolutely committed to children and their well-being. He liked being a leader and he wanted to do well. Bill wanted always to do the right thing. However, he was about to be fired, for good, even if the reasons were perplexing to him.

Bill liked everyone, and he desperately wanted everyone to like Bill. He sought approval when he should have pursued respect. He prided himself on his open-door policy. He was personally accessible, to a fault. He permitted others to intrude on his time. He eliminated the administrators between himself and the district's approximately one hundred principals. He supervised all principals, which, of course, meant he did not supervise any of them. He never met an idea or a person he did not like. Therefore, every idea and every individual was of equal value. He had no priorities. Every possible action was as significant as every other possible action. Every interaction with another individual was as valuable to him as any other interaction. The result was that his energies, his ideas, his authority, his advice, and his time were splintered. He could accomplish little because he strove to accomplish everything. He was ethical, idealistic, generous, selfless, likeable, and useless. He was the antithesis of a strategic leader. His district made no progress toward the goals set for him by the school board. They terminated his contract. Bill just did not get it. Even his firing baffled him.

In order to overcome any possibility of acting in the directionless manner just illustrated, an effective leader should consider carrying two, possibly three, small cards in his or her shirt or blouse pocket. The cards should be ever present, even if not visible to others. One card should contain up to approximately six organizational goals. Every day a leader should examine these, read them on the way to work, and determine what of his or her intended activities that day will likely contribute to the accomplishment of one or more of these goals. If the day's activities do not in some significant way align themselves with the accomplishment of goals, constructing and sustaining an effective school culture, then the day may be wasted, and the time spent may have better been directed toward other activities.

CARD 1: SCHOOL GOALS
• 90th percentile on state academic tests
• 90 percent graduation rate
• No achievement gap by race
• 90 percent daily attendance
• Zero expulsions and suspensions
• 90 percent parent engagement and satisfaction

Card 1 illustrates a possible set of goals for Howard Miller, principal of Martin Luther King Middle School.[1] These goals are the crystallization of his aspirations for his school. Here you can see that principal Miller is concentrating heavily on high academic performance. More important, note that each of principal Miller's goals is quantifiable and measurable. Take a moment to consider which of his goals are ends and which are possibly means to an end.

Being Mindful of Means

A second card should list the principal management strategies in which one believes and for which one strives continually to implement. Presumably, these management strategies comprise the major means through which one can achieve the just-mentioned organizational and school culture goals. These too will serve as everyday considerations to guide action.

CARD 2: DECISION GUIDES
• Academics first
• Hire the best
• Empower subordinates
• Appraise fairly
• Reward results
• Anticipate change

Card 2 lists principal Miller's decision guides. These are the most important management priorities by which he chooses to achieve his previously specified organizational goals. These decision guides are what principal Miller believes will enable him to continually renew his organization and facilitate his school's sustained success. As with the card on school goals, adherence to these guidelines is objectively verifiable.

Personal Values

The third card should be a set of personal beliefs. These are not so much about the school's culture as they are about the leader as a person. These are preferred personal values that guide actions. Cards 1 and 2 are organizationally focused, where a leader says to himself or herself, "I want my organization to be a success (as defined by my Card 1 goals), and I think I know how to get there, (as displayed in my Card 2 decision guidelines). However, in my own actions, I want to be true to my values as expressed in Card 3."

The personal values expressed in Card 3 should be adhered to, regardless of organizational context. They are personal and professional attributes every bit as much as leader attributes. They should be as applicable as much in principal Miller's personal life, with his family, friends, and others with whom he regularly interacts, as with his school colleagues and employees.

CARD 3: PERSONAL VALUES
• Honesty • Professionalism • Collegiality • Optimism • Helpfulness • Humility

In Card 3, principal Miller has listed personal attributes that are important to him. These are the traits by which he ideally prefers to act and the manner in which he would like his peers and those who work for him to think of him. These are aspirational. It is unlikely that principal Miller, or anyone else, is sufficiently disciplined or constantly diligent to the degree of 100 percent compliance with his own high code of conduct. Few individuals always match their aspirations. Still, having the code is a larger guarantee of consistent and thoughtful action than not having such a code.

Progress toward Card 1's organizational goals is measurable. Adherence to Card 2's decision guides is verifiable. Compliance with Card 3's personal values is known fully only to one's self.

PRESIDENT GEORGE W. BUSH AND LEADERSHIP VALUES

The following are the values to which former president George W. Bush publicly subscribes and to which he strives personally to adhere.

- Freedom
- Compassion
- Opportunity
- Accountability

INSTILLING PRIDE: PUTTING LIFE INTO PRACTICAL PRIORITIES

Assuming that as a reader you now have a sense of self and how you want to act and be perceived as a leader and, further, that you have a sense of that which you would like to accomplish, then just what should you do? How, concretely, should you begin to move from a sense of what should be done to actually doing it? Such is the purpose of this section. Your principal tool involves the mnemonic *PRIDE: Policy, Resources (people, money, and time), Incentives, Data (used systematically), and Empowerment.* It is not sufficient for a strategic leader to look at these tools as an either-or option. An effective school leader must orchestrate all five.

Policy

It is important for a leader to specify purposes and expectations. One needs to be careful not to overspecify or overly prescribe these items, leaving no room for subordinates to exercise authority and creativity. Few things are less effective in leadership than to micromanage, or prescribe too intensely. However, those who work with and for you deserve a concrete sense of what is expected. This is what is meant by policy. Good policy also serves to provide a template against which the performance of subordinates can be fairly appraised.

Resources: People, Money, and Time

Upcoming chapters, Chapters 4 through 7, concentrate on the topics of people and resources, including time, and there is no need here to duplicate the principles and prescriptions provided in these settings.

People

When it comes to personnel, there are a few simple, but remarkably practical and powerful, messages to be emphasized here.

- No leader can perform effectively without the help of others. Converting intent into reality calls upon the commitment, knowledge, and skills of others.
- Selecting, motivating, and appraising those "others" is one of the most important practical tools at the disposal of a leader.

Money

Educators are sometimes uncomfortable and reticent in dealing with money matters. They seldom have been trained regarding finance. If a reader recognizes this phobia, then strive to overcome it. An agency's budget process provides a crucial lever for organization influence and change. Only vision and people come first as levers for reshaping an endeavor.

Here are productive steps to pursue in order to take advantage of an organization's budget process as a means for understanding and then influencing the overall organization. Keep in mind that the following steps will likely meet with resistance as budgeting is far more a political and social than a technical undertaking.

- Situate yourself in your organization's budget planning process to occupy a place at the center of this endeavor. When you have a full budgetary understanding and the organization, through its resource allocation, is pursuing the path specified by your vision, you can then return the reins of budgeting to subordinates.
- Ensure that you are fully in the information loop regarding important budget planning matters such as enrollment projections, teacher turnover and recruitment projections, class size assumptions, facility needs, revenue projections, and alterations in government funding procedures.

- Inform yourself regarding federal government regulations pertaining to any program, school, department, or related activity for which as a leader you have responsibility. While the federal funding will not always be a large amount, regardless of magnitude, the federal funding is likely to be the tail that wags your organizational dog. Knowing the rules is crucial, or otherwise the forces of inertia will rely upon them to claim change is impossible.

- Become technically informed regarding any formulaic distributional or allocation decision rules relied upon by your organization to distribute resources from the managerial center to the operating periphery. Such distribution formulae tend to have a coloration of rationality and technical certainty to them when, in fact, they are almost always speculative and arbitrary. To the extent to which you can, and it may take time, rearrange these distributional criteria to more closely link resources with accurate measures of need and in a manner that is able to reward performance.

- However gradually, strive to move your organization away from employee salary arrangements that bear little or no relationship to performance and student achievement (e.g., certificates or credentials possessed, years of instructional experience, and units beyond the bachelor's degree) and establish an incentive system that rewards instructional skills, successful teaching, and elevated student performance.

- Maximize budgetary discretion for subordinates in whom you have confidence. It is a means for empowering them and unleashing their creativity. In effect, as a leader you are trading a conventional but unproductive role of prescribing processes for an emphasis on outcomes. It thus follows, of course, that accurately appraising outcomes is a part of the process thereafter.

- Pursue efficiencies and organizational incentives. For example, place substitute teacher budgets at individual schools and permit the unused funds to be rolled over into a subsequent budget year and used for other purposes at the discretion of teachers and principals. Such small actions have been found to reduce teacher absenteeism. Treat utility budgets similarly. Arrange budgets to shape behavior. For example, by placing utility budgets at individual work sites, and permitting the carryover of unexpended funds, employees are motivated to conserve power, heat, and so on. Permit them to apply such surpluses to instructional programs.

Time

Your time is the most elusive of a leader's resources. It is utterly irretrievable. Once used, it is gone. It cannot be stockpiled. Because of its scarcity, it is a leader's most valuable personal resource, and its deployment should be undertaken with considerable care. Thus, how is a leader's time best used?

There are limited hours in a day. One learns periodically of individuals alleged to need little or no sleep. Generally, sleep deprivation is not a productive way to solve the time scarcity problem. Similarly, time must be set aside for logistical realities such as shopping, personal chores, physical exercise, interaction with family and friends, and, on occasion, vacation. The latter can be a point of remarkable rejuvenation and should not regularly be foregone on grounds that one is too busy. It is often during time off for recreation that significant new and creative perspectives emerge regarding one's work.

A leader can routinely expect to work 50 to 60 hours per week. If working this much or this hard is not part of a reader's life plan, then one might well reexamine one's motives in seeking a leadership position. Long hours, and full days, are simply part of the territory of assuming added organizational responsibility.

Assuming a 50-week work year, this means that there is something in the neighborhood of 2,500 to 3,000 hours per year to be allocated to work matters. However, one cannot assume that all of this is time at a leader's absolute discretion.

For public officials, as most educational leaders are, a question regarding "how to spend one's time" is somewhat rhetorical. There is an air of unreality to it. That is because there is a large part of a principal's job, a superintendent's role, or a teacher leader's position that is unpredictable and subject to the flow of contextual events. A principal, a superintendent, and others of their ilk often are in reactive positions. Their time is not fully under their control. A private-sector CEO such as Jack Welch, Steve Jobs, Indra Nooyi, or Carol Bartz can determine with far greater certainty how to spend time. Even here, however, he or she must, on occasion, react. The stock market can plummet, an employee can unexpectedly run amok, a natural disaster can occur, and the CEO will have to drop all else and pay attention.

For a school official, a predetermined calendar of events can easily fall prey to a public disaster, a school bus accident, a racially motivated student or staff conflict, a violent act at a school, the misbehavior of a school official or teacher, or the unpredictable actions of a crazed individual or criminal element such as was made famous by the shootings at Columbine High School, outside of Denver, Colorado. An interruption can occur due to something so mundane as the mayor phoning and expressing a desire to have lunch that day because of something he or she would like to discuss.

When faced with unpredictable conditions to which one is expected to react, how does one plan a rational allocation of one's time? For example, a public-service leader should know that he or she is unlikely to be able to fill an entire day's or week's schedule with predetermined appointments, presentations, conversations, classroom visits, and central-office conferences and realistically expect that such can happen for a fluid uninterrupted 10-hour span during the day. Rather, a leader might think in an alternative fashion. A leader should consider flexible or block scheduling. That is, think of time in macro modules of a day, a week, a month, and a year. Consider disaggregating goals and activities and fitting them to available time blocks. The result is a distributed focus.

Your Own Block Scheduling

Here is a somewhat overly simple illustration of how a leader might think of using block scheduling. Imagine that there are three major functions during the day, a week, or a month. One function is to achieve a predetermined organizational goal. Disaggregate the actions needed to fulfill such a goal into component parts that lend themselves to incremental action. Fit the increments into your predetermined schedule over a period of time.

For example, elevating student performance in one's school to the 90th percentile on state achievement tests can be taken as a goal. Assign 30 percent of one's discretionary time to activities aligned with this goal. However, do not be insistent upon precisely what 30 percent of your time that will be. Also, do not assume for a moment that the 30 percent will be routine or uninterrupted.

Now, imagine further that part of a leader's job is to react to conditions that are not always predictable. Simply assume in your daily, weekly, and monthly block schedule that about a third of your time is going to be occupied by unpredictable and uncontrollable events. If few or no emergencies or urgent conditions come about, then use the unanticipated free period productively to undertake actions consistent with your larger goal, elevating student achievement, for the block of time involved.

Finally, in order to maintain one's organization, to just manage the status quo, it is necessary to engage with employees and subordinates and keep one's ear to the organizational ground. Here the technique of "management by walking around" is useful. One can allocate the remaining time block to engaging in this activity.

Walking Around

This need not be done at the same time each day or each week. Indeed, there are advantages to moving through one's organization at different points in the daily or weekly cycle of events. Often if you walk around your school, or drive around your district, at the same time each day or each week, you may encounter only the same individuals. Also, your visits become predictable, and those you meet with have anticipated or even prepared for your arrival in advance. You are less likely to encounter them at candid moments. By relying upon a more random schedule, you may expand the spectrum of employees, subordinates, students, and clients you encounter, and you may expand the sample of their work lives and behavior you are able to observe.

The point of walking around is to engage with people wherever possible and, while not disrupting instruction, to talk to as many individuals as you can. The agenda is not formed or formal. Topics are whatever is on people's minds. In the course of the conversation a leader should continually be attuned to events and conditions that appear to be emerging and with which he or she may subsequently have to deal. It may also be a time when a leader can inspire subordinates and provide them with added information useful to their performance of assigned tasks. Being visible, sharing insights, commiserating where appropriate, congratulating when there is something to celebrate, and making note of what needs to be fixed or added are all events that provide subordinates with a sense that their leader is present and cares.

A leader should not feel guilty, as if he or she was wasting time, when walking around and interacting with subordinates and clients. It is somewhat easy to feel guilty about such actions because for most leaders it is enjoyable. Talking to people is an activity from which many leaders themselves derive energy. However, there is an important balance here. Too much time in the field almost assuredly means too little time devoted to focused efforts at improvement and too little time devoted to reflection.

Gimmicks

What time of day should a leader do what? Some claim to be more alive early in the morning; others claim to be better later in the day. Whatever your circadian rhythm, it makes most sense to tackle that which you find most challenging at the time of day you feel most alert. That leaves for consideration the issue of paperwork. There is a quantum of paperwork, virtually no matter what one's role. Some corporate CEOs claim to hold all meetings while everyone is standing. No sitting is permitted. The proclaimed consequence is that meetings are more focused, everyone allegedly gets to the point quickly, decisions are made more expeditiously, and gossip and informality are reduced to a minimum. This idea is silly. If the decision is where to go to lunch or what team to back at a tournament, then fine. However, if the issue is where geographically to locate a new school, which candidate to employ as a new principal, or which textbooks to use in elementary mathematics instruction, the topic justifies sitting down and taking the issue seriously.

A former big-city superintendent gained a measure of media fame by claiming he never touched a piece of paper more than once. Presumably, to read a memo, a notice, a letter, or a request was immediately to formulate a response. Such an action probably is foolish. Some, usually trivial, items can be disposed of rapidly. Others are deserving of careful consideration and added thought. Strive to avoid falling victim to ill-conceived work gimmicks claiming to save time.

Incentives

Forthcoming Chapter 4 concentrates on personnel and incentives. What is important to understand here is that individuals working for and with you are likely to undertake those activities for which they perceive there are rewards and punishments. Consequently, one must exert great care to ensure that whatever is being incented in your organization is that which will contribute to an effective school culture. Beware of "goal displacement," the tendency of the easily quantifiable to displace that which, while complicated and perhaps not easily measured, is nevertheless important.[2]

Data Used Systematically

Within America's new era of heightened expectations for schooling, growing societal complexity, and increasing instructional sophistication, school leaders are looked to as individuals who can identify, define, and solve problems. While there are many approaches to making decisions and solving problems, a critical first step in solving problems is to identify and fully understand them, and one powerful mechanism for specifying and comprehending problems is to collect and analyze data. (See Chapter 6 for more detail.)

When strategic education leaders compile, assess, and use school and community data, they are in a better position to serve as catalysts for problem solving within school communities. While some problems clearly present themselves, others are not immediately evident or explicitly defined and thus must be discovered, fleshed out by careful analysis of data. Given the nation's current policy context, educators increasingly recognize the value of data and the need to obtain a greater comprehension of data analysis and decision making.

Empowerment

If you are not prepared to delegate sufficient authority to "others" so that they can freely and fully do their assigned job, then you have wasted your resources in hiring them. If you cannot trust subordinates to do their job, then you might as well do it yourself.

COMMUNICATING PURPOSES, CREATING IMPRESSIONS, CONFRONTING CONFLICT

Leaders make decisions. They create vision, determine priorities, select subordinates, and allocate resources. However, once they have determined the right thing to do, virtually all else a leader accomplishes will likely take place by persuading others to take action. Leaders are badly handicapped, probably hopelessly handicapped, if unable effectively to communicate preferences to audiences such as the general public, parents, professional peers, and subordinates and persuade them of the utility of pursuing necessary tasks.

By creating a favorable impression, particularly from the outset, a leader may establish a predisposition among targets of communication, a predisposition that can assist in gaining acceptance of the message, making persuasion easier. However, sometimes a favorable impression and effective communication are insufficient. Sometimes something goes wrong, and an uncomfortable conversation is a necessity. These difficult exchanges can operate two ways. One can initiate them, or one can be the target or recipient of someone else's negative judgment. Regardless, there are ways to handle unpleasantness that defuse the negative and may even salvage something positive. Confrontation need not result in irresolvable conflict and can, on occasion, be converted to a constructive outcome. This section is about these and related topics.

Communicating Purposes

Previously cited Harvard psychologist Howard Gardner situates communication at the heart of effective leadership. His assertion is that effective leaders, particularly public leaders, have an unusual capacity to frame stories that fall upon followers' ears with the ring of authenticity. A story, speech, or message that resonates with the recipients' reality has a chance of triggering allegiance and agreement. These stories enable a follower to identify with the leaders personally or with the leader's purposes. The more effective the story, the wider the believing audience and the more intense the possible follower commitment.

Communication can take at least three forms: oral, written, and informal or nonverbal. As a leader, or aspiring leader, one should consciously craft an ability to speak effectively to audiences, both large and small. It will take practice, and there are ways to gain help. This is another place where watching and analyzing the styles of others can be of assistance. Still, regardless of how acquired and honed, effective public speaking is a must for a leader.[3]

Second, one should hone writing skills. Different audiences necessitate different writing formats and styles, and this is not the place to identify and review each of the various kinds. Suffice it to say that an administrative memorandum to subordinates is different from a congratulatory letter to a recent high school graduate or the winner of a teacher-of-the-year award. Most writing is intended to be persuasive, either of action or of feeling. However, audience matters greatly. A budget message based solely on emotion, and devoid of facts, is less likely to be effective than one that stresses fiscal conditions and likely budgetary trajectories. A reader might keep in mind the difference between the Declaration of Independence, intended to inspire, and the United States Constitution, intended as a charter or regulatory document. The former was lofty and vague; the latter was declarative and specific.

Handwritten notes, for selected purposes, convey a special message, and a reader should consider his or her ability to undertake this medium. Good penmanship is ever more rare. Still, a handwritten note at a special time of commendation, commiseration, or celebration can have a disproportionate effect upon a recipient. What it says is important, but the medium is here also the message. Taking the time to render communication personal means that you, the leader, thought sufficiently of the recipient that you were willing to allocate your personal time to the matter.

Nonverbal and Informal Communication

This topic is accorded special emphasis here because of the capacity for a leader to underscore or undo much by mindlessness. One can harm that which is good by thoughtlessly conveying a separate or antithetical message through informal activities and nonverbal actions such as body language. Anyone doubting this should watch an accomplished elected official such as former president William Clinton weave his way through an audience, shaking hands, exchanging pleasantries, and conveying to virtually each individual that he or she is special to him. A picture of concern and engagement emerges that would be almost impossible otherwise to convey in writing or in spoken words alone.

Conversely, attending a major meeting and acting in a callous or flippant manner can convey, even if mistakenly, to those present that you as a leader are unengaged in the activity that is taking place.

Influencing Follower Impressions

Others inevitably will have an impression of you as a leader. It may be a snap judgment. It may be modified over time, as an observer gathers more evidence and has more interactions. It may be a superficial, unflattering, or incorrect impression. Nevertheless, observers and those with whom leaders interact will form an impression. Consequently, given this inevitability of follower judgment, it is advantageous to consciously strive to shape impressions, to create a favorable predisposition. Creating a favorable impression is analogous in marketing to creating brand identification and brand loyalty. A leader can benefit from a wellspring of favorable regard, which proves invaluable to counter or dilute the inevitable episodic downturns when events and results are less than what the leader would want.

LINK TO CASE STUDY 3

Every school and school culture undergoes challenges. Think back to a time when your school underwent a challenging situation. Drawing upon the list of 10 leadership dimensions presented in the case study, can you propose any particular leadership traits that were most essential or influential in helping the school community grow and move forward?

There are many means by and material components of which a favorable image can be constructed. What follows is intended to be illustrative, not exhaustive. Also, what follows assumes that the characteristics of leadership and the leader being promoted are authentic. They are actions and attributes the leader aspires to when constructing an image, but to be an authentic and successful image, the underlying facts, portrayals, and interpretations need to be accurate.

The following is a set of activities and items that are grist for constructing a leadership impression. These are the vehicles from which an image or persona can be constructed. The content or coloration to be placed within each vector is a matter of selection for the individual leader. However, what follows is a list of image-shaping vectors contributing to follower impressions and amenable to shaping.

Vectors of Personal Impression (Initial and Lasting) Amenable to Influence

- Website appearance and content
- Personal resume[4]
- Office and personal stationery
- Telephone answering and messaging protocols
- Office (and outer office) size and décor
- Office staff greeting and behavior
- Personal handshake, greeting, eye contact, and recollection of names
- Bearing, posture, projection of energy level
- Personal attire and its condition (shoes shined, tie tied, accessories matching)
- Office trappings (books, awards, diplomas, photographs)
- Evidence of connection to persons of power and to luminaries
- Evidence of public and professional recognition and office holding
- Media management and publicity
- Use of language
- Evidence of tastes
- Public and professional venues where seen by others
- Humility and self-effacing demeanor
- Humor
- Compassion

Difficult Conversations

Regardless of a leader's success, image, or preferences, sometimes something goes wrong. If the "wrong" is a function of a person's errors or systematic failure to perform, then a difficult interpersonal conversation may be in order. If the failing individual is aware of the shortcoming or willing to acknowledge the deficiency, then the conversation may be less difficult in that he or she may be apologetic and not defensive. Nevertheless, it usually is a good idea to discuss the failure so as to ensure that the individual understands that you, as leader, are mindful of the deficiency, and, whereas you are perhaps forgiving, you still do not want the incident or phase to go unnoticed. It is important to discuss it to ensure that it is understood as failure and is not to be repeated. Moreover, open acknowledgment of and discussion around failure may be cathartic for all involved, even for the overseeing leader. Finally, discussions of failure may lead to corrections that benefit both individuals and the entire organization.

If you anticipate that the failing or deficient individual is unaware or will be defensive, then your posture should be firm, convincing, and possessed of fact, after fact, after fact. Your record, and your ability to convey the record, must be resolute. If you have any reason to believe that the conversation will become confrontational and that threats or retribution may be implied, you should arrange for a witness to be present or within earshot.

What if the difficult conversation is about you? What if you as a leader or aspiring leader are perceived as having made an error, an error of sufficient consequence to warrant a conversation or some kind of corrective action? In such an instance, you should play out the conversation in your mind in advance of the actual event. If you believe you are in some way at fault and either deficient or contributing to deficiency, then it is almost always best to acknowledge the condition and put forth means by which the situation can be reversed and avoided in the future. The rule of thumb by which you should act is to imagine yourself in the accuser's role and behave in a manner you would wish to see in the event roles were reversed.

LEADER ETHICS AND CONSISTENT BEHAVIOR

Two things can interrupt an ambitious leader's otherwise brilliant upward ascendancy quickly. One is unbridled personal arrogance. The other is falling prey to the myriad unethical temptations strewn in the day-to-day path before successful leaders. A leader's long-run effectiveness may well stem from his or her ability to resolve these tensions and resist such temptations.

Ethical issues are sometimes difficult for leaders. So is consistent behavior. This is because there can exist an inherent tension between many of the traits and qualities that render a leader effective and ethical and consistent personal behavior. Moreover, ironically, the more successful a leader becomes, often the more attractive and extensive the opportunities are to behave unethically. Once accruing power, overcoming adversity, and having tasted success, it is tempting to deviate from one's previously determined path and seek personal gain.

To gain acceptance for an idea, in order to mobilize support for the pursuit of a vision, a leader may well develop traits of unusual persuasion and trustworthiness. These very traits, so crucial to leader success, need deviate only by but a few degrees before they can be distorted to the pursuit of personal and unethical ends. Witness, again, the persuasive prowess of Hitler. The problem was the ends he pursued. Had he pursued world peace, he might have been one of the greatest moral figures of all time. Moreover, the gregarious charm that may enable a leader to mobilize support for otherwise difficult-to-accomplish goals can be misdirected toward personal gain or short-run selfish pleasure. This was a weakness of former president William J. Clinton.

Constant personal vigilance and self-criticism is the first line of defense regarding unethical leader behavior and arrogance. An internal gyroscope is a far more effective guide to ethical behavior than detailed knowledge of a complicated set of external strictures.

Often it is nuanced issues that pose the greatest ethical challenges to a leader. Stealing organizational assets for personal gain, embezzlement, or perpetrating personal or physical harm upon others are well-understood felonies and constitute a clear path to personal destruction. Overt and obvious crime almost invariably leads to a leader's downfall. However, it is the gray areas where judgment becomes more clouded, and it is in the interstices of indecision that the ethical standards of a leader more likely will be tested.

What follows is an illustrative list of gray areas, leadership decision dimensions not immediately subject to the scrutiny of others but that can contribute to a leader's ethical decay. In each of the following instances there is, conceivably, a reason for a leader to distort the truth or to be misperceived as having acted appropriately. As such, each of the following illustrative dimensions involves matters of judgment important for a strategic education leader to consider.

- Possibly withholding or distorting information needed by others to judge a leader's performance or an organization's success
- Taking, perhaps unduly, credit for the accomplishments of others
- Appropriating, or perhaps misappropriating, organizational assets for personal comfort or individual material gain
- Invoking organizational authority on behalf of, perhaps, inappropriate purposes
- Possibly taking advantage of insider knowledge to advance personal, rather than organizational, goals
- Using one's position of authority, maybe unfairly, to extort material items or personal favors from others

THE UNSUNG SIGNIFICANCE
OF PREDICTABLE LEADER BEHAVIOR

In addition to acting ethically, it is important that a leader's behavior be consistent or, within reason, even predictable. If a leader is given to unexplainable mood swings and shifts in outlook, if the same behavior from a subordinate provokes widely different reactions in a leader from time to time or from person to person, if the criteria being used to judge proposals for action or personal performance vacillate from one moment to the next or from one subordinate to the next, then a leader is contributing to an atmosphere of emotional instability. In such circumstances, organizational instability may not be far behind.

When surrounded by instability or unpredictability, subordinates will minimize personal risks and react by curtailing initiatives and creativity. In an effort to reestablish equilibrium, to render their working culture stable, employees will revert to rigid rules, a condition that inevitably diminishes the capacity of an organization to elevate its overall performance. Such debilitating conditions can be avoided by the conscious efforts of a leader to establish and maintain a predictable pattern of action and style.

CONCLUSION

This chapter highlights the importance of a consciously crafted and authentic leadership style that requires school leaders to identify their core values and consider them in relation to the school community. By addressing considerations in the operationalization of PRIDE, the chapter provides school leaders with suggestions for how to implement the components of an effective school culture.

QUESTIONS FOR DISCUSSION

1. Consider the organization at which you are currently employed. Spend a few moments constructing a goal card for this institution. Based on your experience with the organization, create a card of decision guides that would help the institution achieve these goals. Finally, create a card of your personal values that guide your actions, both within and outside of your current organization.

2. Recall a few instances of employment hiring successes or failures, whether by you or other leaders you have known. Is there anything, upon reflection, that you can see was undertaken correctly or incorrectly during the hiring process? Are there actions, in retrospect, that would have made the selection of employees more effective for the particular position within the organization?

3. List approximately five or six questions that you could ask of a budget official that would begin to situate you, as an educational leader, within the central activities of an organization's resource allocation decision-making process.

4. What do you now feature in your professional resume? Can you imagine changes that you might productively undertake in order better to convey your strengths to a potential employer?

5. Imagine that a subordinate has repeatedly failed to accomplish agreed-upon achievement goals for her or his school or department. Script your part, as a leader, in a difficult conversation with a subordinate.

6. To what degree would you offer unsolicited criticisms of a colleague's administrative performance if doing so held the prospect of providing you a competitive advantage in filling an upcoming leadership position?

7. To what degree do you feel like your colleagues would describe your professional behavior as consistent and predictable?

8. One ELCC standard is devoted entirely to school vision. To what degree is your personal vision, or philosophy of leadership, in alignment with your school or district vision?

SUGGESTED READINGS

Beeman, T. E., & Glenn, R. (2005). *Leading from within*. Franklin, TN: Providence House.

Bennis, W. (1989). *Why leaders can't lead*. San Francisco: Jossey-Bass.

Blanchard, K. (2007). *Leading at a higher level*. Upper Saddle River, NJ: Pearson/Prentice Hall.

Burns, J. M. (1978). *Leadership*. New York: Harper & Row.

Dubrin, A. J. (2001). *Leadership: Research findings, practice, and skills* (3rd ed.). Boston: Houghton Mifflin.

Gardner, H. (with Laskin, E.). (1995). *Leading minds: An anatomy of leadership*. New York: Basic Books.

Howell, J. P., & Costley, D. L. (2006). *Understanding behaviors for effective leadership* (2nd ed.). Upper Saddle River, NJ: Pearson/Prentice Hall.

Kouzes, J. M., & Posner, B. Z. (1987). *The leadership challenge*. San Francisco: Jossey-Bass.

Lawler, E. E., III. (1986). *High-involvement management*. San Francisco: Jossey-Bass.

Wren, J. T. (Ed.). (1995). The leader's companion. New York: The Free Press.

NOTES

1. The text boxes are not intended to be emulated, only illustrative and provocative. An individual reader's cards might well be very different. Moreover, what is on the cards is not as important as having given thought to their content. One's cards should not be fixed for all time. They should change as one's goals change, as one's job changes, as one's vision changes, and as one's personal circumstances change.

2. See *Teachers, Performance Pay, and Accountability: What Education Should Learn From Other Sectors* (2009) by Scott J. Adams, John S. Heywood, and Richard Rothstein on the dangers of establishing mindless incentives that propel people to undertake activities in opposition to an organization's larger purposes.

3. One of the most moving and effective public speeches of all time is Abraham Lincoln's Gettysburg Address. Every reader should familiarize himself or herself with the wording, cadence, and precision of this uplifting set of remarks. Also, a reader can learn quickly the difference between a consciously inspirational set of remarks and a declarative or analytic speech by going to the website that follows and viewing the consequence of turning Lincoln's Gettysburg Address into a modern PowerPoint presentation. For some purposes, PowerPoint is inappropriate. http://www.norvig.com/Gettysburg/index.htm

4. There is no perfect resume. If you are well educated but lack experience, stress education. If you are experienced but not schooled, stress experience. Build your resume around your strengths. The one *must* is contact information—address, title, phone number(s), e-mail addresses, and possible references.

Case Study 4: Warren County School Board Performance Pay Cram Down

Can a Productive Culture Withstand an Unexpected External Pressure?

Warren County was a school district of about 1,000 students situated in one of the nation's most desirable skiing and hiking recreational venues. High, craggy mountains and lush valleys contributed to its Alpine feeling. It had opulent resorts and spas, famous golf courses surrounded by architect-designed mansions, and a homeowner community that included many of the nation's most prominent business CEOs. It housed, among other groups, a substantial retirement community of industrial tycoons, high-ranking military officials, and foreign investors. Its airport served the personal jets that brought the weekend residents and recreational guests.

Warren County also had another side, a set of low-price houses, mobile homes, and barely legal shacks that housed the working class and immigrant populations providing the labor force for Warren County's restaurants, hotels, ski resorts, luxury spas, golf courses, and infrastructure maintenance. Between these income extremes was a stable middle class of managers, professionals, and longtime residents who, historically, had provided the municipal and school district elected leadership.

Despite this bimodal student population and bifurcated community, Warren County's K–12 school was remarkably successful. It was a large school, but it had an elementary and secondary school division within it. The school's value-added testing results suggested that all kinds of students—rich and poor, young and adolescent—made progress in the district. The school had an academically oriented curriculum, but it also had English-as-a-second-language offerings and sufficient and effective remedial courses to bring low-income, recently migrated worker populations into the school system. The curriculum was rich with electives, and students were deeply engaged in both athletics and community projects. The district had no difficulty in recruiting teachers, either at the elementary or secondary level. Moreover, once employed, if identified as good teachers, there had been no problem with turnover. Teachers and administrators liked to work in the Warren County schools.

Note: This case study, as with others associated with other chapters, is about an actual school, actual people, and actual conditions. Nothing is fabricated. All cases are about situations school leaders routinely encounter. However, in each instance, names of people, schools, and locations have been altered to ensure confidentiality.

Brenda Johns was the Warren County superintendent of schools. She had come to the area after college as a ski bum. She fell in love with the physical beauty of the area and when not skiing could be found hiking, running, or cycling. She supported herself initially as a substitute science teacher. Over time, and after several knee operations, she forwent serious skiing and took up serious teaching. She eventually became known as one of the best biology teachers in the state, and she exercised substantial leadership in overseeing a redesign of the state's learning standards. She obtained advanced leadership degrees through executive programs and summer courses. She married and had three children. All the while, however, she maintained her commitment to the environment, to the outdoors, to her family, and to her career as a professional educator. She was confident in her abilities, civil and assured in her manner, and committed to her profession.

Brenda's state leadership role had whetted her appetite for administration. She had never before quite seen herself as a superintendent, but increasingly she was thrust before the Warren County school board as a presenter and advocate of various initiatives. She knew the school board members. One was a highly visible ski resort operator; another was a prominent housewife whose husband was the town banker. The third was an investor whose family had long lived in Warren County and whose family name appeared on many of the county's parks and civic monuments. Brenda interacted easily with these individuals both socially and professionally. Thus, it was not a huge surprise to her when the board president asked her over a dinner one weekend if she had ever considered being a superintendent. She acknowledged that the idea increasingly crossed her mind and that she was certified for the position. However, she quickly said that, perhaps, she should have some time as a principal before operating an entire district, albeit one consisting of only one school. She knew that she was particularly naive regarding the day-to-day operation of elementary grades and would have to get up to speed.

The school board president talked to the superintendent, who acknowledged that he too thought Brenda was ably prepared for a leadership role. She was encouraged to apply for the elementary school opening in the district. She prevailed in the competition and served four years as a principal. She was widely acclaimed by her parents and teachers, all of whom were quick to testify regarding her intellect, broad knowledge of education, management skill, and community awareness. Thus, it was no surprise that, when the long-serving superintendent announced his retirement, Brenda, upon her 50th birthday, was named by the school board as his successor. She was proud to have been selected and eager to take over the reins. She admired her predecessor, knew she could count on him for advice, and was somewhat anxious regarding all the responsibility, but she was eager to put her imprimatur upon the district. She knew its strengths and its weaknesses. She wanted to preserve the former and quickly address the latter.

Shortly after Brenda assumed her new leadership duties, the complexion of the school board changed substantially. Her ski resort–owning acquaintance was unseated in a hotly contested election, and in his place as president came a retired executive of a major manufacturing firm. At the same election the chairman of the local chamber of commerce replaced the long-serving prominent community icon. The principal issue in the election had been the district's stagnant state examination scores, and the allegation that Warren County's teachers were insufficiently motivated by what was claimed to be an outmoded compensation system.

Brenda thought she knew the answer to the state test score issue. The district had become the home of a large number of Hispanic students whose parents were employed in Warren County resorts. The school district, until then, had not adapted well to the need for English language learning programs and to the need for new reading materials. Brenda was confident that she could cooperate with the two principals and teachers and address the language issues, and, in time, these changes would be reflected in high state scores.

Brenda was far less confident regarding the teacher motivation issue. Her experience as a teacher left her with the impression that most of her colleagues worked diligently, were professional, desired that their students succeed, and were continually striving to improve their instruction. From where did this view come that Warren County teachers needed to be more intensely motivated? Brenda acknowledged that there had always been and probably still were a few slackers; free riders willing to do the minimum and take advantage of their harder-working colleagues. However, her view was that there were few of these and that, in time, she and the principals could counsel them out of the district. What was the crisis, and what did the new board want?

At the first public meeting with the new board president and majority, Brenda and the district testing director made a presentation regarding the state test scores and proposed a multipronged plan to address the low reading scores of the district's Hispanic students. The board applauded her efforts in this regard and quickly adopted the proposed plan and accepted its budgetary implications. Then the surprise came.

The board president altered the agenda through a set of technically correct but otherwise provocative parliamentary procedures and then explained the educator performance pay plan that he and his newly elected chamber of commerce ally proposed be adopted that night. The audience comprised principally of district employees, central-office administrators, and interested parents sat in stunned but attentive silence. The local reporters took notes furiously.

Brenda too was surprised and felt a profound sense of betrayal. She had been polite to the new board members. She had gone out of her way to appraise their interests and to make clear that she wanted to cooperate with them. She took offense at the means by which they had sprung their idea on the public, on the staff, and upon her. It would not have been difficult and certainly would have been professionally appropriate for the board president to inform her ahead of time of his plans. That way, she would have been prepared for what followed and would not have been made to appear foolish before her staff, the public, and the press.

Brenda was not happy with what she was hearing. For a brief moment, as all of this unfurled before her surprised eyes, she thought of simply standing up, announcing her resignation, and departing. However, she bit her lip and sat through the board member's presentation. It did occur to her that if she resigned she would be forfeiting an enormously comfortable $250,000-per-year salary, an amount that was even more than her husband was paid and an amount that ensured her three children would be able to attend college.

The board president's proposed new educator compensation plan was heavily influenced by his private-sector experience. It involved a mixture of performance bonuses and market-oriented financial inducements based upon the test scores of individual teacher's students, premiums for teachers in hard-to-staff subjects such as physics and mathematics, and bonuses for effective teachers who voluntarily moved to or agreed to remain in the district's hard-to-staff schools.

A part of Brenda was attracted by the compensation ideas. She had long lamented the single-salary schedule upon which Warren County had conventionally relied in determining teacher pay. She did wish that the president had not pushed his ideas upon the school community in such a surprising and abrupt manner. She feared that the message might be lost because of the means by which it was presented.

When the board president had completed the presentation of his ideas, Brenda took the microphone and informed all those present in a most controlled voice that she had not known of this proposal before the meeting and that she was sorry that the board president had chosen to release his ideas in this manner. She said openly that such behavior was far from the civil precedent that had long characterized Warren County School District discourse, and she feared that a persistent confrontational pattern of this nature would result in a dysfunctional separation between the board and the professional educators in the district, a separation that would likely result in many losers and certainly no winners. She also reminded the board that, to the extent to which the proposed pay plan touched upon the existing salary schedule and did not involve only added bonuses, the district's collectively bargained contract was assuredly involved and that any changes would require the district to return to the bargaining table.

Then Brenda surprised the board president. She stated that there were parts of his plan that were unusually intriguing to her and that she hoped that there might be a way in which the ideas could productively be explored. She explained that, whereas she believed in performance pay in the abstract, and had virtually insisted with the prior board that her own contract with the district possess performance pay provisions, she was less sure of the means by which this principle could be applied to teachers, principals, and other professional educators. She said she had many questions, none of which were intended to be confrontational or derogatory, but all of which would take time and conversation to answer. Off the top of her head she illustrated these issues to be resolved:

- How would principals be paid under the proposed performance plan?
- By what means might teacher cooperation still be retained under a performance pay plan? Would teachers necessarily have to compete with one another for bonuses? Should bonuses be awarded to individuals, groups, or both?

- Who will be charged with evaluating teachers and selecting which ones earn bonuses? Who will teachers trust to do a comprehensive and impartial job?
- How would teacher performance be measured? Standardized test scores? Observations? Portfolios? Some other way?
- If teacher performance is to be measured with standardized test scores, would attainment, value-added, or subject matter achievement gain be the measure of performance?
- Which actions taken by teachers should be rewarded? Higher test scores? More creative teaching? Higher attendance rates? Better grades?
- What about teachers who taught in subjects for which there were no state or district test scores; that is, language teachers, P.E. teachers, counselors, etc.?
- How would teachers who taught in schools with high student turnover and a preponderance of low-socioeconomic-status students be treated fairly?
- What kinds of changes to the district's data collection and information system would have to be made?
- What would be the financial magnitude of proposed bonuses?
- How would teachers and the broader community continually be engaged in the design process?
- Once effective teachers were identified, would all parents want their children in such classrooms?

Once Brenda finished, to her further surprise, the audience clapped for her. The school board president was himself taken aback by her posture on the issue and her eloquence in explaining possible drawbacks.

The school board president asked Brenda how she suggested they proceed. She asked if she and her staff might have until the next scheduled public meeting to study the issues and report back to the board regarding added steps. The board president and others acknowledged that this was a productive direction, and the board meeting came to a close.

FOR DISCUSSION

1. What is or should be the role of the school board and the district central office in shaping school culture?

2. Was Warren County broken? If so, how?

3. Was the school board jeopardizing the already existing productive culture or just trying to tweak it to an even higher performance level?

4. Did the school board make a mistake in employing Brenda, an individual without central-office experience or outside-the-district experience?

5. Did the school board president act illegally in bringing forward the pay-for-performance issue?

6. Did Brenda respond appropriately? Should she simply have resigned? Was she rendered timid and ineffective by her personal material needs and enslavement to a high salary?

7. Should Brenda better have rejected the board president's proposal out of hand?

8. Would Brenda have been better served had she known more regarding the history of American education? Could not she have said to him that such merit pay plans have been previously tried and failed?

9. Has Brenda posed the correct questions of the board president's plan? What other questions might she have asked?

10. By what steps do you think Brenda and her administrative staff should proceed in attempting to wrestle with the board president's pay-for-performance plan?

11. What do the board president's actions, his pay plan itself, and the manner in which he presented it portend for the cultural trajectory in Warren County's schools?

CHAPTER 4

Personnel and School Culture

In this chapter a reader will learn about the following:

- Recruiting, selecting, training, and compensating effective employees
- Creating positive teacher/administration relationships
- Creating positive parent/staff relationships

INTRODUCTION

One of the most complex challenges embedded in the concept of school culture is concretely creating and maintaining the type of culture that one desires. Culture as a concept and a reality is embedded so deeply in the details and actions of all participants in a school community—what they say, what they do, what they think, what they expect, and how they express what they think and what they expect—that it is a daunting proposition to change the collective tone and direction of all these individual thoughts and interactions.

This chapter discusses one concrete dimension, the people dimension, by which a school leader can proceed to create the type of school culture that he or she desires. This culture-building activity begins with identifying and successfully recruiting able teachers, and it proceeds through a description of related matters such as induction, professional development, motivation, and personnel compensation. Subsequent chapters explore the means by which personnel can be evaluated and incented, crucial components in the construction of a productive school culture. Finally, yet other chapters explore actions, in addition to personnel, by which a leader can productively shape the culture of a school.

IDENTIFYING, RECRUITING, SELECTING, AND CONTINUALLY DEVELOPING EFFECTIVE TEACHERS

The most influential part of a culture is the people that comprise the school, and the most influential people (at least in relation to student achievement) are usually teachers (Hanushek, 1986). Hence, the first step to creating a highly effective school is to recruit, select, retain, continually develop, and motivate able teachers.

Recruiting Candidates

The first step, personnel recruiting, will vary widely based on the situation of the school. In larger districts in particular, a school may have few levers for influencing which teachers apply for a job. Depending largely on the district in which the school resides, the school may be inundated with applicants or struggle greatly to fill positions. For school leaders in the latter position, recruitment becomes a large issue; for leaders in the former position, selection is important.

School districts that routinely find they are unable to attract sufficient numbers of high-qualified education school graduates often resort to preparing their own teachers. Districts such as Houston, Texas, operate alternative-certification programs in which they actively recruit retired or experienced individuals with bachelor's degrees, particularly in hard-to-staff subjects such as science and mathematics, and then provide instructional training that fits the district's curriculum and performance expectations. Houston has found recruiting among retired government and business executives, retired military personnel, and mothers whose children have matured and left home to be a productive source of able instructors.

Education school proponents often are critical of alternative-certification pathways into teaching careers. However, researchers cannot discern any difference in the student achievement accomplishments of alternatively certified teachers from those who have received more conventional education school teacher preparation.

Houston is one of the nation's largest school districts. It has sufficient economies of scale to undertake expensive projects that would elude smaller districts. Hence, it may be to the advantage of a small district, particularly rural districts, to cooperate and engage in collective recruitment efforts. Also, state education departments sometimes assume leadership in small and rural district recruitment.

When recruiting applicants, it is important that a school presents itself in a positive light as a place where individuals will have a chance to evolve professionally. Principals should ensure that job openings are accurately posted as soon as possible and use any opportunities they have to accentuate the positives of the school that make it stand out from other schools. Nashville, Tennessee, has produced videos of recent school district accomplishments that are of a high professional nature, the viewing of which is likely to stimulate interest in at least exploring a job in the district. A local music production company contributed the expertise to construct the videos. The vigor and tone with which one recruits obviously depends on the ease with which their school normally attracts applicants.

Selecting From Among Applicants

For those who are in schools with large applicant pools, or who successfully recruit a large number of applicants, selecting the best applicants is an important step. However, selecting the most effective teacher prospects is not an easy task, and the task is apparently becoming more challenging. Researchers have, for years, tried to discern means for predicting who will be the most effective teachers given various data about them (e.g., test scores, grades, certification, etc.) and have, for the most part, struck out. This means that there is no easy way to examine standardized portfolio information about potential teachers and select from among applicants the ones who will be the best. In other words, potential teacher quality is not easily observable.

It is difficult to overemphasize the significance of teacher selection. Researchers increasingly confirm that a good teacher can make a significant difference in the academic achievement of students. For example, Nye, Konstantopoulos, and Hedges (2004) report that up to 21 percent in the variation of students' academic achievement is attributable to differences in teacher characteristics.

There is a caveat here. Teaching in the United States, beginning in the twentieth century, has been a feminine undertaking. For more than one hundred years it has not been an occupation to which large numbers of males are attracted. Nothing about this latter situation has changed. Today, about 80 percent of public school teachers are women, and the vast majority of men in the profession are secondary school teachers.

Something has changed regarding women and teaching. Apparently, at least until the onset of the 2008 economic recession, the pool of qualified female potential teachers is shrinking (Bacolod, 2007). This trend has been evident for more than a half century, ever since professional workforce opportunities for educated women expanded beyond being a teacher, librarian, or nurse. With ever-larger numbers of women graduating from law, engineering, medical, and other professional schools and entering such well-paying occupations, the number of unusually able women interested in teaching has diminished (Corcoran, Evans, & Schwab, 2004).

So, for what traits should school leaders look when selecting applicant teachers to hire and retain? Keep in mind, in responding to this rhetorical question, that not only is one searching for effective teachers, one is also searching for teachers that will fit the school culture vision that is desired. Thus, one should seek candidates who are intelligent, well-educated generally, expert in their subject areas specifically, passionate about the profession, enthusiastic about teaching, likely to be dedicated to their craft and their school, and willing to learn continuously.

PERSONNEL PRACTICES: AIRLINE INDUSTRY EXAMPLE

If you have ever flown on Southwest Airlines, you may have noticed the unusual, sometimes infectious, enthusiasm of their flight attendants. Southwest has a remarkable capacity to attract, select, retain, and motivate flight attendants who are a bit quirky and humorous and still completely competent when it comes to the safety and service features of the flight attendant job. Southwest is attentive to an individual candidate's capacity, to ensure that all the ability measures are intact in successful candidates. However, the airline goes further; it is obsessed with the idea that successful candidates also appreciate and fit into the "Southwest culture." This can-do and will-do culture reflects the spirit of its offbeat and passionate cofounder, Herb Kelleher. Southwest has been more successful than most commercial airlines because of its avant-garde business model and personnel culture of innovation and cooperation. So, a candidate who can easily smile, tell a tasteful joke, spin a tale, provide evidence of willingness to help, and display an ability to empathize with passengers regarding the vagaries of modern airline travel is likely to have a leg up on being hired.

Intellect

Raw intelligence is the principal indicator of a potentially good teacher. Researchers consistently confirm that instructors, at all grade levels, scoring higher on the distributions of standardized tests, of all kinds, routinely are associated with students whose academic achievement is higher (Clotfelter, Ladd, & Vigdor, 2007; Ehrenberg & Brewer, 1995; Ferguson, 1991; Ferguson & Ladd, 1996). One should acknowledge quickly that individual intelligence by itself will be insufficient. Other relevant qualities to which attention is paid on the following pages count a great deal also. However, a smart instructor can sense and adjust to students' needs quickly, acquire larger amounts of subject matter as needed, be inventive regarding new ways to instruct, and create materials that may enable more students to learn than otherwise would be the case.

However, how can a principal, personnel officer, or other school official identify an intelligent candidate? Conventional IQ tests are seldom required of applicants and, even if they were, they are far from an infallible litmus test for intelligence. It is possible to request of applicants whether or not they have an SAT,

ACT, GRE, LSAT, or other standardized college or graduate school admission test score. If such is available, these test score can be good proxies for intelligence.

There is no substitute for a face-to-face conversation, or a telephone conversation or videoconference if meeting in person is difficult or impossible. In a personal conversation it is possible to ask questions, follow up upon feelings, sense nuances, test humor, pose hypothetical problems, and determine the manner by which a candidate thinks his or her way through to a conclusion. One can even engage in some standardized interviewing, to gain greater inter-rater reliability, by posing identical or similar hypothetical situations to individual candidates. Responses can be videoed or recorded and held for others to review, should such be helpful to those engaged in the decision-making process.

When time and other resources permit, there is an additional productive means for appraising the raw ability of a teacher candidate. It is possible to place the candidate in a school or even in a classroom for a day or two and, subsequently, engage in conversations with the individual to inquire regarding what he or she saw, thought was productive and artful teaching, viewed as being a problem, and what changes he or she would make had they been the teacher or teachers viewed.

Education

A candidate's education is an easily reviewed qualification. However, what traits or experiences are desirable on this dimension? What should a personnel officer or principal be searching for in reviewing a candidate's education experiences and college and university transcripts? There are at least two answers. First, do the undergraduate and graduate courses a candidate has completed form a coherent and significant pattern, and do they align with what he or she is expected to teach? If it is a biology teacher that is needed, and a candidate has had little or no courses in that subject, then the fit is unpromising.

Second, if one has the luxury of recruiting from highly selective colleges, then do so. There are approximately 25 colleges and universities in the United States that undertake unusual care in their admissions processes and rely upon rigorous appraisals of applicant ability. Some big names here are Harvard, Stanford, Princeton, Yale, Vanderbilt, Williamson, Southern Methodist University, and Duke. There are others. A teacher applicant who has graduated at the bachelor's-degree level from one of these selective institutions should be given careful scrutiny. It is likely that admission to such elite institutions is a proxy for intelligence and ambition. It does not mean that these colleges are unusually effective in adding value to their graduates as they pass through four or five years at the institution. It is more likely that these selective colleges attract and accept such able individuals that they emerge well educated as much for the quality of their raw material as for the institution's instructional efficacy.

Credentials

Public schools are legally required to ensure that teachers hold state licenses consistent with the requirements of their instructional and related professional responsibilities. (Nonpublic schools and some charter schools operate under far fewer constraints.) Hiring officers have to ensure that such qualifications are met and authentic. However, do not be deceived into believing that there is a relationship between credentials held and instructional ability. No reliable empirical study has ever found a systematic positive relationship between the presence of state credentials and elevations in pupil achievement.

Experience

Does added experience in teaching result in better teaching? Not necessarily. Empirical studies of teachers and seniority suggest that the contribution of experience to instructional ability of teachers peaks somewhere in the range of five to ten years. Having 15 years of teaching experience is, by itself, no guarantee that an individual will be more effective as an instructor than another candidate with only five years of experience. Critics allude to the experienced individual who, in reality, has had the same first-year experience 15 times, without any cumulative effect. Most school districts pay a substantial salary premium for teachers with experience. Available scientific evidence suggests they are wasting their money (Ehrenberg & Brewer, 1995).

Commitment to Learning

Some have argued that the most important trait of a successful teacher is simply a passion for learning (Fried, 1995). Passion not only allows teachers to make it through rough patches, but it also leads to more enthusiastic students. Students who see that their teachers are passionate about learning are more likely to become passionate about learning themselves. Passion cannot solve all problems, but it is certainly a good place to start. The challenge, of course, is identifying reliable means for appraising passion, commitment, and desire for added learning.

Another related trait to look for is dedication, both to the teaching profession and to a particular school. This trait is easier to identify among current teachers than prospective teachers. Prospective teachers who are dedicated to the profession will be more confident in their career choice and more assertive about their goals as an educator. Current teachers who are dedicated will put more time and effort into their jobs.

It is often little things that set apart the most dedicated teachers: helping a student after school; forming a club or team; creating a new worksheet instead of copying one out of a book; offering advice to new teachers; communicating effectively with parents; volunteering to undertake weekend, afterschool, or summer tutoring; planning and carrying out effective field trips, and so on. Besides being dedicated to their job, it also helps if teachers are dedicated to their current school. Teacher mobility is high in numerous places, and many teachers leave for schools they perceive as more attractive each year. Indeed, approximately 10 percent of America's teachers change jobs each year. Working to retain these teachers may be counterproductive if they are not concerned about and dedicated to their current school.

Openness

The last major trait to appraise when selecting teachers to hire and retain is a willingness to learn continuously. It is teachers with this trait who will create a culture of continuous learning. Teachers and prospective teachers who are willing to learn benefit a school in two ways. First, they become better teachers because they work harder and smarter at enhancing their craft. Second, they are less likely to become recalcitrant and more likely to work with other staff to effect change. Teachers that are both more willing and more able will influence the culture and, ultimately, the success of any school.

Persuading a Highly Qualified Candidate to Accept a Position

Selecting the best applicants to hire does not necessarily mean that those candidates will choose to work, or remain, at a school. A large part of a school leader's challenge, then, is not only selecting the correct teachers, but also making sure that he or she can hire these teachers and keep them working in a school.

Many factors that affect hiring and retention (e.g., location, student body composition, size of school, salary, etc.) are sometimes out of the immediate control of a principal. Thus, a leader needs to concentrate on dimensions that can be controlled in order to convince teachers that the school in question is the best one for them.

A useful initial step for a school leader to take is to ensure that the school has a consistent and clear commitment to specified learning and other student outcome goals and that progress can be both measured and rewarded. For a prospective teacher, clear goals are a sign that a school is organized and well managed, as well as an indication that the school strives to be the best it can.

Few teacher candidates are likely to want to sign up at a school that does not seem committed to student success. For current teachers, a continued commitment to goals reinforces the idea that the school is effectively organized and consistently operated. Rewarding progress made toward these goals reinforces these notions as well as makes teachers feel that is there is something tangible toward which they are working. A feeling that one's work is meaningful is a major contributor to satisfaction among employees.

Induction

An important step for a school leader to take in recruiting able faculty prospects is to give thoughtful consideration to the manner in which new teachers are effectively inducted. Attention paid to ensuring that new teacher candidates understand district and school goals, are informed regarding instructional materials and auxiliary services, are aware of opportunities to explore alternative pedagogical practices, have access to more experienced teachers, and are given assurances of reasonable assistance may all prove useful in persuading new recruits to accept a teaching position.

Mentoring

Research suggests that appropriate mentoring programs for incoming teachers increase both effectiveness and retention (Ingersoll & Smith, 2004; Smith, 2007). Prospective teachers will be looking for a situation in which they can be successful and have an easy transition from whatever they formerly were undertaking. The knowledge that a mentoring system is in place will assuage some fears. For current teachers, an effective mentoring system will make success more likely and frustration less likely. In addition, it may create strong relationships among faculty members that may decrease the odds that a teacher will seek employment elsewhere.

Professional Growth

Prospective teachers need to feel as though they can accomplish a great deal if they choose to work at a certain school, and current teachers need to feel as though they have more room to grow. Various schools and districts attack this issue in numerous ways. The idea of teachers serving as coaches, mentors, or lead teachers has expanded in a number of districts. In New York City, for example, lead teachers earn a large bonus in addition to their regular salary and teach half time while mentoring new teachers half time. Knowing that there are added professional opportunities toward which one can aim down the road will decrease the chances of a teacher feeling stunted professionally and increase the chances of a positive outlook.

Motivating Teachers and Others

Viewed through the most cynical of lenses, to get ahead in America's current public school system is to put distance between yourself and pupils. The most pay, the most prestige, the most interaction with other adults, and the most control over one's time accrues to those who have left classroom teaching and have assumed positions such as teacher specialists, counselors, school administrators, principals, central-office managers, superintendents, state officials, or education school faculty.

The motivational message is clear and regrettable. For a teacher to get ahead professionally and financially, one must leave the classroom. At each stage of the conventional promotional pyramid in education, one has less direct contact with students. In professions such as medicine, architecture, law, and engineering one can be paid more, even be promoted to levels of greater professional responsibility, but still engage with the principal purposes of the organization. In few other professional endeavors are the highest rewards so clearly reserved for those who forsake the principal function of the profession—instruction. Correcting this dysfunctional condition necessitates the formation of a credible professional ladder for teachers, a means by which promotion is possible but through which neglect of instruction is not inevitable.

Inert Incentives

Dysfunctional consequences are not limited to teachers' promotional opportunities. The conventional means by which classroom teachers routinely receive pay raises is itself wasteful. The single-salary schedule rewards added years of teaching experience and college course credits beyond a bachelor's degree. Whereas, in a historic context, these pay dimensions are reasonable, they now prove to have little or no empirical basis of support.

The reigning econometric research on the topic of teacher compensation suggests that when student characteristics such as socioeconomic status and prior academic achievement levels are accounted for in statistical models, there remains the significant residual effect of classroom teachers. That is, as emphasized earlier, even when student characteristics are controlled, one can identify an important effect of teachers upon student achievement. These effects are found most systematically for teachers who attended highly selective undergraduate colleges and who scored high on SAT, ACT, GRE, and other standardized tests to determine eligibility for college admission.

Regrettably, research-identified teacher effects are almost completely unrelated to the single-salary schedule and state certification dimensions upon which classroom teacher pay is presently based.[1] Experience as an instructor does appear to be related to student achievement, but only the initial years of experience are key. Little relationship between experience and student achievement appears after that. No significant relationship appears between post–bachelor degree college credits and student achievement. Further, there is no discernible relationship between certification and teacher effects upon student achievement. An exhaustive examination of New York City beginning teacher certification and student achievement, conducted by Kane, Rockoff, and Staiger, (2006) resulted in the following quote from their report:

> There is not much difference between certified, uncertified, and alternatively certified teachers overall, but effectiveness varies substantially within each group of teachers. To put it simply, teachers vary considerably in the extent to which they promote student learning, but whether a teacher is certified or not is largely irrelevant to predicting their effectiveness.[2]

Performance Pay

A subsequent chapter, Chapter 5, concentrates on resource deployment and the role of resources in constructing an effective school culture. Suffice it to say here that performance pay and financial incentives are an increasingly growing practice in America's public schools. In 2010, more than 20 percent of the nation's public school teachers were employed in a school system that uses performance pay or incentive pay as a portion of remuneration determination.

LINK TO CASE STUDY 4

Case Study 4 deals with the tenuous topic of performance pay. In what ways do you think performance pay can enhance the culture of your school? In what ways does performance pay hold the prospect of damaging your school culture? What can school leaders do to minimize the negative consequences and magnify the potential benefits of this increasingly popular policy?

Pension as a Part of Pay

Beginning teachers are seldom focused on the pensions that accrue to publicly employed professional educators. However, pensions are a part of remuneration, even if youthful teachers are somewhat unaware of them. Relative to private-sector employees, teachers usually enjoy high fringe benefit levels. These include items such as pensions and health insurance. The former are usually part of a statewide system, including either all teachers in a state or all public employees in a state. In either instance they are likely to be what is known as a defined benefit plan. This arrangement provides a more secure pension than its counterpart, the defined contribution plan, which overwhelmingly characterizes private-sector employees. In the former, for each pay period, an eligible pension plan participant makes a financial contribution, usually a combination of employee and employer payments, to the state pension system. A participant is eligible for drawing upon the capital amassed in the pension plan after a specified number of work years, usually about seven. When the required period of employment has occurred, the individual is said to be vested. Under these arrangements, an individual teacher's or administrator's annual pension payment is a function of three conditions: (a) salary at time of retirement multiplied by a percentage derived from summing, (b) years of service, and (c) individual age at retirement.

For example, if Ms. Jones decided to retire at age 60, and she had been a teacher in the retirement system for 35 years, she would be eligible for a pension equaling 95 percent of the salary she was being paid in her last year, or an average of her salary over the last three years that she taught. If Ms. Jones was being paid $70,000 in her last years, she would have been eligible for an annual pension of $66,500.

Fringe Benefits

In addition to pensions, teachers are also usually accorded handsome fringe benefit packages, particularly medical and dental insurance. Medical costs have continually risen faster than the overall cost of living. The existence of third-party payers (insurance companies), the inventions of costly new pharmaceutical and treatment technologies, and the widespread vulnerability of physicians to tort liability for malpractice have combined to send health costs to meteoric levels. One of the means for exerting cost control is through what are known as copayments, asking the insured personally to defray some of the costs and attempting to provide a disincentive for frivolous doctor visits. Fringe benefits are estimated to cost the employing school district approximately 30 percent on top of the salary of an employed educator.

ENSURING EFFECTIVE STAFF PERFORMANCE

Once high-quality teachers are in place within a school, the second half of the battle is to make sure that they perform up to their abilities. This requires aiding them in improving their practice as well as monitoring and rewarding staff.

Two main ways exist for staff to improve their practice: receiving appropriate training and collaborating with others. Training staff, often known as "professional development," is potentially the most crucial step toward ensuring teacher effectiveness in a school. This only applies, however, if the training is done well. It is quite easy to operate ineffective professional development in a school; it is much more challenging to implement effective training sessions.

The fact that many professional-development sessions are of such poor quality is ironic considering that they are usually operated by individuals who are or were teachers; people who have been trained effectively to engage and educate an audience. In the end, overseeing an effective professional-development session is not as different from running an effective classroom as some would believe. One still needs to have a plan of attack, to engage the audience, and to demonstrate and explain clearly and concisely. Unfortunately, this plan is not well executed in too many schools.

The two complaints that may be heard most frequently among critics of professional development (usually the teachers who feel their time has just been wasted) are that it is disorganized and irrelevant. These problems are far from insurmountable.

It is easy for the planning of professional-development sessions to fall by the wayside when school leaders are inundated with other, seemingly more pressing, tasks and obligations. Unfortunately, many school leaders forget to take into account how their handling of professional development reflects on their leadership abilities and affects the perceptions held by other staff members. Ensuring that professional-development sessions are well planned and organized far in advance can only increase the effectiveness of a school leader and the teachers who are being trained.

No matter how well-planned professional-development sessions are, however, they will still be resented by participants if they are not perceived as relevant and helpful. Having staff members that are motivated and willing to learn helps enormously in this regard, but even the most enthusiastic staff member will become disaffected of sitting through repetitive lectures. Teachers must believe that the training is valuable in order for it to be effective. First and foremost, professional-development sessions must, therefore, address topics about which teachers have indicated they need more information. Which topics should be addressed? This will differ by school, by teacher category, or even by individual teacher, but some possible sources of ideas include a professional-development committee, surveys, informal conversations and observations, and reactions to previous professional-development sessions.

Teachers cannot rely upon professional-development sessions exclusively to aid them in improving their practice. In most places, these sessions are simply too infrequent or too general to be the sole source of influence. Another potential fountain of knowledge lies in collaborating with other staff members, either formally or informally.

Collaboration with other staff members can take myriad forms, and multiple forms should be present in any one building. Some of the ways in which collaboration can take place include informal sharing of ideas among teachers, group lesson planning, peer observations, peer walkthroughs, grade level/department/ other designated group meetings, peer critiquing, and mentoring. Multiple forms are present in the most successful schools because collaboration is so critical to the formation and maintenance of a positive school culture.

High-quality training and widespread collaboration are both essential to the effective performance of school staff, but they are also an essential part of creating a positive school culture. High-quality training leads to both a more positive view of furthering practice and more respect and trust in school leaders while collaboration leads to better relationships throughout the school.

The most effective means for ensuring that professional development is useful and relevant for a teacher is to undertake a diagnosis of her or his students' performance and progress toward learning objectives. Where deficiencies are evident, perhaps determined by formative or value-added testing results, then professional development can be tailored to instructional or content areas in which it is evident that the teacher is weak.

Monitoring Staff

Even if staff members work well together, it is still a principal's responsibility to ensure that they are performing effectively as instructors. *Accountability* is a term often bandied about when discussing failing schools, but it is also present, if not frequently discussed, in the most successful schools. Even with the most able staff, it is still incumbent upon school leaders to monitor the actions of their staff.

In a school where relationships are based on respect and trust, it is not necessary for school leaders constantly to look over the shoulder of every teacher, but they still need to know what is happening. In these types of circumstances, the best way of monitoring staff members is simply to engage in frequent conversations with them. This will both build relationships and provide information on what that individual is doing and what they have noticed about their peers. Frequent informal conversations make staff members feel more important and respected while also providing valuable information.

Conversations, of course, can never give a complete picture. Observing happenings within a school, particularly inside classrooms, adds much-needed depth to the picture. School leaders are usually required to observe teachers formally, but there is nothing stopping them from observing informally as well. A principal who stops by for a few minutes and encourages students will gain much insight as to the workings of that classroom but will also likely earn the respect of the teacher (and increase motivation levels among students). Some principals have even been known to stop by and teach a lesson in order to give a teacher a break (imagine the gratitude of the teacher and also how well the principal would know the knowledge level of the students).

It is important to note, however, that informal observations should focus mostly on positive facets during the duration of the observation. It is, of course, the job of a school leader to find a solution to anything he or she sees that might be troubling, but there are various ways to solve these problems. Teachers will not appreciate frequent informal observations if they feel as though they are being constantly watched and judged. Instead, they should feel as though their school leader is interested in what is taking place in their classroom. It is imperative that in all but the direst situations a school leader says nothing but positive things to a teacher while their students are present.

Consider the following two examples for an illustration of the different techniques used by different school leaders.

> *Mr. Cobb was a new teacher in a large, urban middle school. He worked quite hard at his craft, but he still struggled sometimes, particularly with classroom management. Due to the size of the school, his immediate supervisor was the assistant principal on that floor—Ms. Gordon—and he rarely saw the principal.*
>
> *Ms. Gordon liked to keep a close eye on her teachers, particularly the new ones with whom she was not yet comfortable. She would often drop by Mr. Cobb's class to see how it was going. She had explained to Mr. Cobb how his classroom should be run and would get very upset if she saw something different. When she walked into the room she always demanded to see a lesson plan so that she knew what was happening. She would then walk around the room to see how the students' work looked. Sometimes, however, she would simply watch from the doorway for a minute. She noticed that the class got quite a bit quieter when she would enter the room.*
>
> *Mr. Cobb lived in constant fear of a visit from Ms. Gordon. He knew he was doing what he should, but he, and the entire class for that matter, would freeze up when Ms. Gordon came into the room. He was open to her ideas and suggestions, but her criticisms were starting to grate on him. One day when he was having particular difficulty with his class, Ms. Gordon stepped into the doorway. "Mr. Cobb, can I see you for a minute?" she asked. Mr. Cobb stopped the lesson and walked over to her. "They need to be quiet while you're teaching the lesson" she said, and then promptly walked away. Mr. Cobb was frustrated and embarrassed. He knew they were supposed to be quiet—he wasn't an idiot—but now every single student in his classroom knew that Ms. Gordon thought he was.*

> *Mrs. Robinson was a new teacher at a small school in a small town. She enjoyed her job and looked forward to coming to school each day. As a new teacher, she knew that she had not yet figured everything out and welcomed help from others. The principal of the school, Mr. Johnson, seemed particularly concerned with making sure that things were going smoothly in her classroom.*
>
> *Mr. Johnson believed that it was important to be as involved as possible in the day-to-day happenings within the classrooms in his school. Not only did he enjoy working with the students, but it also gave him better insight into how the various teachers were performing. When he dropped by a classroom he would make sure not to interrupt the lesson but would smile when students looked at him and remind them to pay attention. He would help any students who appeared to be struggling and, when there was a break, ask if the teacher needed any help. Occasionally teachers would request his assistance with a particularly complicated lesson in which two adults were needed to lead an activity.*

> *Mrs. Robinson had a great deal of respect for Mr. Johnson. He seemed both competent and concerned. She especially liked that he stayed very up-to-date on what was happening in her classroom. At first, she was a bit nervous when he would come into her classroom, but he was always encouraging and helpful during his visits and would offer advice afterward. She had even asked him to assist with a lesson on a couple of occasions. She knew that she always had to be on the top of her game, because she did not want to disappoint Mr. Johnson, but she had never planned on being a poor teacher anyway.*

- How do Mrs. Robinson and Mr. Cobb feel when their supervisors enter the room?
- Which supervisor is more effective? Why?
- If you were a student in each of the classes, what would you think the motivation was behind each of the principal's visits?
- What could Ms. Gordon do differently?

Ms. Gordon and Mr. Johnson both have similar concerns but very different styles. As such, Mr. Cobb and Mrs. Robinson react to these styles very differently. It is quite easy to see that Mr. Johnson is aiding the effectiveness of Mrs. Robinson's teaching while Ms. Gordon is creating a negative environment in her section of the school. While each principal is attempting to monitor teachers and improve instruction in their respective schools, only Mr. Johnson takes into account the way that his actions may be perceived. Both principals have every right to expect that teachers are well prepared and are teaching effectively, but both teachers and students likely view Ms. Gordon as a hindrance and Mr. Johnson as a help. As such, only Mr. Johnson is truly helping foster more effective instruction. In other words, perception matters more than intentions in this case. The human interaction that is inevitably part of observing always serves to complicate matters, but there are other ways to monitor teachers.

LINK TO CASE STUDY 4

Teacher evaluation is invariably an integral element of the performance pay programs at the heart of Case Study 4. How does the culture of your school encourage productive conversations and support professional growth in ways that are aligned to the faculty evaluation system?

The last facet, and the one that is growing most rapidly, of monitoring staff is the use of data. This includes test results, attendance, report cards, and other routinely completed administrative forms. Data help supervisors maintain an unbiased picture of what is happening inside their school. The use of data serves both to raise red flags and to assist in determining which staff members deserve more recognition.

With high-stakes testing nearly ubiquitous, it is all the more important for school leaders regularly to analyze data on the performance of their school. Many districts now have multiple tests per year that are used as practice assessments before the mandated state testing occurs. Results from these tests can be used to monitor which teachers have the most and least growth among their students as well as to learn in which areas students are struggling the most. In order to make the greatest use of this data, it must be used to guide future instruction in addition to using it to gain a clearer picture.

Attendance data can be another rich source of information. Depending on the circumstances, frequent absences and lateness may reflect poorly on a teacher or signal that there are students that need immediate intervention. Attendance also reflects on the school as a whole. In some schools attendance is not an issue, but in others it may be the largest obstacle to learning. Absenteeism varies greatly by school and by grade level, but the importance of a student's presence in school cannot be underestimated.

Report cards are another source of data. If an efficient data system is in place, it is easy to compare the performance of students across various classes and teachers. Though it must be noted that judging teachers based on how many students fail or make the honor roll is as much a fair evaluation tool as it is a way to induce illegitimate grades. Test and attendance data in addition to data gathered during observations are crucial to ensuring that teachers do not simply award high grades in order to make themselves look better to students and parents or escape pressure from above.

In successful schools, all staff members are monitored and held accountable by other staff members because they all have high expectations for each other. The monitoring that takes place, however, is geared toward improving practice rather than identifying the weakest link. Rather than hiding, staff should request evaluation so that they can better learn regarding the instructional dimensions upon which they need to work. When this happens, it is a sign of a positive school culture.

Rewarding Staff Symbolically and Ceremonially

Monitoring will serve little purpose other than intimidation unless those who perform well are rewarded in some way. Rewarding staff members is important not only because of the incentive it adds for success, but also because of the effect that it has on morale.

The easiest way to reward staff, at least with psychic benefits, is simply through positive feedback. Whether a simple "good job" or a formal letter, a little praise goes a long way toward boosting employee morale. Positive feedback is essential to the construction of and maintenance of a positive school culture because it has a trickle-down effect. Somebody who is praised is more likely to praise somebody else. In this way, a positive comment from an administrator can lead to the reception of positive comments by students and other teachers.

Sometimes, however, actions speak louder than words. Over the course of a long school year, in particular, people enjoy being rewarded in minor ways. There are a number of "little things" that a supervisor can do to reward staff that can make all the difference. Perhaps a school leader brings in donuts and juice for staff to share before the start of the school day, or maybe he or she makes sure to bring a birthday card every time a teacher has a birthday. Whichever little things an administrator does, they are sure to be appreciated.

Rewarding staff members by increasing their autonomy is another method. In this sense, the reward is that teachers are implicitly told they can be trusted and that their abilities are respected. For example, teachers may be allowed to design their own curricula, their own course, or pick their own textbook instead of following the usual school procedures. This is empowering for the teachers and potentially powerful for both staff morale and the effectiveness of instruction within a school.

There is, of course, no one right way to reward staff members. Different things work for different people. The following are strategies used by three different principals to recognize positive achievements and boost staff morale.

Ms. Clark had been principal of Adams High School for 25 years. During her tenure, she had done her best to make the school a positive place for everybody to be. She had learned during the early part of her career that frustrated teachers could wreak havoc on the culture of a school and create administrative nightmares when they quit. Since then she had tried to make everybody feel appreciated. She kept a large calendar of every staff member's birthday and made sure to present each one with a card and a smile. Occasionally, she would buy donuts and juice for the staff to have on their way into school in the morning. She did not like to make a show of praise, eschewing staff appreciation days for doing the little things.

Staff members universally praised her as a tough but fair school leader. Her leadership was steady, and teachers knew they were appreciated without Ms. Clark having to say a word. As a result, the climate within the school was calm and noticeably upbeat.

Mr. Frank had just begun his second year as principal of Washington Middle School. The first year had been rocky as he struggled to gain control of a chaotic situation. Particularly frustrating was the fact that so many teachers were ineffective; either because they were inexperienced or because they were burned out. He decided to focus more attention during his second year on monitoring these teachers to make sure they were doing their best. He focused most of his attention on teachers that he believed were shortchanging students and made sure to document their transgressions and let them know that he was dissatisfied and expected more.

The school staff had been through a lot in the past few years. Washington had never been an easy school to work in since the kids came from a rough neighborhood and brought a lot of their problems to school with them. To make matters worse, they were on their third principal in the past four years. Mr. Frank looked like he would be the first principal to serve two consecutive full years in quite some time. The staff, however, was far from happy about this. Though he was a hard worker and seemed determined to turn the school around, nothing ever seemed to be good enough. Teachers openly complained among themselves that they had never heard the words "good job" from his mouth. More and more teachers talked about how burned out they felt and noticed that they just did not have the enthusiasm for teaching that they once had. Though Mr. Frank was determined to change it, the quality of teaching in the school never seemed to improve as efforts were swallowed by a culture of negativity.

Ms. Simpson has worked at Wilson Elementary for five years. During that time she felt as though she had made the school a more positive place. She always made sure that staff knew they were appreciated. She constantly stopped by classrooms to let teachers know how nice their bulletin boards looked, how nicely their students were lined up, and how much she appreciated their effort. She was constantly smiling and encouraging every person in the school.

Teachers appreciated that Ms. Simpson made the school a pleasant place to be, though they were never sure how seriously to take her when she was congratulating them on something. Teachers sometimes whispered that they wished she would spend more time tackling problems and less time telling people how well they had done. Overall, however, the school was a positive place to be. Students gained self-confidence and teachers worked hard.

- What are the strengths and weaknesses of Ms. Clark's strategy? Mr. Frank's? Ms. Simpson's?
- How do these different strategies affect the culture of the school?
- How would you react if you worked in one of the buildings just described?

Positive reinforcement and rewards are a vital part of any successful school culture, but there are a myriad of ways in which they can be implemented depending on the personality of the school leader(s) and the climate within the building. Regardless of whether rewards are verbal, physical, or simple actions it is imperative that staff in a school feels valued.

CONCLUSION

Understanding the components of a successful school culture is important for any administrator, but creating a culture with personnel dimensions described earlier is the most difficult challenge. In order to achieve success, administrators need to ensure that their staff is of the highest quality by recruiting, hiring, and retaining the most effective staff members and then encouraging them to perform well. Even the most talented staff, however, cannot succeed when negativity dominates the relationships in a school. It is imperative that students, teachers, and parents all feel that they are valuable contributors and feel positively about their peers and leaders. When positive relationships are created, talented people can create a successful school.

QUESTIONS FOR DISCUSSION

1. What traits are most important to look for in prospective teachers? Why?

2. What are some strategies to use in order to ensure high levels of teacher retention?

3. What types of things make a school a more pleasant place to be?

4. Why is it important that students not make excuses for their actions?

5. How are the needs of students, teachers, and parents similar?

6. What are some common traps that administrators fall into when trying to ensure staff effectiveness?

7. How does coercion negatively affect relationships? How can coercion be avoided?

REFERENCES AND SUGGESTED READINGS

Bacolod, M. (2007). Who teaches and where do they choose to teach: College graduates of the 1990s. *Educational Evaluation and Policy Analysis, 29*(3), 155–168.

Clotfelter, C. T., Ladd, H. F., & Vigdor, J. L. (2007). *Teacher credentials and student achievement in high school: A cross-subject analysis with student fixed effects.* NBER Working Papers 13617, National Bureau of Economic Research.

Corcoran, S. P., Evans, W. N., & Schwab, R. M. (2004). Changing labor-market opportunities for women and the quality of teachers, 1957–2000. *American Economic Review, 94*(2), 230–235.

Darling-Hammond, L. (2003). Keeping good teachers. *Educational Leadership, 60*(8), 6.

Ehrenberg, R., & Brewer, D. (1995). *Did teachers' race and verbal ability matter in the 1960's? Coleman revisited.* NBER Working Papers 4293, National Bureau of Economic Research.

Ferguson, R. F. (1991, Summer). Paying for public education: New evidence on how and why money matters. *Harvard Journal on Legislation, 28*(2), 465–498.

Ferguson, R. F., & Ladd, H. F. (1996). How and why money matters: An analysis of Alabama schools. In H. F. Ladd (Ed.), *Holding schools accountable: Performance based reform in education* (pp. 265–298). Washington, DC: Brookings Institution Press.

Fried, R. L. (1995). *The passionate teacher: A practical guide.* Boston: Beacon Press.

Hanushek, E. A. (1986). The economies of schooling: Production and efficiency in public schooling. *Journal of Economic Literature, 24*(3), 1141–1177.

Ingersoll, R. M., & Smith, T. M. (2004). Do teacher induction and mentoring matter? *NASSP Bulletin, 88*(638), 28–40.

Kane, T. J., Rockoff, J. E., & Staiger, D. (2006, April). *What does certification tell us about teacher effectiveness? Evidence from New York City.* NBER Working Paper Series. Available at http://ssrn.com/abstract=896463

Nye, B., Konstantopoulos, S., & Hedges, L. (2004). How large are teacher effects? *Educational Evaluation and Policy Analysis, 26*(3), 237–257.

Smith, T. M. (2007). How do state-level induction and standards-based reform policies affect induction experiences among new teachers? *American Journal of Education, 113*(2), 273–309.

NOTES

1. This book, generally, eschews formal citations to research studies. There would be so many as to render the book one vast footnote. However, in this instance, the topic under consideration, teacher compensation, is possibly so at odds with the experience and intuitive sense of likely readers that an effort is made here to ensure that any interested party has independent access to the empirical findings upon which this section is based. Hence, a reader is encouraged to see Podgursky, Michael J. and Springer, Mathew G. "Credentials Versus Performance: Review of the Teacher Performance-Pay Research," chapter in *Peabody Journal of Education*—edited by Jay Greene.

2. See Podgursky and Springer, pages 9 and 10.

Case Study 5: The Challenge of an (Almost) Brand-New School

Can the Past Be Blended With the New to Form a Productive Culture?

Kent Stallings was unusually excited. The school district's board of directors had recently selected him to serve as the principal of the district's long-awaited new school, a state-of-the-art soon-to-be-opened middle school that would be named after one of the district's most famous former administrators, Karl Kennedy. This would be his initial assignment as a school principal. He knew he would be challenged, but he thought he was well prepared.

The Kennedy school had been designed by a nationally prominent architectural firm, and it was scheduled to have every imaginable amenity and technology system. The district had floated a large public bond issue to finance the school. Its high cost, $60 million, and the resulting elevated property tax rate, had alarmed some in the community who contended that it was a pleasure palace for pouty and overly privileged pupils, "hormone-dominated adolescents," as they were labeled by the new school's opponents. Such critics were clear that they had other priorities, such as a lower tax rate, road and sewer system upgrades, or an expanded senior center. Their challenge, a challenge they repeatedly made clear at public school board meetings, was that any school that was this palatial had quickly better display high levels of academic, artistic, and athletic performance.

Stallings had been a Teach For America volunteer who had fallen in love with education. He had graduated from a highly selective southern university, forgone a richly paying Wall Street job and, for several years, had taught high school physics courses. He routinely took students to state and national science fairs, and his students regularly captured top performance prizes. He had served briefly as a high school science department chair and as an assistant principal. He had acquired high public visibility and a well-deserved reputation for having led a statewide science standards revision team, and he had acquired all the credential qualifications to become a principal. He had married a teacher, in another district, and they had two children. He was young, 37, and self-confident without be overly cocksure. However, some thought him lacking sufficient experience.

Regardless of his age, it was not clear than any experience would have prepared him for the challenges he was about to face.

Note: This case study, as with others associated with other chapters, is about an actual school, actual people, and actual conditions. Nothing is fabricated. All cases are about situations school leaders routinely encounter. However, in each instance, names of people, schools, and locations have been altered to ensure confidentiality.

Kennedy was not scheduled to open for a year. Stallings had time to plan his new school, and he was grateful for that. However, it was not quite a *new* school. To be sure, it would be all-new physically. Still, there was a catch. The Kennedy School was to replace one of the district's long-declining schools, an aging school that was to be closed, a school that repeatedly had failed to meet its No Child Left Behind "Adequate Yearly Progress" goals. It was a school in which the district's board and broader public had lost all confidence, a school the enrollments of which had continually been declining as parents exercised options and selected other public schools or even began increasingly to rely upon private schools.

The new Kennedy School, when viewed through another set of lenses, was a "reconstituted school." The once proud and well-regarded, but now failing, school was to be closed. Its administrators and teachers, while protected by their tenure in the district, were no longer guaranteed a job at any particular school. The board had specified that for any one of them to teach at the new Kennedy School, they would have to apply individually and be selected.

This school closing and reconstitution was a matter of substantial contention in the district. Teacher and administrator advocates claimed it was the students who had changed, not the once well-regarded school. After all, it had once been a premier institution, highly sought by parents. Some said it was unfair to blame teachers for a failing school when they had worked selflessly for years to improve matters, often without any help from the district's central office. Teacher representatives claimed that their constituents were being unfairly blamed and being made scapegoats for changing social conditions, shrinking financial resources, and inept district leadership.

Skeptics repeatedly asked what a new set of teachers would do that the existing faculty had not already done or tried to do. At school board meetings they inquired, rhetorically, as to why if everyone knew with such confidence what was wrong in the past, and what should now be done for the future, they had not revealed this vast truth a long time ago? What difference would a new school and a newly recruited administration and faculty make? What would they do differently?

Kent Stallings, while proud to be selected as the new Kennedy principal, was under no illusions regarding the magnitude of the challenge. He had to determine what kind of school to operate, identify teachers and other administrators that could make it all operate successfully, satisfy the school board's elevated aspirations, assuage the spectrum of doubts and complaints by cynics and skeptics, and find some answer to the pressing question of "What would be different now?" He was glad he had some planning time.

As Kent contemplated what lay ahead of him, these are some of the issues that ran through his mind:

- Was there a quick way to develop a positive identity for the new school, an identity untarnished by the unfavorable reputation of the school it was replacing?

- How could a new school have any culture at all, let alone a productive one?
- What was he to do in the absence of traditions, a history of past success, a record of prestigious graduates, or a politically influential constituency to protect the school against budget incursions by competing schools in its fledgling years?
- How does one compensate for a teacher cadre that has at least a minimum of able and experienced teachers capable of mentoring newly employed teachers?
- How beholden should Kennedy school be to NCLB expectations, state standards, district testing, state teacher credential requirements, and college admissions criteria? Was there any choice in such matters? Did charter schools have more leeway? Could or should Kennedy apply to be a charter school?
- What balance should he strike in determining unique parts of the curriculum? Should he decide the elective parts of the curriculum and use these plans as a dazzling template to recruit and attract new faculty, or should he recruit raw teaching talent and then let the new faculty decide unique parts of the curriculum?
- To what degree could or should the Kennedy curriculum mirror the other middle school in the district? Would students be advantaged by having all grade levels across middle schools standardized?
- What balance should be struck in determining parts of a new culture, items such as a school mascot, mission statement, athletic uniforms, student government, school rivalries, internal traditions, and alumni support? Do these things even matter? Should he concentrate on the academics and let the "softer" side of schooling take care of itself?
- How should he go about selecting teachers and other staff? Were teachers from the old school deserving of another chance at the new school?
- Did he want a mix of youth and experience? He had been a Teach For America recruit. Should he open Kennedy to a cadre of alternatively certified teachers? What would parents think of that?
- Should he have a dress code for students or for faculty? How strict should the rules be regarding student behavior? Should parents be engaged in setting the boundaries for dress and behavior?
- How high tech should Kennedy become? To be sure, the school was both wired and wireless. Did that mean that instruction was to be technology based? To what degree should instruction be linked to the Internet?
- What should be the class schedule at Kennedy? He had heard much about block scheduling and rotating schedules. Were those good things? Should Kennedy be a year-round school?

Initially, Kent had been thrilled at the prospect of becoming the principal of a brand-new school. Now he was having second thoughts. The more he deliberated about these complicated matters, the more confused, bewildered, and anxious he became. He needed some decision rules, or else he just needed someone else to make decisions, and then he would implement them.

The notion of a tabula rasa for a school had initially been attractive. Now, it was less so. He could see that behind virtually every point of choice there was a political constituency that would be either offended or delighted at his decision. How many wrong decisions could he make before he became a target for replacement? How long was his honeymoon? Was there any place to turn for dispassionate and informed guidance?

FOR DISCUSSION

1. Without conscious thought and expert intervention, what would you predict the culture at Kennedy school would become?

2. Was Kent's anxiety justified? Had he lost his nerve? Had he gotten in over his head? Should the board have selected a more experienced person, perhaps one who had previously designed and opened a new school? Was a planning year sufficient?

3. Did Kent have the correct list of issues or was there a different or more significant list of items with which he should be concerned?

4. Was there a different way he should think about the issues he faced? Was there some way of organizing the issues so that they could be addressed in sequence? Were, perhaps, some issues more important than others, and should he not find a way to prioritize his challenges?

5. Is there any overall strategy to which he should turn for resolving his many design and operational issues?

6. Is there anyone to whom you would recommend Kent turn for advice?

7. Does Kent have a prayer of succeeding? What will most enable his success, and what might most hinder his success?

CHAPTER 5

Resource Deployment and School Culture

In this chapter a reader will learn about the following:

- An "investment frame of mind" regarding resources and school culture
- The unique nature of "psychic" resources in shaping organization culture
- The nature of "material" resources possibly available to a change agent
- Processes by which "material" resources are conventionally allocated
- Means for marshaling and maximizing available resources
- The crucial role of performance data and continuously appraising personnel and program effectiveness in directing resources
- Alternatives to which discretionary resources can be put in order to gain a high likely return on investment (ROI)
- Dysfunctional paths to be avoided in allocating resources

ELCC STANDARDS

ELCC standards addressed in this chapter include the following:

- 1.3—Implement a vision
- 1.4—Steward a vision
- 2.1—Promote a positive school culture
- 3.1—Manage the organization
- 3.2—Manage operations
- 3.3—Manage resources
- 4.3—Mobilize community resources
- 5.1—Act with integrity
- 6.1—Understand the larger context

INTRODUCTION

Creating, or re-creating, a productive school culture is always challenging. In order to accomplish this worthy but daunting objective, a principal or other change agent will need to marshal all reasonable resources and then deploy them in a manner likely to result in the highest return on the investment (ROI). A productive school culture is the goal. Thinking smart regarding resource deployment, using virtually every category of resource available to a leader, likely will assist in achieving this goal faster and more forcefully than most other strategies a change agent can undertake.

There is more than one tool that can be used to shape a school culture. But resources—monetary, material, and mental—are among the most powerful. The utility of smart resource investment is easily proclaimed, but it invites many questions. What resources are under consideration, and how likely are they to be available? Even if these resources can be marshaled, which of them come within the ambit of a change agent's discretion? Assuming, however, that useful resources are available and amenable to change agent direction or redirection, where or how should they be invested to generate likely organizational returns toward a productive school culture?

Resource allocation should serve two imperatives. On one hand, resources must be directed toward productive ends, ensuring the organization is doing the right things. In addition, resources must be used to ensure that things are done right. This chapter concentrates on resources with some attention, also, to rewards and incentives. Rewards and incentives stem from and are rooted in resources. However, a distinction is made in this chapter between the two in order to cover both imperatives. Resource allocation can drive an organization to do the right things. Rewards can serve as levers to ensure that things in the organization are done right.[1]

A THEORY OF ACTION

The theory of action involved in productively allocating resources, as well as using performance incentives, is not complicated. The logic here has two prongs. Resources are needed both for personal rewards and for facilitating and reinforcing organizational steps in the right direction and redirection.

A change agent needs consistently and appropriately to reward subordinate or colleague behavior that contributes to a productive culture. This is Pavlovian but practical and powerful. This is the theory of action behind performance incentives. In addition, a strategic or change agent leader must strive to engage resources with operational activities where they will likely have the greatest investment return for creating and sustaining a culture of achievement.

This chapter addresses resource-related issues. The first task in this sense is defining and identifying resources. The second task is determining the degree to which these resources either already are or could be placed at a change agent's discretion. A third focus is to render explicit the need to employ performance data to determine effectiveness of any particular resource investment or reward strategy. The fourth focus is describing alternative investment strategies worthy of change agent consideration. The final focus is upon easily made mistakes to avoid in allocating scarce resources. Before turning to these ends, however, a modest digression regarding resources and a change agent's mental models may prove helpful.

AN INVESTMENT MENTALITY REGARDING ALLOCATING RESOURCES (AND REWARDS)

The "resource allocation mantra" for a change agent is constantly and consciously to comprehend that critical resources are always in short supply, and scarcity compels spending tradeoffs. This goes for ethereal resources such as the leader's time and energy and also includes material resources such as money, personnel, and physical space. Allocating precious resources should always be considered as an investment. If a scarce resource is used for one purpose, at one time, then it is expandable and cannot be used for some other purposes.

Allocating new or incrementally available resources is easier than redistributing existing resources. One can almost always anticipate greater resistance if the plan is to redistribute resources in a fashion different from the status quo. Distributing new resources can be viewed organizationally as someone or some group gaining something. Redistribution is almost always perceived as someone or some group losing something.

There are never sufficient resources to address all the needs an organization can envision. The more labor intensive and professionally oriented an organization, likely the more true is this assertion. Physicians, engineers, military officers, social workers, and other professionals can always think of added ways to do an even better job or help even more people. One can always wish for and think of good ways to use additional resources. Therefore, it is always necessary to think in terms of priorities.

In that all good things cannot be simultaneously addressed, then upon what good purposes should an organization concentrate with the resources likely to be at hand? The question is not simply rhetorical. If one is intending to alter the course of a school through the conscious construction of a productive achievement-oriented culture, then consideration must be given to resource allocation priorities. If one cannot address everything, then from which spending targets is one most likely to obtain the greatest return on an investment?

Educators, as a group, are seldom accustomed to thinking of resource trade-offs. There is much about public schools that is rooted in the status quo—inertia. For example, the principal manner in which school district budgets are constructed is to assume that which is presently taking place should continue to take place in the future. Thus all that is needed by way of budgeting, planning for future resource deployment, is to (1) account for anticipated student enrollment growth or decline, (2) determine personnel needs by applying longstanding or contractually defined pupil-teacher and other personnel ratios to each school's anticipated enrollment, and then (3) adjusting all present operating elements for cost-of-living changes and other inflationary or deflationary factors.

Voila! Once having taken these three broad steps, then next year's proposed operating budget is ready for school board or voter consideration and approval. However comforting this conventional resource allocation process and mind-set, it will not lead to a dynamic and achievement-oriented organization. The creation and maintenance of a high-performing school culture necessitates a continual search for better ways in which to use resources to further the end of added student achievement. The status quo, on this front, is never acceptable. Approaches such as pupil-weighting formulas, which ensure a calibrated and fair manner of shifting resources into schools, are acquiring increasing salience in the domains of both policy and practice.

The professional football player protagonist in the film *Jerry Maguire* repeatedly and forcefully fended off coaches' and employers' rhetorical outpouring of high regard, potential interest, and good intent by persistently and loudly proclaiming, "Show me the money!" His point, however lacking in nuance, was that whereas intentions may be good and quite genuine, it ultimately is the flow of resources, be it consciously intended or occurring by default, that most accurately displays an organization's intentions and priorities. "Show me the money" is a metaphor for determining what an organization fundamentally cares about.

But one might observe that surely school districts are about educating children. Virtually every school district has a mission or goal statement: "We educate the whole child!" "We educate every child to his or her maximum potential," "Education is our most valuable service!" These slogans are usually offered with the best of intentions. Those who frame them, paint them in school hallways, and print them on school and school district business cards, T-shirts, and letterhead may well mean and care deeply for what is said.

However, an organization's real priorities are far more accurately revealed in its budgets. "Show me the money," and one can see what a school or school district genuinely intends. If the organization's resources are not closely aligned with its rhetoric, then one has cause for being skeptical regarding announced purposes.

If subjected to this kind of—some might say cynical—scrutiny, one can see that school districts, at least the majority of them, exist for two purposes: to maximize retention of and benefits for existing employees and to ensure that their future budgets are larger yet. Why else would the component costs of school and district budgets change so little from year to year? Personnel costs almost always comprise 80 percent of a school district budget, year in and year out.

If a school or district was consistently accomplishing its student achievement goals, elevating students' academic performance, closing the achievement gap, successfully preparing students for careers and college, then perhaps a district would be justified in persisting in its conventional budgeting patterns. Year after year we see the same class sizes maintained, the same mix of teachers and aides, and the same salary procedures of rewarding college course credits beyond the bachelor's degree and paying for years of service as a teacher.

However, if a district were falling short of its various achievement goals, then it would seem that a far more radical approach to resource allocation would be in order. In short, if the culture is not now producing a high performance for students, then the time may have come to seek a shift in the deployment of resources. Resources should be reallocated to support other strategies, strategies for which there is a glimmer of hope that they will lead to better student performance.

Therein resides the challenge. In what ways should resources be deployed differently? Also, if reallocated, who will win and who will lose? If students win, that is they learn more, then perhaps it is worth the organizational pain of having some adults either being displaced altogether or at least being asked to alter what they do. Resource reallocation is not simple. Consideration must be given both to how best resources might be used and how best to withstand the inevitable resistance from those individuals or groups who will likely lose some degree of presently allocated benefits.

In short, to alter a school's culture will likely call for identifying, marshaling, and deploying assets differently. However wrenching such a move, by itself, even this is insufficient. Once taking the bold steps of reallocating scarce resources, it is continually necessary to monitor the results of such a move, to measure the return on the investment, to see if the reallocation achieves desired results. If the return is low, then it may be necessary to try yet another reallocation plan. Such a frame of mind, such decisive actions, and such a continuous-improvement mentality, are likely to meet with resistance.

RESOURCES (AND RELATED REWARDS) TO BE CONSIDERED

What resources should be in the mix when considering building or rebuilding a school's culture? There are two kinds: "psychic" and "material." Each category is of substantial significance. Soon-to-be-described school district budget processes conventionally consider only one category of resource, material. However, psychic resources can also be powerful tools for change.

Psychic resources refer principally to intangibles, conditions and efforts aligned most closely with human values and interpersonal interactions. These resources may not involve much, if any, actual material costs. These resources perform their investment magic in the minds of resource and reward recipients.

In the category of psychic resources are ceremonies and ceremonial rewards; allocation of social or organizational status; establishment of professional career ladders; low-cost perks such as office size, subject matter and office assignments, and teaching time of day; team teaching assignments; personal recognition; interpersonal expressions of appreciation; and visible rewards such as parking spaces and classroom or office location.

Material resources refer to more tangible matters such as salaries, promotions, performance premiums, class size, allocation of teacher aides, stipends for added duties or afterschool assignments, a mix of professionals with classified staff, and materials such as computers and textbooks.

The line between the mental and the material is not always an absolute or permanent one. For example, if the awarding of a nicer office requires no net new resources to the organization, that is, the offices are a fixed cost and already paid for, then a corner office with two windows is more a psychic than material reward. The action may have a desired effect, a recipient feels rewarded, but the reward does not cost anything in terms of money. However, if a new office intended as a reward for good performance must be rented or, more expensive yet, constructed anew, this may edge over the line into a material reward.

Keeping matters in perspective, it is not as consequential to determine which resources fall into which definitional category as it is for a leader to recognize that not all resources are costly in terms of money. Not all resources are to be found in a school district budget.

A great deal of organizational change can result from a sincere and deserved pat on the back. This does not mean, however, that nonpecuniary, intangible rewards are always free. If time is taken to reward behavior "X" or "Y," then it may mean that the leader did not have sufficient time remaining to reward some other individual or some other condition or behavior. Again, there are almost always tradeoffs, even with regard to something seemingly so elastic and inexhaustible as a leader's or change agent's time to comment favorably to a colleague.

Psychic Resources

Herein resides the change agent's secret weapon. Psychic resources are not conventionally seen as resources at all. They seldom are featured in education administration texts or professional-development materials for leaders. They often lay fallow, neglected by leaders as a source of exchange in seeking to change an organization. However, if properly conceived and appropriately deployed, psychic resources can provide a significant margin of difference in changing the culture of an organization. Some leaders have an intuitive grasp of the significance of psychic resources. They employ them to good effect and do so with seeming ease. However, they are available to all leaders and should become a conscious component of every leader's organizational change quiver.

LINK TO CASE STUDY 5

In Case Study 5, we find Kent Stallings with the daunting challenge of crafting a new culture for the almost brand-new Kennedy School. In what way might a school principal deploy the resources just described to develop a positive identity and high-performing culture in a school with a tarnished reputation or historical barriers?

There is no claim here that psychic resources are more important than their material counterparts. Rather, the contention here is that psychic resources are often neglected and can be a crucial asset for a principal striving to change a school. This is particularly true if slack material resources are unusually hard to come by.

Recall your youth. Were there not times when a favorable remark from a parent, relative, friend, coach, or a teacher meant a great deal, made you feel good about what you had accomplished, and motivated you to perform as well or better in the future? Psychic resources can be crucially important in influencing members of and shaping the eventual outcomes of an organization. No one seriously believes that General George S. Patton achieved remarkably heroic results in World War II because he offered to pay his troops more for battlefield victories. He was a master of nonmaterial motivation.

Psychic resources are themselves of two kinds: passive and active. The distinction here is the degree to which the leader's or organization's time and effort are engaged to display or enact the reward.

A *passive* resource can be something as simple as a poster, a book, or a casual remark. For example, if desirous of communicating a state of mind, an organizational frame of reference, or a particular view of change, some executives simply place, and from time to time replace, on their desk a visible copy of a recent book that reflects a relevant philosophy or point of view. The CEO may make no verbal reference to the casually displayed book whatsoever. It may prove sufficient for subordinates, in the CEO's office for whatever purpose, simply to see what the boss is reading. In the natural course of wanting to know what one's boss knows or cares about, it might behoove the observer to obtain and read the same book. It never hurts to be informed.

Active psychic resources call for one or more overt, deliberate, purposeful, and directed actions. For example, an awards ceremony is active. Here the achievements of a student, teacher, or other individual can be openly and publicly acknowledged and celebrated. The message is twofold. First, the well-performing individual is openly and publicly acknowledged. Second, what is important as an organizational behavior is made visible and more concrete to others by virtue of the public celebration. Figure 5.1 provides an overview of select active and passive psychic resources available to leaders.

Figure 5.1 Illustrative List of Psychic Resources Often Available to Leaders	
Passive	*Active*
Desk displays, office wall charts, visible office symbols such as awards, degrees, certificates, plaques	Award ceremonies and public individual and group commendations
Leader attire, tone of voice, manner of both public and private speaking, general comportment	Scheduled formal office meetings with groups or individuals to praise culturally desirable performance
Symbols of student and teacher achievement visibly posted throughout school building (school performance on state test scores, number of graduates proceeding to college, graduates accepted to the military, etc.)	Showcasing individual or group performance at an external local, regional, or national ceremony (e.g., Rotary Club, PTA meeting, school district board meeting, or national professional conference)
Visible leader behavior such as routine civility, picking up a piece of trash in the corridor, comforting a grieving staff member, knowing names of students	Newspaper articles or television news releases praising individual or group behavior
Access to an executive lunchroom, use of semiprivate restroom, gym locker for fitness purposes, good athletic tickets	Assigning status rewards such as office space, class assignments, or committee membership to high performers

Source: Compiled by the authors

Caveats

Inappropriate or insufficiently earned rewards, those widely perceived by organizational members or even recipients as undeserved or excessive, either passive or active, can have an unintended or even detrimental effect. If rewards are not perceived as having been earned, either by an individual recipient or relevant others in the organization, the effect can be counterproductive.

A change agent should use psychic resources to reward that which is important, not that which is trivial or would otherwise likely occur. Too many awards of a fatuous or gratuitous nature can be as bad as too few. To be effective in shaping and reshaping organizational participants' behavior, resources used as rewards must be perceived as being distributed for an activity or performance judged to be valuable.

There is an additional caveat in relying upon or deploying psychic resources. These resource exchanges are highly interpersonal in nature, often depending upon the perceptions and tastes of both the target or recipient of the reward and the personality of the change agent, the individual extending the reward. Hence, the reward must be consistent with the personality and management style of the administrator distributing the reward. In this instance, a change agent should ensure that a comment, a commendation, an action, or award is consistent in style and manner with his or her personality. Otherwise, the reward runs the risk of appearing disingenuous, inauthentic, manipulative, or even Machiavellian.

Hard-bitten, curmudgeonly George S. Patton distributed rewards in the form of praise for a task performed well. However, his tight-lipped manner and parsimonious use of words would not have carried over into flowery phrases and effusive encomia. Such was simply not his style and would not have been perceived as authentic by subordinates and recipients.

Material Resources

These are tangibles, resources that involve deployment, or redistribution, of scarce items—money, personnel, time, facilities, or individual perquisites. The nature of these resources engenders the most interest in organizational participants and the most resistance from those who perceive that a resource redistribution will disadvantage or detract from their position or privileges.

Material resources, ultimately, involve money. That is why they are routinely a part of the organization's budgeting and accounting processes. They necessitate expenditures of revenue to happen.

Material resources may manifest themselves as annual salaries or pay, pensions, performance or employment premiums, fringe benefits, added personnel, consultancies, physical space, equipment, and personal perquisites (who parks where, who travels to which conferences, and who eats what and where). These may involve immediate expenditures (such as employment bonuses) or eventually involve expenditures such as construction of a new physical facility.

Fungibility

Money is the mother or all resources because it is fungible.[2] Think of it this way: money perhaps cannot buy love, but it can certainly purchase emoluments that facilitate love or happiness, such as diamond rings, flowers, and trips to beautiful resorts. Similarly, money may not be able to buy added student achievement, but it can be traded for conditions and circumstances that likely facilitate student learning.

A PRIMER ON CONVENTIONAL SCHOOL DISTRICT BUDGETING

School districts usually allocate material resources through budgeting. This is a mystical process for most educators. It is cloaked with complexity and a dash of intrigue. It has a "black box" air to it and a sense that budgeting must be left to experts because its complexity is too daunting for the rest of us.

In fact, however, budgeting is fundamentally simple. *It should involve an organization consciously and routinely taking the opportunity to align or realign its resources with its purposes.* In fact, such seldom happens in a school district. Rather, what takes place is a mechanical and formulaic repeating of past resource allocation practices.

School districts contend they budget by operational "functions." In a sense, they do. However, school district budget code functional categories are so large, abstract, and amorphous as to be of little use. Typical budget functions are administration, instruction, pupil support, food service, transportation, and maintenance. There is insufficient granularity in these categories to signal what is actually taking place with a district's money.

In fact, school districts budget by "object." An "object" is a good or service that is purchased. The major object code categories in a school district budget are professional salaries, professional benefits, classified wages, classified benefits, supplies, consultants, utilities, and assorted items such as legal fees and insurance. These object codes are replicated within each of the aforementioned large-grained functional categories.

The just-described functional and object code classifications will inform a reader about how many people are employed and in the aggregate what they are paid. They will not inform a budget consumer or lay observer about what school district employees actually do, what function they are intended to perform, or which goal they are supposed to accomplish.

A true functional budget would display proposed school district spending by much more finely grained categories such as elementary school reading, mathematics, counseling, science, administration, or transportation. A secondary school budget would include history, language, physical education, art, and so on. In turn, each of these instructional and operational areas would be disaggregated to a fine-grain level so that one could actually see for what ends a school district was spending its money.

Financial detail of the just-suggested nature, when coupled with performance measures such as student test scores, would permit judgments regarding which expenditures were bringing good returns on the investment and which were in need of changing. Fine-grained budget data would facilitate judging the payoff to investment mentioned near the beginning of this chapter.

Getting resources to schools is usually quite mechanical. Schools are not financed, they are "resourced" with teachers, classified personnel, and a small amount of discretionary money for supplies. The number of teachers, classified personnel, assistant principals, and other staff is a function of pupil enrollments. There are districtwide ratios that specify a position for every so many pupils. There is little left over which a principal has operational control.

As illustrated later in this chapter, these seemingly equitable formulaic procedures actually contribute greatly to per-pupil spending irregularities and inequities across schools within the same school district.

There is also a revenue side to a budget, but, in fact, a district's per-pupil revenues change but very little from year to year, and as displayed in Chapter 1, what change there is is usually upward.

IDENTIFYING ADDED MATERIAL RESOURCES

Public education in the United States involves a great deal of money, approximately $11,000 per year per student. However, it is an unusual school district in which a principal has anything approximating this amount at his or her annual spending discretion.

Most school districts budget centrally, leaving but a small amount of revenue at the decision discretion of an individual school principal. Such a highly centralized management precept is outmoded. Among its deficiencies is that it interferes with clear-cut accountability for a school's success or failure. Most private-sector organizations, the military, and nonprofit agencies provide operating officers far greater budgetary discretion.

Regardless of the outmoded nature of most school district management and budgeting, there are places where discretionary revenues can often be identified. The following three segments of this section provide illustrations of possible pools of added material resources. These pools result from (1) inefficiencies within present school district spending strategies, (2) milking intradistrict financial inequities to advantage low-achieving schools, and (3) repurposing present inefficient spending in order to elevate academic achievement.

All three of these conditions result from inequities and inefficiencies that often can be exploited by a knowledgeable and resource sophisticated change agent principal.

Reaping Discretionary-Spending Dividends From Presently Inefficient Practices

Schools, unlike private-sector undertakings, seldom sense an efficiency imperative with intensity. In the private sector, added efficiency boosts profits and wages. Management, labor, and investors stand to reap material benefits if the firm or agency operates with greater efficiency.

In the public sector, there are few efficiency rewards, other than an episodic "green school" plaque or professional association accolade for saving money. No school manager has his salary increased or receives a bonus for being efficient. The same is true for teachers. School board members do not earn a dividend for overseeing efficient schools.

Thus, schools are rife with inefficient practices and behaviors. Schools spend money on activities that do not necessarily produce results. They also may spend more money than comparable private-sector organizations on fixed costs.

Some of these operating inefficiencies are prime candidates for reaping residual revenue from operating more efficiently. Here are three illustrations.

Substitute Teachers

Often, relying upon a substitute during an absence of a regular classroom instructor risks the wasting of instructional time. In all but the more rare circumstances, the presence of a substitute teacher sacrifices momentum. At the least there is a degree of instructional disruption. At the worst, an ineffective substitute, if deployed over a sufficiently long time period, can actually lead to retrogression in student learning.

The point here is not to flog substitutes. Their task is difficult and they are seldom well paid. Rather, the objective should be to reduce a school's reliance upon substitute teachers and, thereby, reap a dual dividend of added student achievement and cost savings.

By what mechanisms can such magic be wrought? The answer is positive "financial incentives." Most districts budget for substitutes centrally. They do not place resources at schools. A central-office staff member arranges for substitutes early each school day in response from principal directives or as a result of early dawn phone calls from teachers proclaiming their illness or other inability to get to their class that day. Sometimes a teacher is encouraged to specify a preference for a substitute. Sometimes a principal can list a preference also. Flexibility in fulfilling such preferences is contingent on the market for substitutes. The more qualified individuals there are available to substitute, the more flexible the ability to match teacher or principal preferences in undertaking substitute assignments.

A substitute is paid a daily wage, sometimes established as a consequence of collectively bargained teacher contracts. Substitutes are paid through central-office arrangements. The budget from which substitutes are paid is generally based on past years' experience of teacher absenteeism. Nationwide, about 10 percent of teachers are absent on any given school day. Mondays and Fridays are days on which most substitutes are needed. The district budgeted reserve for paying substitutes, thus, understandably, can be as large as 10 percent of all classroom teachers salaries.

Only in uniquely bargained circumstances do districts maintain a pool of full-time substitute teachers, individuals routinely drawing annual salaries and fringe benefits. When this happens, often the substitute pool is regrettably comprised of teachers that are least preferred in the classroom but for which outright dismissal from the school system is seen as an overly costly and tiresomely litigious option. More typically, substitutes are part-time workers and do not receive fringe benefits.

One solution to this organizationally, instructionally, and financially wasteful condition is to incent teachers to reduce their absenteeism. One means for accomplishing this goal is to place substitute budgets at school sites, under the aegis of the principal. The daily telephone arrangements for substitute assignments can still be undertaken by the district office so as to retain the economies of scale in central scheduling. However, the pay for the substitute is a draw down from an individual school's budget.

Under this proposed alteration, each year a school's substitute budget would be updated by a dollar amount determined by districtwide past-year usage of substitutes. If an individual school can reduce substitute usage to below the district average, the school and its teachers can share the fiscal dividend, perhaps as a teacher salary bonus, perhaps as a mix of purposes including something that assists students directly. Many ways can be considered for assigning the dividend. The important part is, responsibly, to reduce absenteeism.

If a change agent can succeed in provoking such a savings dividend, it may well have multiple advantages. The school relies less on substitutes and harvests the instructional benefits, and revenue is then released for other more productive purposes.

Utility and Supply Savings

Electricity, heating fuel, school and office supplies, water, and other consumables are recurring costs. Money spent on these items is gone—unrecoverable.

Hence, the challenge is to reduce the use of these items. Savings could be redirected toward functions closer to the core of schools—instruction.

An effective strategy for reducing such costs is to determine a per-pupil average cost for the district, multiply by an individual school's anticipated enrollment, and then place the budgeted amount as a discretionary account at a school site. Savings can be retained by the school or shared with the overall district. The point is to incent a sense of frugality among those employed and schooled at an individual campus site.

Other Imaginative Revenue-Saving Incentives

Likely savings, leading to fiscal dividends that can be redeployed in service to instruction, can be found in virtually every nook and cranny of a school district budget. For example, facility maintenance is a target of opportunity.

Most school districts spend 8 to 10 percent of their per-pupil revenues on routinely maintaining buildings and grounds. The conventional mode of operation is to have a centrally administered set of budget categories supplying the district maintenance office with appropriately qualified personnel (e.g., plumbers, electricians, and painters) and materials. In addition to some regularly scheduled maintenance activities such as inspecting heating and air conditioning and sustaining a cycle of reroofing and painting, maintenance operations respond to "work orders" submitted by individual schools. Work orders are continually prioritized with potential emergencies moved to the top of the list and more routine matters sifted downward. When the work order is reached in priority sequence, a team of correctly skilled technicians goes to the school and addresses the issue.

This procedure, if overseen by competent manners and staffed by qualified and committed workers, can be satisfactory. Good maintenance saves money by addressing operational and physical conditions before they break or wear out and provoke a far more expensive emergency.

However, not all maintenance departments in school districts are efficient. Unlike a private-sector plumber, electrician, painter, or mechanic, in-house maintenance operations do not believe they have any competition. After all, if something breaks at a school, where else can the principal go to get it fixed but to the district maintenance office? There are few market forces to discipline an internal maintenance operation that perceives itself as a monopoly provider.

To counter this monopoly condition, some school districts have moved to establish a set of internal accounts. Under this arrangement, the money for maintenance is not allocated to a central maintenance department but, rather, is placed in the budgets at school sites. All principals are then empowered to outsource a repair among private-sector local vendors or to use the district's maintenance office. Most principals prefer their internal provider and are happy, if receiving good service, to transfer funds from their individual school maintenance account to the central-district supplier. However, knowing that a principal can always seek an outside source provides market discipline and a sense of competitive pricing to the situation.

The details here are less important than the concept. By relying on internal accounts and budgeting resources at individual school sites, a district can establish a set of internal markets and reap the benefits of competition, assisting both service quality and price.

This concept can apply to other school service sectors such as reprographics or even food service. It can apply to central-office professional-development providers and to various subject area and curricular experts. If individual schools choose to purchase the service of central-district experts, then the experts, "service vendors," are paid from individual school budgets. If no school sees the benefit from a central-office "vendor" and chooses not to buy the service, then the district has a market-oriented barometer of the value of the service group or individual provider involved.

Milking Intradistrict Financial Inequities to Advantage Low-Achieving Schools

Districts tend to budget via standardized formulae. They do not allocate a dollar amount per pupil to each school. Rather, most school districts "resource" schools, providing them with a specified number of personnel based on their anticipated enrollment. The putative purpose of such a formulaic personnel position funding is to achieve and maintain equality across schools. In fact, it has an opposite effect. It contributes to what can amount to substantial interschool spending differences within the same school district. However, to the unsophisticated observer, it provides the illusion of equal treatment for each school

Principals, over and above personnel and fixed expenses, such as utilities, typically receive only a small amount of money for spending at their discretion. Here is an example.

If one considers a 2,000-student high school, spending $10,000 per student per year, one can see that a big high school is an approximate $20-million-a-year operation. This is a good-sized business, often the biggest business in a small town. Nevertheless, even given its economic significance and educational importance, it is unusual for a principal to have discretion for more than $100,000, just 5 percent of operating revenues. Not much money to gain leverage for change. That is why a change agent has to scrape for every discretionary penny he or she can identify. Fortunately, there are some places to look for added discretionary money. What follows is an illustration of two possible sources of added money.

Typically, school districts spend 20 percent of total budgeted amounts to purchase nonpersonnel items such as utilities, fuel, office supplies, computers, food, and consultants and other ad hoc experts.

A principal or other change agent may save some money, and such is always a good idea, by reducing electrical usage or having more efficient bus routes. However, these efficiencies will never come close to matching the resources that can be gained from seeking efficiencies in the other 80 percent of the school district budget, those resources allocated to personnel.

Most of a school district's or school's budgeted revenue, 80 percent of budgets, that support personnel are allocated for teacher and classified employee salaries and fringe benefits (which are much more generous for teachers than for private-sector employees with comparable professional responsibilities and occupational requirements).

Thus, the number of teachers, administrators and specialists on a district's payroll makes a huge difference. Also, the seniority of the teacher workforce in a school district is enormously determinative of what is spent. Recollect that 96 percent of America's public school teachers are paid principally for their years of service and number of graduate college credits. Hence, if a school or district has large proportions of its workforce that is heavily experienced, all other things being equal, the district will pay more for its teachers than a district or school with relatively inexperienced teachers. The following example displays the manner in which two schools in a district, all other things being equal, can have substantially different expenditure profiles, depending upon the seniority of their respective faculties.

Illustrating Personnel Policy-Driven School-by-School Spending Inequalities

Assume two elementary schools each have an enrollment of 500 students. Each has 25 teachers assigned to it. Each has a principal and a core of classified staff, custodians, food service workers, and bus drivers. Assume further that the salary schedule for similarly qualified individuals in the schools is identical. Any teacher with the same number of years of district employment and graduate college credits and degrees is paid the same as any other individual with similar characteristics.

The only difference between the two schools is that School A has virtually all newly employed teachers and School B relies upon heavily experienced individuals for its teacher workforce. The district average annual salary may well be at the national mean, $50,000. If that is all that was under scrutiny, there might not be a problem of equity or efficiency. However, if one drills deeper, the picture quickly changes.

Assume a district entry-level teacher salary of $30,000. The salary schedule peaks after 30 years at $90,000. If School A has 25 teachers at close to $30,000 annually, its aggregate salary expenditure will be (25 x $30,000) $750,000. Conversely, if School B has 25 teachers at the top of the salary schedule, the aggregate salary amount will be (25 x $90,000) a total $2,250,000, three times as much as School A. This is a difference of $3,000 per student.

In the foregoing intraschool spending illustration, one school receives massively more financial resources ($1.5 million) than the other. Federal guidelines, accompanying a school district's acceptance of federal funding, are intended to reduce or eliminate such intradistrict per-pupil spending inequalities. However, these guidelines have been watered down over time and are seldom enforced. A few equal-protection court cases[3] have declared these inequalities to be unconstitutional. However, on balance, this type of teacher salary inequity is education finance's dirty little secret. Few members of the public understand this dynamic.

The remedy for this resource inequity is to budget financial resources, not teacher positions, school by school. In instances where inequities occur, they can be remedied by providing a low-seniority school with added per-pupil revenues and placing those revenues at the discretion of a principal.

The even better news is that it is schools serving low-achieving students that routinely are the ones on the short end of the revenue distraction scheme. Seeking per-pupil funding parity might well help achievement if the dividend were productively deployed.

The principal point here is that a change agent, a principal intending to alter the culture of a school and in search of added resources to further the process, should ensure that his or her school is not being financially shortchanged under the illusionary guise of egalitarian formulaic funding. Most district funding ratios only equalize personnel positions, not revenues. It is the latter that possibly can contribute added financial resources to the school relying most heavily upon low-seniority teachers.

Repurposing Spending to Elevate Academic Achievement

Repeated prior reference has been made to the 80 percent of annual school operating budgets devoted to the salaries and fringe benefits of personnel. This amounts nationally to approximately $480 billion each year. Some $300 billion of this is wrapped up in remunerating the nation's four million teachers and administrators. The remainder supports classified workers. These dollar amounts understate the magnitude in that they do not include state-operating teacher pension systems and the health coverage obligations to hundreds of thousands of teacher and administrator retirees.

The point of reciting such remuneration figures is not the precise dollar amounts involved but, rather, to emphasize the overall financial magnitude. Paying educators is a hugely expensive public-sector undertaking. Presently, much of the pay is misdirected and based on factors only marginally related to teacher effectiveness. There probably is no greater opportunity to improve education generally and instruction particularly than by placing educator pay practices on a more productive path.

Technically, this is not difficult, and an illustrative cutover plan from the present day to better pay will be presented shortly. However, if technical change is relatively simple, the politics of any change are daunting. The only likely path to change is to create a two-tier system wherein presently employed teachers have a choice of remaining with the status quo of being paid by virtue of years of experience and college credits or switching over to a more performance-based and career ladder system. Newly employed teachers would not be given this choice but would, rather, fall to a performance- and career ladder–based system.

The problem is that beyond a minimal threshold of some two or three years, teaching experience does not appear to be systematically related to added amounts of student achievement. College credits beyond the bachelor's degree do not display a relationship to student academic growth either.

Putting the politics of resource redistribution aside, there are literally dozens of suggested performance-related teacher pay alternatives.[4] Some involve individual teacher pay premiums for elevated student achievement. Others involve group or schoolwide performance premiums. Regardless of the details, there are plentiful models of strategic compensation systems that move away from the step and ladder system to one based on career advancement and student achievement.

The essential element of this cutover from outmoded to modern pay practices is shutting off the valve by which incoming new or recent teacher hires are paid for experience and added college credits and capturing the dollar amounts that they would conventionally have been paid for these conditions and using that dividend to pay the same individuals on a performance pay plan.

If undertaken adroitly, the transition to performance pay should be cost neutral, no more costly to the district and resulting in no less pay to teachers than the former set of pay procedures. Figure 5.2 displays one-year cost projections associated with the single-salary schedule and a cost-of-living schedule with performance pay elements, whereby the dollars flow, during a transition period, from conventional to modern performance pay purposes.

Figure 5.2 One-Year Cost Projection of Single-Salary Schedule Versus Performance Pay Schedule

Years of Experience/ School Year	Single-Salary Schedule	2% Cost-of-Living Increase	Effective Teacher on Performance Pay Schedule (15% bonus not added to base pay)
1	$341,300	$341,300	$0
2	$134,064	$97,482	$80,070
3	$138,434	$99,428	$81,670
4	$142,804	$101,402	$41,645
5	$147,174	$103,446	$42,485
6	$151,544	$105,504	$43,335
7	$155,914	$107,618	$44,200
8	$160,284	$109,760	$45,080
9	$164,654	$111,958	$45,985
10	$169,024	$114,198	$46,905
11	$173,394	$116,466	$47,835
12	$177,764	$118,804	$48,795
13	$182,134	$121,198	$49,780
14	$186,504	$123,620	$50,770
15	$190,874	$123,620	$51,790
16	$195,244	$128,618	$52,825
17	$199,614	$131,194	$53,885
18	$203,984	$133,812	$54,960
19	$208,354	$136,486	$56,055
20	$1,105,800	$646,360	$228,700
	Year total for 100 teachers: $4,528,862	Year total for 75 teachers: $3,072,274	Year total for 25 teachers: $1,166,770
		75/25 combined yearly total: $4,239,044	
		Balance: $289,709	

CRUCIAL NATURE OF PERFORMANCE AND PROGRAM EVALUATIONS IN DETERMINING TARGETS FOR RESOURCE REALLOCATION AND CONTINUALLY ASSESSING RETURN ON RESOURCE INVESTMENT

The section following this describes several likely targets for high-value return on investment in redeploying resources to achieve high academic performance. Here, however, is a modest digression to emphasize the process by which a change agent principal can determine where to invest and when to convert a nonperforming investment to another strategy.

Sustained appraisal of personnel and performance effectiveness is the overarching key. Under this strategic umbrella, the crucial component is the presence of school-based data systems that continually feed to a principal granular information regarding the academic performance of individual and groups of students in the schools.

Principals need to know with accuracy and regularity how individual and all students in any individual teacher's class, or at any particular aggregate level (e.g., grade level, all of mathematics, all of English, or all students from poverty-level families), are performing in both key academic and nonacademic schooling domains.

Also, it is necessary for a change agent principal to be able to slice and dice performance data to determine how well students using a particular computer-assisted program are performing or how students (both treatment and control-group members) are faring who are engaged in a randomized field trial experiment using a different instructional idea as a "treatment."

It is feedback from student performance, linked to individual or groups of instructors and linked further to various kinds of instructional strategies, that enables a change agent principal to determine if an investment strategy is paying off in academic performance dividends or should be altered or terminated.

WHERE TO INVEST DISCRETIONARY RESOURCES

What follows are descriptions of illustrative investment targets. One involves process, one involves people, and a third involves technology.

Performance Effectiveness and Related Data Systems

If a school does not presently have the kind of comprehensive performance management and evaluation data system to which reference will be made in Chapter 6, such is a high-return investment target.

A performance management evaluation and data system by itself does not immediately contribute to student achievement. However, it is a crucial tool by which a change agent principal can determine which investments are paying dividends in terms of added student academic performance.

There are multiple vendor-provided data systems, and this is not a place to recommend one over the other. However, other items for consideration on this dimension are provided in the following chapter concentrating on data systems. What is crucial in this context is for a change agent principal to ensure that whatever system is purchased fits the needs of the individual school involved. Also, there is an important caveat. *What an evaluation system measures is what employers will do.* Be sure that you are measuring what matters because that is what will shape the efforts of those being evaluated.

Teacher Effectiveness and Remediation

A second major investment target is the evaluation, continual professional development, and, in selected instances, the remediation of teachers.

Here again, the previously mentioned performance management and program evaluation data system is crucial for facilitating the identification of teachers who are performing effectively and others for whom some form of targeted professional development or remediation is in order. For those proving effective, a performance premium may be appropriate.

Technology as an Investment Target

The mindless purchase of computer-assisted instructional (CAI) programs is to be avoided. Inappropriate systems and hardware can be a huge waste of scarce resources. However, if accompanied by tailored inservice training for teachers, selected computer-assisted instructional programs in areas such as reading, mathematics, and science may be an enormous help in two ways. First, if the CAI program has good student learning diagnostics, it can develop branched instructional applications for a student, particularly one who is not learning fast, that may exceed that which a conventional classroom teacher could do. Second, a good CAI may bring to bear upon instruction information and activities beyond that known to a conventional classroom teacher.

DYSFUNCTIONAL RESOURCE ALLOCATION PATHS TO AVOID

What is most to be avoided is the reinforcement of the status quo. If student achievement is not that to which you as a change agent principal aspire, then set your mind to identifying instructional pathways different from those employed at present. The most important attribute in this regard is a questioning frame of mind. Adopt a "show me" attitude when encountering those who claim that what now is in place is what should continue. If some vendor persists in efforts to sell a "silver bullet," be cautious.

The most often repeated change agent mistakes are investing in the following:

- Unproven computerized instructional systems
- Widely advertised off-the-rack or canned professional development that is not individually tailored to the identified remedial needs of an individual or faculty group
- Advice of superintendents or principals who do not themselves have a substantial track record of success. Associate with those who have proved repeatedly they can perform, not those who have failed and continually blame others.

Expect no silver bullets. If something is overly simply, it is highly likely to be wrong.

CONCLUSION

Thinking smart regarding resource deployment, using virtually every category of resource available to a leader, likely will assist in achieving school goals faster and more forcefully than most other strategies a change agent can undertake. There is more than one tool that can be used to shape a school culture. This chapter has explained how school leaders can use psychic and material resources to shape organizational culture and has provided insights about means for maximizing available resources—monetary, material, and mental—in order to continually enhance a productive school culture.

QUESTIONS FOR DISCUSSION

1. Discuss a list of passive and active psychic resources that you can envision using to alter a school's culture.
2. Can you envision how you might use psychic rewards to alter a school culture?
3. Discuss a similar set of monetary rewards and resources.
4. Brainstorm a list of ways in which your school district or school might save money and redirect the dividend to assist instruction.
5. Does your school district budget enable one to see how much is planned to be spent for instructional functions such as reading?
6. How might you reinvest material resources to propel instruction more productively?

SUGGESTED READINGS

Curtis, M. (1976). *The great political theories: A comprehensive selection of the crucial ideas in political philosophy from Burke, Rousseau and Kant to modern times.* New York: Avon Books.

Dahl, R. A. (2005). *Who governs: Democracy and power in an American city.* New Haven, CT: Yale University Press.

Kennedy, J. F. (1955). *Profiles in courage.* New York: Harper Collins.

McGregor, D. (2000). *The human side of enterprise.* Somerset, NJ: Wiley.

Nolan, D. R. (2007). *Labor and employment arbitration in a nutshell* (2nd ed.). St Paul, MN: Thomson.

Webb, L. D., & Norton, M. S. (2003). *Human relations administration: Personnel issues and needs in education.* Upper Saddle River, NJ: Merrill-Prentice Hall.

NOTES

1. Even though some attention is given in this chapter to rewards, as linked to resources, most of the discussion regarding rewards and performance incentives is reserved for Chapter 7 on performance accountability and incentives.

2. *Fungible* refers to an item or service that is tradable or substitutable.

3. Most notably a Washington, D.C., case and a consent decree in Los Angeles (*Los Angeles Unified School District v. Rodriquez*).

4. See www.cecr.ed.gov for a comprehensive set of resources and examples.

Case Study 6: Data, Data Everywhere But Hardly a Drop of Useful Information

Karlene "Karla" Bailiff was the newly appointed principal of recently opened Everett Middle School. She had been an English teacher, had served as an assistant principal in other districts, and, after completing a doctoral program at a nearby university, had been named the principal of Everett, a spanking-new middle school. She was pleased at her career so far and confident in what she knew regarding instruction and management.

In her new job, she received monthly reports from her district's human resources (HR) department. One came at the end of August. The other came a month later. These reports listed, among dozens of other items, facts such as teachers' names; absences that month, if any; afterschool working hours as a coach, afterschool club adviser, and so on; and whether or not the teacher was taking graduate credit hours at night or at other times at a local education school. Teacher salaries were also listed. There was both a lot and little detail. For example, the monthly HR spreadsheet said nothing about the name of the college courses being taken.

Karla dutifully read and filed these reports, but in truth she did not know what to do with them. They did not seem to have actionable information, and little about them seemed to change from month one to month two, the two months her school had been in operation. Still, Karla was not critical. She thought that there was assuredly some logic to these reports and that, in time, she would come to understand their purpose.

Serving as a principal of a new school was more than a full-time job. There were many beginning teachers in need of assistance; the school's reporting procedures and communications had not all been ironed out; the facility, though new, had a few glitches; and Karla was eager to learn the names of students and parents as well. She was happy, but she was busy.

Thus, one can guess Karla's abject astonishment to receive an unscheduled visit from the head of the district's HR department. Karla's assistant called Karla to her office. There sat the HR director. This person was clearly miffed, and that puzzled Karla even more. Karla knew who the lady was, but she did not really know her.

Note: This case study, as with others associated with other chapters, is about an actual school, actual people, and actual conditions. Nothing is fabricated. All cases are about situations school leaders routinely encounter. However, in each instance, names of people, schools, and locations have been altered to ensure confidentiality.

The HR head asked why Karla had not been responding to the monthly reports. Karla decided to be extra polite; after all, she was the newest principal on the block, and she may have inadvertently committed some error or organizational faux pas.

Karla apologized and then asked, "How do you believe I should have responded?"

Karla was further knocked off balance by the look of utter shock on the HR director's face. Karla wondered if she had just asked the stupidest question in the world.

The HR director, close to apoplexy, blurted, "You appear to have taken no action. What about the teachers on your faculty who do not have a required afterschool assignment? All teachers are supposed to coach or sponsor a club after school."

Karla said that she was sorry, but she did not know that. She promised to look into it immediately.

The HR director continued angrily to say that Karla had not commented on the graduate courses that her teachers were taking. The HR director wanted to know if these were courses that Everett teachers should be taking.

Karla explained that she had just started as principal and that Everett had just started as a school. After two months of operation, Karla believed it a bit premature to make judgments regarding the "rightness" or "wrongness" of the kinds of courses for Everett teachers. The HR director dismissed this explanation by pointing out that 60 percent of Everett teachers were experienced and had had their professional experience in the district. In her view, Karla should have followed up with these teachers' prior principals.

Karla started to say to the HR director, "Why did you not mention any of these things during the new week-long new-principal orientation?" but she bit her tongue and simply said that she would certainly follow up on this issue.

The HR director left in a snit, and Karla noted the experience as one of the most awkward in which she ever had participated. Still, she found her district personnel manual and noted that the contract with teachers did indeed specify an afterschool extra duty assignment for all tenured teachers. She examined the HR report and determined that there were two such teachers at Everett who seemed not to have an afterschool activity assignment.

Karla wrote each of them an e-mail that afternoon asking them about their view of the situation and inquiring whether or not they wanted to come to her office and talk over the matter. One of the teachers immediately responded that, though she was a district employee, her salary was fully federally funded and that she was consequently exempt from this contractual provision. She volunteered, moreover, that if Karla gave her such an extra duty assignment she would immediately file a personnel grievance. The next day, the other teacher responded that she was four months pregnant and, thus, for the interim, did not fall subject to the extra duty requirement.

Karla thought she was the protagonist in Bel Kaufman's classic novel *Up the Down Staircase*, about a dysfunctional New York City school's management: Still, she liked most of her job and intended to keep on soldiering.

At the end of her third month as a new principal, Karla received her first quarterly financial statement for Everett. This document's daunting complexity and length was bone rattling. Karla was unprepared for such a dense document. It made the HR report seem like a simple first-grade comic book by comparison. To Karla the whole undertaking seemed like drinking water from a fire hose. It was data overkill. Still, she slogged through the document with the image of the HR director confrontation still fresh in her mind.

The Everett quarterly financial statement contained the following:

- What was owed in publicly issued bonds to finance construction of the building (this included the fluctuations in the interest rates surrounding the bonds)
- The total spent over the last month for maintenance and operation at Everett (This figure was then disaggregated into personnel-classified and -certificated, personnel benefits-health, pension, and other vendor services, cafeteria food costs, per-meal-served food costs, cafeteria revenue, athletic revenue, athletic operational costs, transportation costs, per-pupil mile transport costs, maintenance costs, maintenance costs per square foot, maintenance costs paid for hourly employees, maintenance costs paid to vendors, supplies, consulting fees, professional-development costs, PTA revenue, federal revenue, state categorical revenue, district general-fund revenue, philanthropic-contributed revenue, and on and on it went.)

Karla had no idea what all of this was about. She could not imagine why she needed this informational detail.

Karla searched intensely for data she could use. What she wanted was an annual or monthly salary figure for each of her teachers, counselors, administrators, and classified staff. That was nowhere to be found. She also looked, in vain, for accounting information in areas where she believed she had decision discretion. By piecing together about 10 accounts she could tell that in supplies and in a few other expense areas, she was spending on track, assuming that she could multiply each month by 12 to see what the trajectory for the year would be. She found it strange that nowhere were Everett's utility costs mentioned. There was nothing about electricity, water, gas, reprographics, or telephone. Surely these items were accounted for somewhere. They could not be free.

Karla wished she had some Rosetta stone that would crack the financial statement code. What did all of these figures mean anyway? Were there not some benchmarks somewhere that could suggest to her what she *should* be spending, not just what she *was* spending?

Would the district business manager soon visit her and ask her why she had not taken some action about something about which she now knew nothing? Karla thought she would talk to some of her fellow principals and try to learn more.

Fortunately, from Karla's viewpoint, the business manager never said anything to her. However, right after the end of the first semester, the district director of testing and measurement came to visit her, carrying envelopes, each with the name of one of her teachers on it. Karla was asked to sign a receipt for the conveyance of each envelope for each teacher. Karla was tingling with excitement to find out what was in each envelope. She felt like maybe she was going to win a lottery, as if these were all from the Publisher's Clearinghouse.

Once the paperwork was complete, the testing director explained that the envelopes contained value-added testing results for each of her 100 teachers. However, Karla was cautioned that while she personally had the information, and she could share it with the individual teacher involved, she could (1) not share the information with other teachers, (2) could not share it with parents in the individual teacher's class, and (3) could not use the information for evaluating the teacher at the end of the year or disciplining or dismissing a teacher.

Given these restrictions, Karla wondered, "Why bother?" However, being a newbie, she said nothing.

When the testing director had left, Karla selected and opened a few envelopes. There was Ms. Jones, one of the school's most experienced teachers, with 25 years of teaching seventh-grade math. Ms. Jones was a legend in the district. Thus, Karla was surprised to see that Ms. Jones's value-added score was "MINUS."

Conversely, when Karla opened the envelope for Mr. Smith, the second-year English teacher, his value-added score was "PLUS." What was going on here? Everything was backward.

Karla looked further. She wanted to see where Ms. Jones was weak and where Mr. Smith was strong. Surely there was more to the scores than PLUS or MINUS. Was there not some granular detail that would enable Karla to meet with each of her teachers and counsel them about their instructional weaknesses and congratulate them on their strengths? Alas, no envelope had such detail. Worse yet, there were a number of envelopes with no information at all. They were for teachers in nontested subjects such as PE, woodshop, art, and music.

Again, after reading the content of each envelope, envelopes for which she had signed a very official-looking receipt, Karla wondered what she was to do with all of this.

The one thing she did conclude, however, was that she had better lock up all the envelopes very safely.

What Karla kept reflecting upon, in the following days, is why all the data she was receiving couldn't come in a format that helped her. Why couldn't the financial data be meshed with the personnel data and the personnel data meshed with the student performance data? That struck her as useful. However, she did not talk about this. She thought she would gain a little more knowledge and a little more seniority and then speak out. She also wished her doctoral program had offered a course on performance management data systems.

In June, upon completion of her first year as Everett's principal, Karla was requested to visit with the district's supervisor of middle schools for her year-end evaluation. This was a tense time for Karla. She knew not what to expect.

The meeting went well. Karla was congratulated for having had a most successful first year, and her contract was to be renewed. She was told that she was popular with her teachers and her parents, her teachers thought she knew a great deal about instruction, the school climate seemed productive and pleasant, she had few discipline problems, the cafeteria food was rated highly, the facility itself and the building grounds and playfields were in good shape and pleasant in appearance, and she had (somehow, she wondered) stayed within her budget.

The one place where Karla was rated negatively was in using data to construct a climate of continuous learning in her school.

Hmmm, how could that be?

FOR DISCUSSION

1. What is going on here? What is the disjuncture between data and performance management that is taking place at Everett?

2. Are these problems of Karla's making?

3. How does Everett compare to a well-run private-sector business?

4. Why is Everett different from Wal-Mart?

5. What would you do next, if you were Karla? Seek a new job, talk to the superintendent, something else?

6. In what ways is your school the same as or different from Everett?

7. What would you consider an ideal data prototype for a school for which you were responsible?

CHAPTER 6

Data-Driven Decision Making and School Culture

In this chapter a reader will learn to do the following:

- Recognize the importance of data-driven decision making for education leaders
- Use a systematic process for making data-based decisions that can lead to school culture enhancements
- Use performance data in the design and operation of instructional programs and in guiding staff development
- Consider data infrastructure requirements to support school and district data-based decisions
- Identify various ways that school leaders can use data to guide program, personnel, and resource allocation decisions

ELCC STANDARDS

ELCC standards addressed in this chapter include the following:

- 1.1—Develop a vision of learning
- 1.2—Articulate a vision of learning
- 1.3—Implement a vision
- 1.4—Steward a vision
- 1.5—Promote community involvement in the vision
- 2.1—Promote a positive school culture
- 2.2—Provide an effective instructional program
- 2.3—Apply best practices to student learning
- 3.1—Manage the organization
- 3.3—Managing resources
- 4.1—Collaborate with families and other community members
- 4.3—Mobilize community resources
- 6.1—Understand the larger context

INTRODUCTION

Within America's new era of heightened expectations for schooling, growing societal complexity, and increasing instructional sophistication, school leaders are looked to as individuals who can identify, define, and solve problems. While there are many approaches to making decisions and solving problems, a critical first step in solving problems is to identify and fully understand them, and one powerful mechanism for specifying and comprehending problems is to collect and analyze data. When strategic education leaders compile, assess, and use school and community data, they are in a better position to serve as stewards of school culture and catalysts for problem solving within school communities. While some problems clearly present themselves, others are not immediately evident or explicitly defined and thus must be discovered, fleshed out by careful analysis of data. Given the nation's current policy context, educators increasingly recognize the value of data and the need to obtain a greater comprehension of data analysis and decision making. The provision of such enhanced understanding is the aim of this chapter.

Consider for a moment what might be possible in American education if student level performance data were systematically linked to corresponding grade level and subject area classroom teachers and those data were linked to professional-development allocations for those teachers, which were in turn linked to key classroom level demographic indicators. While pondering this possibility, consider the following two illustrative scenarios.

> *Mike McGee has been feeling a bit sluggish recently and decides to visit the local Veterans Administration hospital for a checkup. When accounting for habits and genetic factors, it is understandable that his level of anxiety is a bit high. Yet, as each test is conducted, specialists have immediate access to the resultant data through a real-time local area network (LAN). These specialists, located in several separate buildings of the large hospital complex, are able concurrently to analyze and assess the test data and assemble a composite diagnosis for the patient. Throughout this process, nurses, who also have access to the test data and specialist analyses, are able to provide periodic updates and assurances to Mr. McGee. Results of early tests lead to subsequent follow-up analyses until all necessary data have been gathered. Within five hours of admittance, Mike McGee has undergone a thorough assessment and is provided with a data-based diagnosis crafted by a team of specialists. The diagnosis forms the basis of a plan of treatment that, fortunately, will remediate Mike's situation in a matter of weeks.*
>
> *Karen Evans has been experiencing car trouble, and recently the check-engine light of her Lincoln Town Car has been illuminated. She rearranges her Monday work schedule to drop her car off at Friendly Auto for a checkup. However, the lead mechanic tells her that they only conduct diagnostic engine assessments on the last Thursday of each month. He warns that these reports, which are sent from the Friendly Auto headquarters, sometimes take a few weeks to arrive at storefront franchise locations. Further, he specifies that headquarters furnishes a report from these monthly diagnostic tests that lists all of the possible ailments for all of the cars at the garage on that given Thursday, making it difficult to pinpoint a specific problem with her car. Perplexed, Karen leaves Friendly Auto still uncertain if her car is capable of making the 400-mile-roundtrip journey to a business conference later in the week.*

Whether it is listening to the morning weather forecast, turning the radio dial to the afternoon traffic report, determining how to invest retirement funds, or keeping abreast of a favorite sports team, data keeps citizens informed and appropriately influences decisions. Yet, there are few twenty-first-century operations as outmoded as public school data systems. For example, which of the two scenarios just listed, Mike McGee at the VA hospital or Karen Evans at Friendly Auto, more closely resembles the data capacity of your school or district? What influence does this reality have upon the ability of school leaders to make well-informed, timely decisions?

In order to equip current and aspiring school leaders with increased knowledge of how to use data to make informed decisions, this chapter engages the challenging issue of (1) why it is important for school leaders to collect and analyze data, (2) how school data can be approached in a systematic manner, and (3) what specific types of data should be collected. Recall from Chapter 1 the discussion of 14 research-based leadership practices impacting school reform efforts. Several of these practices relate directly to the collection, analysis, and interpretation of data and the communication of issues and solutions that emerge from this collaborative process.

When done collaboratively, data analysis and problem solving can become powerful levers to instill a culture of continuous improvement. As Hawley and Sikes (2007) contend, effective problem solving in schools brings all constituents together to look at data, formulate a shared theory or understanding, consider potential responses, identify needs for new resources and capabilities, and move into action in response. A skillful education leader ensures the school community collaborates in the process of problem solving so that the process is widely regarded as legitimate, different perspectives are welcomed, actions resolved upon are widely accepted, and the move to implementation is embraced wholeheartedly. Throughout the process of decision making, the aim is to develop a shared understanding of the problem(s) and to mobilize the school to respond wisely and vigorously.

STRATEGIC APPROACHES TO DECISION MAKING IN EDUCATION

Why is data-based decision making so critical for establishing a culture of continuous school improvement? Why should school and district leaders turn to data to help inform leadership decisions? While there are many good answers to these questions, four key reasons will be provided here for why data-driven decision making is important.

First, however, we offer a working definition. Data-driven decision making is the reliance for analyses and decisions upon systematically and reliably collected information regarding multiple performance and status characteristics of school operation. These facets can involve individual and collective student performance (e.g., academic achievement, attendance, extracurricular participation, or course taking), personnel (e.g., teacher characteristics, attendance, or professional-development status), parents (participation, attendance at functions, responses to school communication), or fiscal matters such as spending within important categories (e.g., personnel, supplies, and instructional materials).

Careful collection, analysis, and use of data help schools to do the following:

- Progress toward continuous student and organizational improvement
- Focus upon and establish priorities for instructional and staff development efforts and monitor individual and collective progress
- Meet district, state, and federal accountability requirements
- Develop a sense of community through sustained collective learning

Continuous Improvement

Systematic collection, analysis, and use of data can serve as a catalyst to propel organizational learning. School leaders can harness the regular information flow from data to sustain a culture of learning for both students and teachers within their schools. Data can provide leaders with continual feedback regarding mechanisms critical to supporting individual and collective learning in educational organizations.

In order for school leaders to sustain a culture of continuous improvement, questions such as the following should constantly be pursued: What are school and community data telling us? How can we change our practice in response to the data? What additional data need to be collected? How does data from standardized assessments compare with teacher-created measures of student performance and development? The greater degree of access that teachers and school leaders have to such information, the better able they will be to sustain cycles of inquiry that will enhance professional climate and organizational learning.

Focus Efforts and Monitor Progress

Multiple types and sources of data are necessary for a school leader to understand a school's strengths and weaknesses, set priorities for improvement, concentrate change efforts, and establish a baseline from which to monitor progress. As will become clear later in this chapter, data play an integral part in planning and implementing focused improvement strategies. School and district level data are valuable tools to evaluate policies and programs, to develop and improve curricular offerings, and to monitor teaching and learning. Yet, in many settings, this valuable tool is underused. Take, for example, Sunnybrook Elementary School.

At Sunnybrook, there are currently four isolated supplemental reading initiatives in progress, five different reading textbooks being used, and two quite different approaches taken to developing students' reading comprehension skills. Yet, if detailed data were not collected on the reading program at Sunnybrook, one might be puzzled about the recent decline in reading scores. This is a good example of the fact that data are an excellent problem-finding tool. Yet one often does not have to look far to uncover a multitude of issues needing attention in schools. Here is where strategic education leaders can play a critical role in helping the school community approach problems in a systematic manner. Too often, schools and school systems try to do too much, and all at once.

One common problem in schools is a lack of programmatic focus and alignment. Strategic education leaders, however, are in a position to take a comprehensive view of programmatic data and thus assist schools to develop a more focused and integrated approach to instruction improvement. When used in this manner, data not only provide a valuable means of discovering school problems, but also provide the information necessary for a school to monitor progress in addressing those dilemmas.

Meet Accountability Requirements

Within the current policy environment, one of the most widespread reasons that data-based decision making is so important for school leaders is to meet accountability requirements. The No Child Left Behind Act (NCLB) legislation requires states and localities to collect, analyze, and report data on student demographics and achievement. Much of the accountability pressure that school leaders encounter is external; those outside the school such as district, state, and federal governing bodies determine benchmarks and standards. In order for school leaders to ensure they are meeting these external accountability requirements, they must use school data to answer questions such as the following: Is the school meeting various requirements outlined in the state standards? Are all students making adequate yearly progress? What proportion, and what subgroups, of students are scoring at or above proficiency levels as determined by state achievement tests?

School leaders must also use data to ensure their school communities meet other forms of accountability. NCLB has enhanced the market accountability facing school leaders by requiring students enrolled in persistently failing schools to be given the option to transfer to more successful schools in their district. To address such competition-based pressure, schools need to be able to compare themselves to other schools and to highlight improvements as a vehicle to attract parents and students.

While market-based and externally imposed accountability systems attract most of the headlines, internal accountability is also an important domain influenced by data collection and analysis. Here, school groups develop goals based on local norms and aspirations for growth and then collect data to monitor instructional progress toward the school-based goals. As teacher motivation resides squarely within schools, where individual effort and collaboration can directly affect teaching and learning, internal accountability can play an important role in enhancing classroom practices.

LINK TO CASE STUDY 6

In Case Study 6 you are introduced to Karla, the new principal of a brand-new middle school. Within the first weeks of the school year she is inundated with data, but none of it seems to be really useful. From your personal experience, what sources and types of data are most helpful in divining instructional improvement? What types and sources of data do you think would be most helpful to a school leader seeking to create and sustain a high-performing school culture?

Build Community Through Organizational Learning

Data can be an important lever for creating and supporting the professional relationships and sense of community at the center of organizational learning. An emerging view of teaching, referred to as the "new professionalism" of teaching, sees teaching as part of a communal endeavor, moving away from traditional egg crate classroom autonomy toward new forms of interactive relationships with colleagues. Within and outside of schools, greater dialogue surrounding the collection and interpretation of data provides an opportunity to bridge the traditional divide that exists between key school actors and constituents, such as between middle school and high school teachers, parents and teachers, and schools and businesses. Gone are the days when schools serve an elite population subset. It is now imperative that schools take efforts to broaden the scope of what and who counts within the educational community. This necessary organizational learning is an excellent opportunity to build a sense of community inclusive of the growing demographic diversity facing schools.

SYSTEMATIC COLLECTION AND USE OF SCHOOL DATA

Having discussed several of the many good reasons why data-based decision making matters for school success, it is now important to situate data collection, analysis, and use within the context of an overall school improvement cycle. At its core, the reason for employing data in school decision making is to foster growth and improvement. A typical school improvement cycle is provided in Figure 6.1.

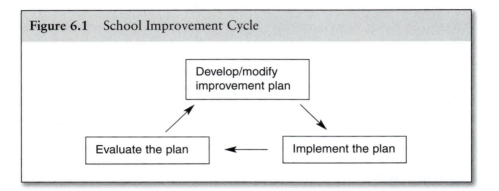

Figure 6.1   School Improvement Cycle

The systematic collection and use of data play key roles in school efforts aimed at continuous improvement. When one develops a school improvement plan, data can provide insight and focus for school goals. Data patterns can reveal strengths and weaknesses within the instructional program and thus provide excellent direction for growth. When one evaluates a plan, data allow the organization to assess if the plan is being implemented as designed and determine the impact of the plan on student achievement or other organizational goals. Of the three components of the school improvement cycle, evaluation is the domain where the process often deteriorates. Yet, to secure continuous, synergistic school improvement, data-based evaluation is critical. Reflections upon the data provided throughout the evaluation process provide a basis for either adhering to an existing plan or modifying the plan better to meet organizational goals.

The use of data throughout the school improvement process, rather than relying upon intuition, tradition, self reports, or one-shot observations or convenience to drive decisions, leads to benefits such as those highlighted in Figure 6.2.

Figure 6.2 Comparison of School Processes	
Decision Making Based on Intuition, Inertia, Tradition, Self Reports, One-Shot Observations, Prejudices, or Convenience	*Data-Driven Decision Making*
Budgetary decisions based on prior practice, priority programs	Budget allocations to programs based on data-informed needs
Staff meetings that focus on operations and the dissemination of information	Staff meetings that concentrate on improvement strategies and issues raised by a local school's empirical data
Grading systems based on each teacher's criteria of completed work and participation	Grading systems based on common student performance criteria that report progress on the standards as well as work skills
Scattered staff development programs	Concentrated collective and individual staff development programs as an improvement strategy to address documented problems/needs
Reports to the community about school events	Organized factual reports to the community about the learning progress of students
Periodic administrative team meetings focused solely on operations	Administrative team meetings that focus on measured progress toward data-based improvement goals

Although the particular manner in which data are collected, analyzed, and used will vary from school to school, the key elements of an effective data-based decision making program include (1) a data leadership team, (2) purposeful data collection and analysis, and (3) a plan for using data to enhance instructional practice.

Data Leadership Team Appropriately Supported

In order for school and community data to be used effectively to enhance student learning, a number of infrastructure and support activities need to be in place. One important support is a data leadership team. A team, rather than an individual, is ideally suited for this work for a number of reasons. To begin, principals and other school leaders have been given a difficult charge: take an abundance of student and demographic data, provided from a variety of sources and in various formats, and turn these data into targeted information that can be used to enhance educational practice. The sheer magnitude of this task would make it difficult for even a "superhero" principal single-handedly to accomplish. Fortunately, discussions are richer and less biased, and potential solutions are more diverse and complete when numerous points of view are considered. When findings are ready to be presented, the dissemination of information benefits from a team that can ensure no constituent groups are overlooked. The tremendous effort needed to sustain a culture of continuous school improvement through data-driven decision making is much easier when tasks are divided among a team of committed people.

For these reasons, strategic education leaders should strive to develop a data leadership team. The goal of collaborative data teams is to cooperate in the design and analysis of data to improve the educational experiences and performance of students. These teams can exist in a variety of forms. They can be made up entirely of teachers, administrators, and various school specialists. Additionally, the teams may include members from the wider community, including parents, business leaders, and others with a vested interest in schools. These teams can be formed with a purposeful inclusion of members across grade levels or subject areas. Certainly, within a given school there may be multiple data teams—from a schoolwide team with representatives from each grade level and curricular area to smaller grade level or subject area teams. Regardless of their composition, these teams all serve the purpose of successfully using data to enhance the educational experiences and performance of students.

Time is one of the most important supports that the data leadership team, and other staff members, need in order to use data for decision making. In order to sustain the infusion of data into school improvement efforts, significant time is necessary to engage staff members with data on a continual basis. While many data-based activities can be embedded within faculty meetings, other activities, such as developing improvement strategies, will require substantial inservice or "release" time to construct thoughtfully. Monthly meetings will be necessary for a data leadership team that has primary responsibility for coordinating data collection, analysis, interpretation, and reporting efforts. School leaders can create time for these meetings through means such as providing substitute teachers for team members, by arranging team members' schedules so that meetings can occur during planning periods, or by compensating team members for their time to meet after school hours.

In many ways, a data management system upon which school personnel rely will either provide a tremendous support for a data leadership team, or it will bring the data-dependent goals and intentions of school personnel to a grinding halt. One major assumption of the benefits of data-driven decision making is that reliable, timely, and accurate data will be available. As such, a primary step for strategic education leaders to take within the domain of data-based decision making is to assess the scope, quality, and availability of data to support instructional decisions. In order to assess the usability of existing data, strategic education leaders should examine data along the following five dimensions: (1) availability and accessibility, (2) timeliness and completeness, (3) accuracy, (4) consistency, and (5) alignment.

The *availability* of data refers to how easy it is for teachers and administrators to access student, teacher, and school level data on demand. Is a special administrative code needed to access data? Is real-time data available, or is information only uploaded weekly or monthly? The *completeness* of data refers to how much pertinent data is available for analysis. Do some teachers and students have data files that are missing significant amounts of relevant demographic detail? What percentage of available student data is entered into the school data system? *Timeliness* and *accuracy* of data refer to how often and how correctly student and faculty data are entered into the data system and are updated. Are recent changes in student and teacher data profiles reflected in the available data? The *consistency* of data refers to the uniformity in which data are entered. Are all similarly situated special education students represented in the data system in the same manner? Are there differences in the way students of various ethnicities are represented in the data system? The *alignment* of data refers to the degree to which data are able to be linked to other data in the system. Is student level data linked to faculty data? Is teacher demographic data linked to payroll data?

Data usability is a function of both the databases and data system used by a school or district. A database is an organized collection of information or data elements, stored electronically, that can be searched, sorted, reorganized, and analyzed rapidly. A data system is a collection of computer programs that facilitates the storage, modification, and extraction of information from a database. It is no surprise that both are integral to the provision of usable data for school leaders and teachers. Consider the degree to which your school data allow you to link teachers to students to educational activities at the elementary, middle, and high school levels. To what extent is your data management system able to link individual students to multiple teachers (such as in team teaching, shared positions, or multigrade teaming)? Does your data system link professional development data to teacher course loads and curricular responsibilities? If you can answer yes to these questions, your school benefits from usable data, likely a product of thoughtfully constructed databases and a high-quality data system. If not, efforts need to be undertaken by school and district personnel to construct a data system capable of accurately evaluating instructional activities and related outcomes.

Unfortunately, America's public schools do not uniformly code, collect, and assemble data with the instructional activities of classrooms linked to student performance. Something as important as linking individual students' test scores to their grade- and subject matter–appropriate teachers and, then, linking that data to key teacher characteristic variables, school demographic variables, and resource levels presently occurs in only a few states and local school districts. At the local school level, strategic education leaders can provide a useful service to school communities by insisting on the availability of high-quality data. This begins by ensuring that usable data is entered into the system in a systematic manner; otherwise, the adage "garbage in, garbage out" may be all too true.

Purposeful Data Collection and Analysis

The acquisition and analysis of school data should be a planned and purposeful process. When data are collected in a purposeful manner, educators are better able to identify patterns of outcomes and design strategies to enhance student learning. Purposeful data collection and analysis is concerned with targeting identified needs and goals that are almost always linked to enhanced student and organizational performance. Currently, most data collection at the school level is externally driven and is primarily used to establish compliance with standards. By taking ownership of school data at the local level, school leaders can move beyond compliance to an authentic school improvement effort.

By focusing on domains of practice to which the school community is committed, school leaders can increase the likelihood that insights provided by data will have a sustained impact on teachers' instructional practice.

Purposeful data analysis is focused on using data to make decisions about programs and students. In order to make informed decisions about programs, data may need to be analyzed across multiple contexts or over multiple years. In order to make appropriate decisions about students, data may need to be analyzed across classes and teachers, disaggregated by gender and ethnicity, and drawn from multiple sources. For example, to determine how various student groups are performing in reading, one needs to collect data on student demographics, teaching practices, student learning (on both standardized and teacher-generated tests), and program features (such as classroom materials used and teacher proficiency with the curriculum) and analyze these data over a multiyear period. By moving beyond simplistic or token data analysis (examining one data source for one year) to in-depth, purposeful analysis (examining the interaction of multiple data sources over multiple years), educational leaders can determine the impact of their programs and practices and modify them to improve the performance of all students.

As the foregoing example illustrates, in order purposefully to collect and analyze data, one must consider multiple types of data. Four types of data are helpful to create the composite picture necessary for answering complex questions. These types of data include student achievement, demographic, school program, and perception data. These four types of data are highlighted in Figure 6.3, and each will be described here.

Figure 6.3   Multiple Data Types

Student Achievement	Demographic
• Standardized tests • Norm-referenced tests • Criterion-referenced tests • Writing samples • Authentic assessments • Portfolio items • Teacher observation	• Enrollment • Attendance • Grade levels • Free and reduced lunch • Race • Ethnicity • Gender
School Program	Perception
• Texts and materials used • Library holdings • Technology • Curriculum • Supplemental programs • Content standards	• Community values • Beliefs • Attitudes • Satisfaction with program • Strengths and needs of school • Skill level of graduates

---

Student Achievement Data

In many ways, student achievement data are the ultimate source of insight regarding educational program effectiveness. Fortunately, there are multiple forms of student achievement data in addition to that which is provided from standardized tests. Standardized achievement data are an example of annual large-scale assessments. Additionally, educators can employ periodic assessment data and ongoing classroom assessment data to determine the efficacy of the instructional program. These three types of achievement data vary in purpose, frequency, type of feedback provided, and targeted audience. This information is summarized in Figure 6.4.

Figure 6.4	Comparison of Assessment Types		
Feedback	**Assessment Type**		
Purpose	Annual large-scale tests	Periodic grade level and subject area tests	Ongoing classroom assessments
Frequency	Infrequent ←——————→ Frequent		
Type	Broad ←——————→ Specific		
Target	Community, policymakers, administrators, general accountability audience	Administrators, teachers	Teachers, students

Annual large-scale assessment data are designed primarily for accountability purposes, providing a broad indicator of school effectiveness. While these data can be of some use regarding curricular program efficacy, their utility is limited because these tests are designed to sample broad domains of student knowledge. As such, these assessments are insufficiently helpful when seeking to determine a specific area of student progress, and they provide only limited utility during a given school year.

Periodic grade-level and subject-specific assessments provide immediate results of student performance on key standards-based skills. These assessments can be used to establish entrance-level performance benchmarks for students at the beginning of a school year. By continuing to use these assessments throughout a school year, teachers and administrators can determine students' progress, as well as uncover strengths and weaknesses in particular content areas. These assessments are able to provide insight regarding which students might need enrichment or special assistance during a school year. Additionally, by examining classroom or grade-level aggregate data, one is able to uncover patterns in content coverage or student success that may require alternate instructional strategies or content-specific professional development for a particular teacher. Ideally, these data are aligned with end-of-course assessments and standardized tests. In this way, one attains data on student and programmatic progress throughout a school year that is consistent with the perspective gained from annual, summative achievement tests.

Ongoing classroom-based assessments can be a powerful tool to help educators understand the depth of each student's knowledge and skills. In order for this data to bear fruit however, the result must be used to make decisions for improving student achievement. Strategic education leaders must challenge teachers graphically to depict data from daily assignments in a way that clearly shows who is excelling, who needs enrichment, and who is performing on target. When data buried in grade books are charted, displayed, and used when constructing lessons, the richness of ongoing assessments is harnessed to the creation of responsive, student-centered learning experiences. The key here is how these formative data are used. If no instructional or programmatic modifications are made, then the potential benefits illuminated by data have been lost. Here again, data can pinpoint a problem, but solutions often require a change in teacher practices.

Demographic Data

In an era of market-based accountability and increasing school choice options, school leaders must continue to develop a solid understanding of their communities. In some locations, this is tantamount to hitting a bull's-eye while riding a Brahma bull, as demographic conditions can be a swiftly moving target. To help facilitate this quest for community awareness, school leaders are advised to take a longitudinal approach to the endeavor. In this manner, an educational leader can begin to view trends and make predictions. When determining which demographic data to collect, the goal is thoroughly to know the school population in order to clarify problems and needs. Dimensions of demographic data that should be collected include the following: neighborhood characteristics, parent involvement, behavioral and social problems of students, key demographic characteristics of students enrolled in school and their parents (e.g., age, gender, race, ethnicity, SES), mobility patterns in and out of grades and schools, student transportation needs, and enrollment rates in special programs (e.g., ESL, special education, or afterschool programs).

The collection and analysis of demographic data allow school leaders better to understand the social context in which students, parents, faculty, and administrators are situated. By assessing trends within the student population, and analyzing factors outside of school that influence student learning, educational leaders are better able to craft a purposeful, relevant, and responsive educational program.

School Program Data

Rich sources of information about the quality of school programs are often hidden in dusty binders or not contained in written documents at all, making this potential source of data difficult to collect and use. To guide the collection of program data, one might consider how successful school programs are in bringing about the academic excellence articulated in the school mission, goals, and content standards. At the outset of a school year, plans should be made to collect program evaluation data. The collection of these data throughout the school year, which can be seen as a form of action research, will inform decision making about programs, curricula, and supporting materials.

For example, if a school is concerned regarding the impact of the band program upon the academic performance of band members, one would collect information about the time demands of the instrumental music program, both within and outside of school, as well as assess students' success before, during, and following their involvement in the band. This latter assessment might be conducted both by looking at student grades and by interviewing students regarding their experiences with juggling academic responsibilities while in the band program. In this case, a mix of quantitative and qualitative data would provide a well-rounded picture of the impact that this program is having on the broader achievement level of students. The successful use of in-house program level data may require a culture shift in some education organizations. The shift involves a commitment thoroughly to examine educational practices with a disposition to determining how such practices might be changed to benefit the academic performance of students.

Perception Data

A fourth type of data to collect and evaluate from various stakeholders in the school community is perception data. These data, similar to demographic data, are enlightening because they turn the attention of school leaders to the important ideas and opinions of the school community. It is no surprise that the opinions of parents and community members influence students profoundly. Therefore, it is essential that school leaders are aware of the perceptions of the school that exist in the community. In order to assemble a reasonably complete composite of perception data, school leaders should include the following members of the school community: students, parents, instructional and support staff, local businesses, school board members, regional colleges and universities, and other citizens with a vested interest in education. Perception data help school leaders understand such things as how the members of the school community feel about the school, how satisfied community members are with the educational programs, what community members perceive to be the strengths and needs of the school, and what the community thinks about the knowledge and skills of graduates.

Mechanisms by which perception data can be gathered include surveys, polls, analyses of local newspaper editorials, and unsolicited letters to the school. This data, which are often seen as diffuse and intangible by members of the community, can be drawn together to provide an essential portrait of a well-rounded and honest portrayal of school progress.

LINK TO CASE STUDY 6

Considering Figure 6.3, how can principal Karla use the four types of data just listed to ensure a pay-for-performance plan is constructed that is tailored to the local context and community?

Using the Four Data Types

As achievement, demographic, program, and perception data are each unique, proper analysis will require slightly different methods. After the various types of data are analyzed through their own lenses, a next step is to bring key insights from each domain together to create a more holistic view. Because the primary emphasis in school improvement is on student learning, analysis of achievement data often forms the basis of school improvement plans and strategies. As a data leadership team sorts through additional data sources, patterns and relationships among the data may begin to emerge. Once these multiple perspectives are pulled together, it is important to step back from the fine-grained analyses and look at the composite picture from a distance.

At this stage, a summarizing and ranking of observed strengths and weaknesses from multiple data sources is beneficial. Based on all the data that have been studied and the patterns that have been observed, a data leadership team can synthesize the overarching problems that have been identified. In doing so, the data leadership team moves from data analysis to interpretation. As data are interpreted and understood within the context of the broader school program, they are able to inform questions about the instructional program to produce the desired results, whether they focus on increasing student performance in tenth-grade math or enhanced parental involvement in elementary school.

Crafting a Data-Based Plan to Enhance Practice

The time-intensive undertaking of collecting and analyzing multiple types of data in a purposeful manner, and the hard work of synthesizing and interpreting data, are wasted tasks if the data are not used to form a plan that will link these insights to appropriate programmatic and pedagogical changes. In some schools and districts, the problem with data-driven decision making is a lack of usable data. In other schools and districts, the problem is one of *having* too much data and not *using* it appropriately. This section provides instructional leaders with suggestions for using data to craft a plan for improvement by generating hypotheses, developing goals, designing strategies, defining evaluation criteria, and communicating with stakeholders.

Generate Hypotheses

One way to move closer to identifying root causes of student, classroom, or school performance problems is to generate hypotheses. A hypothesis is a possible explanation for observed patterns in data. Crafting a hypothesis enables school leaders and teachers to take specific actions aimed at enhancing, or somehow altering, patterns in data. In this way, generating hypotheses is a first step in determining the reasons for observed data patterns. To guide the generation of hypotheses, a data leadership team will create and ponder alternative explanations for why students are performing the way they are and consider what school practices and approaches are contributing to current levels of performance.

For example, considering that the previously mentioned Sunnybrook Elementary School has experienced consistent declines in student reading comprehension levels in Grades 4, 5, and 6, the data leadership team proposed the following hypotheses.

- Hypothesis 1: The reading texts and workbooks are out of date and do not follow a logical, grade-by-grade sequence.

- Hypothesis 2: There are more ESL students in Sunnybrook classes each year, and their low level of English understanding dilutes scores.
- Hypothesis 3: Upper-elementary teachers have not had sufficient training to teach the revised reading comprehension standards.

Having generated several hypotheses, the next step is to collect evidence to either support or reject these possible explanations. Certainly, the kinds of data that are generated, analyzed, and interpreted prior to generating hypotheses will influence both hypothesis formation and subsequent evidence collection. For example, to uncover evidence pertinent to the hypotheses, one would conduct classroom observations, disaggregate achievement data by subgroups of students, and assess lesson plans and homework assignments. For illustrative purposes, data collection efforts linked to each hypothesis could produce such evidence as that highlighted here.

- Data-based evidence regarding Hypothesis 1: Current reading text and workbooks used in Grades 4, 5, and 6 were adopted between the years 1996 and 2000 from three different publishers.
- Data-based evidence regarding Hypothesis 2: Enrollment levels for ESL students at Sunnybrook do show slight increases in Grade 6 but have been stable in Grades 4 and 5.
- Data-based evidence regarding Hypothesis 3: All of the teachers in Grades 4, 5, and 6 do have the appropriate reading credential. However, neither the school nor the district has provided professional-development activities for elementary teachers in reading comprehension during the past seven years.

Assessment of the illustrative evidence for each hypothesis would likely lead to the following conclusions. Hypothesis 1 would be accepted as a possibility, as the texts are both out of date and, since they are from three different publishers, potentially out of sequence. Hypothesis 2 would be rejected due to the fact that ESL levels have been stable for both fourth and fifth grade and only slightly increased in sixth grade. Hypothesis 3 would be accepted as a possibility, since no new professional development has occurred since the reading comprehension standards were revised.

Develop Goals

Obviously, the solution to be pursued is a function of the accuracy of any particular hypothesis. After data patterns have been interpreted and plausible hypotheses have been generated and tested, it is time to develop goals for improvement. When confronted with multiple problems and hypotheses, it is important to focus on developing goals for the most important or urgent issues first. Bear in mind that it is realistic for an education organization to focus on only three to five important goals at any one time. As such, the issue of prioritization cannot be overstated. The process of developing goals is about articulating desired outcomes, be they short term or long range. When developing goals, one must consider the capacities of both faculty and students and be cognizant of barriers that must be overcome. Human beings, by nature, can be quite resistant to change. Therefore, an educational leader must be able accurately to assess the institutional climate when considering a major change effort. A strategic education leader is able to assess the level of commitment to a goal and consider the resources necessary to reach the goal. Once a goal is set, many resources are deployed to attain the intended outcome. As such, crafting meaningful goals is an important endeavor. The following acronym, SMART, can assist in developing well-written goals.

- **S**pecific—Goals should be focused and clearly stated. A specific goal has a greater chance of being accomplished than a vague, general goal.
- **M**easurable—Goals should specify a desired outcome in tangible, quantifiable terms.
- **A**chievable—Goals should be able to be attained. The achievement of goals may require stretching, but leaders should avoid setting goals that are simply unrealistic.
- **R**esearch based—Goals should be directly linked to patterns observed in the data.
- **T**ime sensitive—Goals should reflect sensitivity to the urgency of the problem and the current status of the organizational culture.

To provide examples of school improvement goals, return to the two plausible hypotheses for the recent decline in Sunnybrook Elementary School's reading comprehension scores. The following is a potential goal statement targeting Hypothesis 1:

> To adopt an aligned set of reading text and workbooks for Grades 4, 5, and 6 by the fall of 2008 school year so that by the spring of 2010, 80 percent of fourth-, fifth-, and sixth-grade students score at proficient or advanced levels in reading comprehension.

Similarly, the following is a goal statement targeting Hypothesis 3:

To provide all Sunnybrook reading teachers with four days of inservice professional development regarding the revised reading comprehension standards during the 2008–2009 school year so that by the spring of 2010, 90 percent of fourth, fifth, and sixth graders surpass the median scale scores on the reading comprehension component of the state's annual criterion-reference assessment.

Design Strategies

Once well-specified goals have been formulated, it is necessary to determine what operational actions need to occur in order for the goal to be met. Goals, by themselves, are useless. Action-oriented strategies are necessary to move an organization toward intended outcomes. To determine the appropriate strategies for meeting a particular goal, a data leadership team might begin by brainstorming. The process of brainstorming provides a multitude of potential actions that might move the organization toward attaining a particular goal. In the brainstorming process, it is important to keep the hypotheses in mind, as specific strategies might flow naturally from these plausible explanations of organizational conditions. An additional source of potential action steps exists in the form of best-practice insights from other schools that have grappled with similar challenges. As another means of mitigating the tendency to focus on intuitive strategies, education leaders are encouraged to draw upon research-based and time-tested approaches.

When defining specific strategies, it is important to remember that these proposed actions are the vehicle by which an organization will move from where it currently stands to where it hopes to go. As such, it is important to consider certain guidelines when developing strategies. A successful strategy should have the following characteristics:

- Clear and understandable to all constituents
- Based on best-practice insights and mindful of the existing organizational culture
- Observable and measurable
- Target one specific, attainable action that will lead to accomplishing the goal
- Broad endorsement by data leadership team members
- Implemented and continually evaluated

Strategies represent commitments to carrying out action. As such, it is important for school leaders to discuss the level of dedication and hard work that strategies will require. Additionally, it is helpful to establish timelines for strategies to be carried out and to assign duties to individuals who are responsible for specific strategy components. To the benefit of everyone involved, these arrangements must be noted on a documented version of the plan. It must be stressed that the absence of a written plan for attaining goals through the implementation and evaluation of strategies will significantly hinder improvement efforts.

To provide examples of defined strategies, return again to Sunnybrook Elementary School. The following is one of many possible strategies related to the goal statement for Hypothesis 1:

A reading comprehension committee, chaired by Ms. Jones, and including representatives from Grades 4, 5, and 6, is charged with making textbook and materials adoption recommendations to the curriculum subcommittee of the school board by the end of next semester.

Similarly, the following is one possible strategy related to the goal statement for Hypothesis 3:

The district reading specialist will organize and conduct a professional-development workshop for all reading teachers at Sunnybrook Elementary School during the November inservice day that will address the knowledge, skills, and competencies required of teachers by the new reading comprehension standards.

Define Evaluation Criteria

While strategies provide a vehicle for attaining the intended outcomes articulated in school goals, it is important to assess the degree to which goals are in fact being met. As such, it is crucial to establish measures that will be used to evaluate the success of individual strategies. When determining these criteria it is helpful to consider how the success of each strategy can be measured and what evidence will confirm the success of these actions. As an intermediate step, it is also significant to assess the degree to which individual strategies have been implemented. Without a clear understanding of the degree of implementation, one can never be certain if observed changes can be attributed to the reform strategy. What often fails are not necessarily the reform strategies themselves but rather the degree to which they were implemented.

To determine the impact that implemented strategies have had upon the educational organization, it is necessary to consider multiple data sources, as outlined earlier in the chapter. For example, to assess the degree to which the strategy pertinent to Hypothesis 3 was met, one would evaluate at least the following sources of data: standardized test scores, criterion-referenced assessments, faculty observation forms, evaluation data about staff development activities, select portfolio items, and grade book entries. This example highlights the importance of establishing specific measures for each strategy. To the degree that goals and strategies are measurable, evaluation data will provide targeted insights regarding the degree to which the strategy was implemented and successful in creating the desired results.

Communicate With Stakeholders

Communicating to a broad base of stakeholders about the purposes, results, and ongoing plans for data analysis is important for schools that want to sustain improvement efforts. Similar to communication about student progress and key school activities, communication about data-based findings should occur throughout the school year. It is not sufficient for stakeholders to receive sporadic or annual updates if a strategic education leader hopes to encourage greater understanding of and support for data-driven decision making.

Further, data leadership teams should discuss which particular data-based updates could be disseminated without a conversation and which warrant an opportunity for stakeholders to engage in a conversation about the results of data analysis. Such forums would provide an opportunity to discuss results, patterns, interpretations and responses to trends illuminated by data. While affirming the school's commitment to the challenging process of using data-driven decision making to enhance student performance, these efforts also endorse the commitment of school leaders to engage the community in meaningful dialogue.

Analyzing Data Integral to School Effectiveness

Having described a systematic process for how education leaders can use data within the context of ongoing school improvement efforts, it is now important to provide practical examples of data analysis in domains important for school effectiveness. While there are many pathways to creating successful schools, the pathways share the common theme of a schoolwide focus on teaching and learning. Toward that end, strategic education leaders need to attend to the school's mission and goals, rigorous content standards, curricular and instructional alignment, teacher professional development, culture and climate for student learning, professional community of teachers, and community relations. In this section, various sources of data that can be used to gauge how well a school is implementing select pathways to school improvement will be discussed. Examples of student achievement data analysis will also be provided. Together, these insights provide school leaders with important knowledge regarding the continuous monitoring and evaluation of progress toward achieving school goals.

Mission and Goals

For quite some time, educators have pointed to the importance of school mission and goals in guiding the activities of schools. Since the school mission and goals play a pivotal role for the organization, it is important that school leaders understand the degree to which these aspirations are being attained. A first step in this process is to consider the measurable components of the school mission. Next, one must determine what types and sources of data are currently available and what data must be collected in order to evaluate each component of the mission statement.

For illustrative purposes, consider the mission of Sunnybrook Elementary School:

> The mission of Sunnybrook Elementary School is to provide a safe and nurturing environment with opportunities for all students to learn. All students will reach performance goals at or above grade level in reading, writing, mathematics, social studies, and science while demonstrating responsibility and self-control.

When considering the measurable components of the Sunnybrook mission statement, the following three measurable goals come to the surface: (1) provide a safe and nurturing environment, (2) all students will reach performance goals, and (3) all students will demonstrate responsibility and self-control. To guide the analysis of what data are currently available for each component, and what data are needed, the matrix provided in Figure 6.5 is helpful. As an example, two components of the mission are included in the matrix.

Here, one can see that data regarding whether the school provides a safe and nurturing environment are currently available. However, before one can accurately assess the degree to which the school currently provides a safe and nurturing environment, more data analysis is needed. The matrix encourages the

Figure 6.5	Mission Statement Planning Matrix				
Mission statement components	*What we want to learn from the data*	*Data we already have*	*Data we need to collect*	*Sources of new data*	*Who should be involved in data collection*
Safe and nurturing environment	Do students, parents, teachers, and staff feel school is safe and nurturing?	Number of discipline infractions, office referrals, suspensions; results from annual district parent survey	Input from students, parents, teachers, staff, and administrators	Student focus groups; parent town hall meetings; faculty, staff, and administration discussions	Student Council, homeroom teachers, PTA, administration
Perform at or above grade level in reading	Are all students meeting performance goals in reading?	End-of-year standardized tests; course grades, formative assessments	Level of reading in content areas, usage of library, time spent reading at home	Assignments in science and social studies, books checked out from library, accelerated reading, parent survey	Librarian, curriculum specialists, teams of teachers, PTA, administration

specification of what additional sources of data are necessary and encourages discussion regarding who should be involved in data collection.

For example, where components of the mission are not being assessed by existing data, the leadership team may decide to construct data-gathering instruments to pinpoint these domains. If insufficient data exist regarding the degree to which students feel safe at school, an instrument can be crafted to directly address this issue. Typically, such surveys are constructed by asking specific questions and then providing a scale either to assess to what degree goals are being achieved or practiced or to assess the teacher's, student's, parent's, and principal's level of satisfaction with goal achievement. For example, level of goal achievement can be measured using a four-point scale such as "fully," "mostly," "somewhat," and "not at all." One also can frame the questions around people's perceptions about how well the organization is doing to achieve goals using scales such as "excellent," "good," "fair," and "poor." Armed with these insights, a data leadership team could follow the just-outlined steps to establish goals and strategies for collecting and analyzing the desired data in order to conduct a data-based assessment of the degree to which the school is attaining the components of the mission statement.

Professional Development

Given the rapid pace of change in contemporary educational policy and practice, the elevated expectations now held for schools, and the heightened focus on student achievement, a renewed emphasis has been placed on professional development. Improving the operational and instructional capacity of teachers and other professionals should be a priority of schools and districts. By focusing on what works, school leaders can encourage professional-development opportunities that empower teachers to make a positive impact on student performance. As described in Chapter 2, much research has been conducted on what makes professional development effective. As a means of assessing the quality of professional-development experiences that teachers are participating in, and as a means of linking participation in professional development to the attainment of faculty goals, school leaders can use a data-gathering form like the one provided in Figure 6.6. This form provides an example of how school leaders can assess the degree to which faculty participation in professional development is linked to the correlates of effective professional development.

This form uses eight core components of effective professional development. An educational leader might create a template, similar to this proposed model, for each individual teacher, grade level team, or departmental unit. The form includes a place for the teacher and leaders to discuss professional goals for the year. These goals will likely be linked to the mission and goals of the school, to state and school standards for a particular content area, and perhaps teacher evaluation data from a previous school year.

The column on the focus of the professional development will allow school leaders and teachers to track what particular domains of classroom experience are being targeted. This focus might include enhanced content knowledge (to help bolster low performance in a particular content domain from prior achievement test results) or pedagogical techniques that may have a more broad application. The final column of the sheet allows data to be collected regarding the degree to which individual teachers, teams, and an entire faculty are taking part in professional-development experiences that are aligned with correlates of effective professional development.

Figure 6.6	Professional-Development Record		
Teacher / Team Member	Annual Professional-Development Goals	Focus of PD Activities	Degree of Alignment With Correlates of Effective Professional Development
Jones	1. 2. 3.		___ Linked to student learning outcomes ___ Job embedded ___ Ongoing and sustained, with follow-up ___ Incorporates authentic, active learning ___ Includes subject matter content ___ Encourages reflection ___ Incorporates collaboration w/colleagues ___ Measures impact on student achievement
Rodriquez	1. 2. 3.		___ Linked to student learning outcomes ___ Job embedded ___ Ongoing and sustained, with follow-up ___ Incorporates authentic, active learning ___ Includes subject matter content ___ Encourages reflection ___ Incorporates collaboration w/colleagues ___ Measures impact on student achievement

Culture and Climate of Student Learning

Similar to the other domains of effective schools, it is important to set measurable goals regarding school climate. Yet before goals can be established and data collected, efforts to construct a shared vision of a safe and orderly school climate and culture must be established. In the absence of such consensus-building conversations, the collection and reporting of data will lose a measure of impact. The most efficient manner to collect information about the school's climate and culture is through surveys, which will capture respondents' perceptions, attitudes, and feelings. Survey data should include parents, students, teachers, and interested community members. It is important for a large percentage of each group to have the opportunity to respond. This will mitigate the skewed picture that might prevail if only the most vocally dissatisfied or involved and supportive members responded.

There are many factors that can impact respondents' opinions and feelings. These include the stress of starting a new school year, end-of-year testing anxiety, and so on. Therefore, when collecting data regarding school culture over the course of several years, it is important to collect responses at the same time each year. Consider again the mission of Sunnybrook Elementary School, which aspired to provide students with a safe and orderly environment. Figure 6.7 provides hypothetical data from the annual survey of student perceptions of the school climate.

Figure 6.7   Sunnybrook Elementary School Climate Survey (Students)

GOAL: 95 percent of respondents on an annual student survey will indicate the following (actual percentage reported at right):

1) They feel safe at school   58.0%

2) They believe students are well behaved   94.6%

3) They know the rules for appropriate behavior and consequences for any infraction 92.2%

Analyses of the results of the school climate survey illuminate an interesting condition. While nearly 95 percent of students believe students are well behaved, only 58 percent feel safe at school. These data indicate that students feel unsafe at school for reasons other than student behavior. The faculty and leadership at Sunnybrook are now equipped to deal more substantively with possible root causes of students' feelings regarding safety. In this case, the data do not necessarily provide an answer but do suggest a reframing of the question.

At Sunnybrook, data are routinely collected at school regarding discipline, such as in-school and out-of-school suspensions, office referrals, and other pertinent infractions. These data are tallied and graphed as important indicators of the school climate. Figure 6.8 provides data regarding the number of

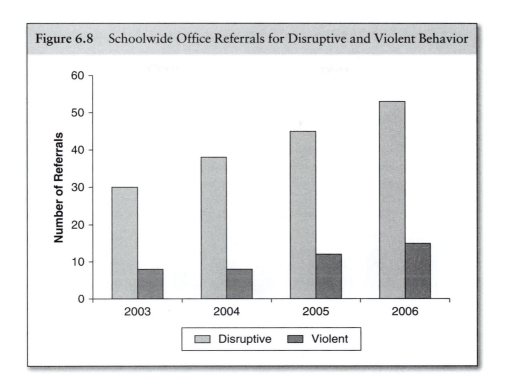

Figure 6.8 Schoolwide Office Referrals for Disruptive and Violent Behavior

office referrals for disruptive and violent behavior across four years. This figure suggests that the climate is becoming more disruptive at Sunnybrook, as there are increasing numbers of office referrals each year.

This graph in Figure 6.8 raises a number of questions. For example, is the increase in the number of office referrals a result of more students enrolled, more students being sent to the office, or the result of a small number of students being sent to the office numerous times? Are some teachers more likely to send students to the office than other teachers? Ultimately, a discussion must occur throughout the school community about the discipline policy and behavioral expectations.

The next step is to dig deeper into the data. This is accomplished by disaggregating data at the individual teacher and student levels. In this way, one is able to gain a deeper understanding of this issue, which is of central importance to a positive school culture and climate. The disaggregated data is provided in Figure 6.9.

This disaggregated data begs the question: Why is there such a difference among the teachers in the number and types of office referrals? Does the faculty have a uniform behavior system? Is it desirable to have misbehavior handled as much as possible in the classroom by the classroom teacher? Using

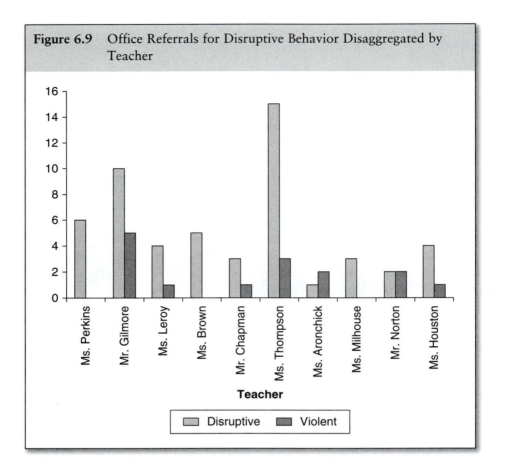

Figure 6.9 Office Referrals for Disruptive Behavior Disaggregated by Teacher

these data as a springboard for discussion, an educational leader might inquire about the various teacher intentions in sending students to the office. These types of questions can form a basis for careful deliberations among the school community, providing opportunities to clarify policies, set goals, and monitor progress on one of the key pathways to school improvement and student achievement; namely, a safe and orderly learning environment.

CONCLUSION

Well-informed decision making is a central component of constructing a successful school culture and effective leadership profile. It is the process by which educational problems are articulated, analyzed, and addressed. However, as described in this chapter, the good intentions of educational leaders are not sufficient to guarantee good decisions. Rather, successful solutions require data analysis and efficient action based on reflective collaboration and sound strategies. Decisions made by school leaders directly influence the culture of the school and impact the instructional experience of students. As such, it is imperative that school leaders engage in reflective and systematic data analysis so that difficult decisions are made wisely while accounting for nuances within the school community. To do so requires education leaders to draw a school community together around a prioritized list of goals amidst the complexities of school life. The information in this chapter provides helpful action strategies for school administrators who are often confounded by the sheer pace and volume of their work. There are many approaches to problem solving within education organizations, yet all of them are enhanced by the thoughtful use of data. While data-based decision making does not guarantee effective outcomes to educational challenges, it certainly improves the likelihood of sustaining a high-performing school culture.

QUESTIONS FOR DISCUSSION

1. Four important reasons for engaging in data-based decision making were described in this chapter. Of these four, which do you feel is the primary reason stakeholders in your school community would cite? What might parents say? Students? Faculty? Administrators?

2. Briefly critique the degree to which your current education organization is successfully pursuing the three components of the school improvement cycle provided in Figure 6.1.

3. In Figure 6.2, comparisons are made between school processes guided by intuition versus data. Drawing on your experience, add two rows to this list, specifying how data *have* or *could* elevate the way decisions are being made.

4. Comment on the current degree of usability of your school level data, providing insight for how your data stacks up along each of the five dimensions of availability and accessibility, timeliness and completeness, accuracy, consistency, and alignment.

5. Figure 6.3 provides examples of the various types of data school leaders can use to guide decisions. Choose one source of data from each quadrant and describe how those data are used to evaluate the quality of the instructional programs or organizational climate at your school.

6. Consider one of your personal or one of your school's current goals. Describe the degree to which the goal is SMART—specific, measurable, achievable, research based, and time sensitive.

7. List the ways that your school currently communicates with the community regarding the purposes and results of data collection and data-based decision making. Propose two additional methods.

8. Using Figure 6.5 as a guide, evaluate your current educational organization's mission statement. What most notable or action-worthy insights emerged from this exercise?

9. Using Figure 6.6 as a launching point, design a form that would help an education leader at your school analyze the grade level and subject area investments in professional development.

10. If you were the principal of Sunnybrook Elementary School and were presented with the data in Figure 6.9, what would your next steps entail? Would you conduct added analyses and create different displays using this data? What additional data would you collect regarding behavioral issues at your school?

11. To what degree are multiple formats of data available to teachers at your school? What concrete steps can be taken to facilitate this practice?

12. Using school data to inform decisions and solve problems cuts across several ELCC standards. Choose one component of one ELCC standard and describe how the use of data can help you be a more effective leader.

REFERENCES

Hawley, W., & Sikes, G. (2007). *The keys to effective schools: Educational reform as continuous improvement*. Thousand Oaks, CA: Corwin.

Case Study 7: "My Way" Ray and the "New" Accountability

Raymond "Ray" Brown was a remarkable person. His very presence exuded authority. However, in his critic's eyes, and he had a number of such eyes focused on him, he was a know-it-all who thought he was correct all the time. And, as his critics were quick to say, it followed that all others were wrong all the time. Ray's cocksure attitude was annoying to some. However, others saw in him a great deal of self-assurance and natural authority and took it to be the sign of a strong leader.

Whatever his critics thought, Ray had admirers too. More to the point, Ray had just been hired by the Metropolitan Independent School District (MISD) school board, with a three-year contract, as the new superintendent. The board, on a four-to-one vote, had chosen him. For a big-city school board, renowned for its contentious meetings and widespread public disagreements, this positive vote was a big signal to all who cared that change might be coming.

Ray made his first large-scale public appearance, addressing all teachers and administrators, at the beginning-of-the-school-year assembly. The entire undertaking appeared to be planned in great detail, down to new and colorful inspirational banners on the walls, tight timing, scripted movements of those on stage, mood lighting in the auditorium, and an opening processional with marshal music. The district's longtime employees were a bit stunned by it all. This was a touch of drama and a sense of hierarchy they had never before experienced.

The meeting opened with a 10-minute forcefully delivered greeting from the school board president. She explained that in her recent reelection campaign she had pledged to school district voters, and they had overwhelmingly agreed, that what was needed was a new era in American education, an era where outcomes, not inputs, counted. "Trying was fine. However, winning was what counted," she reminded the audience. Her job, as the school board president, was to ensure that the district had purpose and that purpose translated into "products," higher levels of student achievement. No longer was trying hard sufficient.

Note: This case study, as with others associated with other chapters, is about an actual school, actual people, and actual conditions. Nothing is fabricated. All cases are about situations school leaders routinely encounter. However, in each instance, names of people, schools, and locations have been altered to ensure confidentiality.

High achievement was the new school district goal. Ray Brown was the leader selected by the school board to reach this goal. When she concluded what the audience could see was a set of prepared remarks, there was polite but hesitant applause.

Ray followed immediately and began his remarks with a self-deprecating joke. He spent time describing his military and private-business background and mentioning his prior professional successes. He continued with an explanation of his leadership philosophy. To some in the audience, it sounded as if Genghis Khan had been reincarnated, this time not to consolidate an empire of far-flung Mongol tribes but to conquer them as independent and creative teachers and principals. Others found his lustrous background and forceful delivery style inspiring and refreshing. They said, at least to themselves, "at last we have a leader who is ready to lead."

Ray explained that he believed the school board had hired him to impose accountability. He emphasized his point by saying *accountability* loudly and then spelling it, A-C-C-O-U-N-T-ABILITY, emphasizing the "account" at the beginning of the word.

Ray explained that accountability depended crucially on specifying expectations. Therefore, all job descriptions in the district would be reexamined and, where necessary, rewritten. He wanted to ensure that everyone knew precisely what they were supposed to do and that they further realized that they would hereafter be judged on the extent to which they performed their duties and met their centrally specified performance goals. He would personally oversee redrafting of all professional job descriptions.

Ray proceeded to proclaim that his kind of accountability had three simple and easy-to-remember parts, all beginning with *P*: "planning," "procedures," and "performance." The audience then understood the three large banners hanging from the ceiling of the stage, each with one of the three words Ray was now emphasizing.

He went on to say that

planning is what we are doing right now. *Planning* is the specification of expectations. *Procedure* is however you as professionals decide to achieve these expectations. *Performance* is my measurement of your progress.

Ray completed his statement regarding accountability by saying, "I will set expectations. You will determine your professional path for achieving those expectations. You are empowered, but I will measure your success."

He concluded with what was intended as a motivational message about his faith in them, a faith illustrated by his granting them discretion to design their particular school's and classroom's path to progress. He would not dictate methods. Mission and measurement was his assignment. Means to ends were theirs. Methods were their challenge.

Ray then left the stage with what some thought was an exaggerated and bullying swagger and what others perceived as the confidence of a bold warrior.

When the meeting was over and audience participants assembled outside in the late afternoon sunlight, there was an unusual quiet for a large group of educators, back from the summer and about to start a new school year. This assembly was different from what had ever before occurred and vastly different from what they had expected. Few showed any signs of new-semester excitement or camaraderie. There was no backslapping or high fives, no discussion of the beginning of preseason football or the end of the baseball season. There was no talk of "what did you do on your vacation?"

Rather, reaction to what they had just experienced was subdued and hushed. They were a bit awestruck and uncertain about what they had just heard. Were their district, their school, and their way of professional life about to change? Were they about to be told what to do? Were they about to be evaluated? Would there be consequences? Would the evaluations be fair? What was to be evaluated anyway? Why had Ray Brown made such a big deal about their having discretion regarding their own procedures? Could they not always do that in the past? Was he making a big bluff? Would this be a set of fads that would blow over quickly as had all others in the past? Would the school board actually stand behind him as he made drastic changes?

In the days immediately following the fall assembly, Ray issued memos to his staff and press releases to the media that further specified his plans for change. He initially targeted the central office. He referred to the "downtown" staff as comprised of "bloated has-beens." He stated that, "if needed, we will carry out excess bureaucrats in body bags." There was no doubt that tough-talking Ray had captured everyone's attention.

Newspapers and television programs were full of Ray. Op-ed pieces supported his tough talk. Talk show hosts repeatedly invited him to come on their daytime programs. (When he appeared, their ratings soared.) The chamber of commerce featured him at their annual dinner, and the business audience applauded as he made his "get tough" accountability speech. Like him or not, Ray was good theater.

For his part, Ray was perfectly consistent. Education mattered most for children. His assignment was to ensure that they were well educated. He said that the goal of elevated student achievement was but an extension of the 1960s civil rights movement and that high academic performance was the new measure of a fair and just society.

The school year began, and first principals and then teachers received their new job descriptions. While those in different roles did not receive the same job descriptions, they had many elements in common. Each now perceived a clear message: reading and mathematics scores were to be the coin of the accountability realm.

As the semester unfolded, the community seemed to divide into supporters and opponents of Ray Brown. Opponents, mostly teacher union officials, referred to him as "My Way Ray." Supporters, which continued to include the school board majority that hired him, the media, and the business community, cheered him on. His fans labeled him "Right Way Ray." Parents had mixed feelings, not sure yet about the consequences of the bold new superintendent in town.

FOR DISCUSSION

1. Have you ever known anyone like Ray Brown? What do you think of him? Would you be drawn to him or feel negatively toward him?

2. What do you think of Ray's top-down approach to constructing an accountability culture in the MISD? Would you have advised him to take a longer-term view, work from the bottom up, and perhaps be less flamboyant?

3. What do you think of Ray's three accountability "P's" of planning, process, and performance? Does he have it right, or is something missing?

4. Is formal and highly structured accountability actually needed in schools? Will not principals and teachers, simply out of professionalism, perform at their best regardless of whatever systematic accountability scheme is put into place?

5. Will the teacher union's opposing view, claiming that children are already tested too often, eventually prevail? Will teachers seek jobs in other districts?

6. Can there possibly be unanticipated consequences from measuring only reading and mathematics? Might the MISD real curriculum, what children are actually taught, become warped and constricted as a consequence?

7. Will Ray Brown last? For how long will he enjoy school board and community support?

8. Would you work for Ray Brown?

CHAPTER 7

Measurement, Performance Accountability, and Reward Structures

In this chapter a reader will learn about the following:

- The meaning and present-day practical translation of "accountability" as used by state, federal, and many local education agencies
- Various issues and operations involved in measuring students' academic performance
- State-of-the-art efforts to determine the value a teacher, or an entire school, is adding to what students' learn
- A spectrum of incentives that can be structured to reward teachers and shape personnel behavior
- An array of actions and sanctions appropriate when encountering poor performance
- Illustrative means for weaving measurements, incentives, and accountability into a coherent personnel performance management strategy at the school level

ELCC STANDARDS

ELCC standards addressed in this chapter include the following:

- 1.3—Implement a vision
- 2.1—Promote a positive school culture
- 2.2—Provide an effective instructional program
- 3.1—Manage the organization
- 3.2—Manage operations
- 6.1—Understand the larger context

INTRODUCTION

As a noun, *accountability* is defined in dictionaries as "responsible," "answerable," and "explainable." In modern U.S. education parlance, *accountability* has evolved to refer to sets of strategies intended to motivate, and possibly intimidate or coerce, school personnel into elevating student achievement. Accountability can take various practical forms, stretching from timid tactics such as simply publicly releasing academic achievement scores by school or by classroom all the way to more intense threats of school closure and educator job loss. The purpose of this chapter is to explain modern school accountability ideas and to illustrate the manner in which a successful school leader can use accountability to assist in constructing a productive and cohesive school culture.

CONTEMPORARY EVOLUTION OF ACCOUNTABILITY AS A SCHOOL MANAGEMENT IDEA

Accountability, at least financial accountability, has long been a feature of American schooling. School districts have come under state fiscal reporting and auditing codes for almost a century. Moreover, starting in the mid-1960s, schools began to be held accountable for complying with burgeoning federal and state rules. This was a kind of regulatory accountability with emphasis upon procedural compliance. Regulatory accountability paid little attention to student performance outcomes.

Also flowering in the 1960s, and stemming from civil rights abuse cases, schools became subject to far higher levels of judicial scrutiny, a kind of legalistic accountability. In these instances, attention was paid by court monitors and plaintiff advocates to assurances that school districts would live up to court-imposed conditions, usually regarding finances.

However, for most of the nation's schooling history, the quality of a school or judgments regarding its effectiveness has been centered upon its level of resource inputs. The more it spent annually per pupil, or the higher the socioeconomic status of its enrolled students, the more likely it was thought to be a good school. During this period, testing data were neither sufficiently widespread nor uniform to facilitate accurate interdistrict and interstate school quality comparisons. Hence, dollars, or dollars per pupil, one dimension that could be measured with a degree of specificity, was the coin of the accountability realm.

A Nation at Risk

Modern school performance accountability began to emerge forcefully in 1983 with the Reagan administration publication of the report *A Nation at Risk* (National Commission on Excellence in Education, 1983).

This slender but bombastic document, characterized by alarmist rhetoric, captured nationwide newspaper and television headlines and acted as an intense siren call for American school change. Its thesis was that low school performance and tepid academic expectations were disadvantaging the nation in the emerging era of economic global competition, defense, and international regard. The report suggested that America's schools had somehow altered their historic course from some unspecified halcyon past where schools were thought to be far more rigorous.

In fact, no evidence was provided in *A Nation at Risk* to prove schools were any worse or even different from those in earlier times. Evidence aside, the policy system was propelled into high gear, and literally dozens of blue-ribbon panels, task forces, and legislative committees came into being, each with a slate of reforms intended to correct the deficiencies. It was a wonderful period of advocates' long-held solutions at last finding problems to which they might be attached.

National Education Goals

In the intervening three decades since issuance of *A Nation at Risk*, much has changed in America's schools. President George H. W. Bush initiated the standards movement via a rare convening of the nation's governors at a summit held in Charlottesville, Virginia, in 1989. This summit resulted in the elevation of a set of national education goals. These goals were highly aspirational; for example, the United States would be first in the world in math and science by the year 2000. However, even if unrealistic, the goals served to galvanize additional school reforms.

No Child Left Behind (NCLB)

Almost immediately upon his 2001 inauguration, President George W. Bush submitted an enormously significant bill to Congress, the No Child Left Behind Act. The bill attracted bipartisan support and was quickly enacted. It went into effect in 2002.

The significance of NCLB is that, for the first time on a national scale, schools' effectiveness was to be determined by student performance, not by regulatory or judicial compliance or resource inputs. Moreover, no longer would schoolwide average student scores suffice as a metric.[1] Under NCLB, schools were assigned annual performance targets, and students were to be classified by race and ethnicity so as to render possible determinations about subgroups' academic performance.

NCLB, in its initially enacted form, was imperfect. The concept of Adequate Yearly Progress (AYP) was awkward to measure. The bill had other provisions, such as proclaiming that every child should have a "highly qualified teacher," that were elusive in their enforcement. The act also contained provisions by which persistently low-performing students were to be provided with "special educational services" (e.g., afterschool tutoring), and if a school failed over several years to meet performance goals, parents of its students were given the option of switching schools, even attending private schools at government expense.

However, the significance of NCLB was more in its overarching concept and widespread consequences than in any of its myriad operational details. Now it was students' academic performance that mattered, and it mattered everywhere in the nation. Virtually every state was quick to adhere to the new federal guidelines (and collect the attached federal funding). Accountability was now formidable, writ large, and packed with significant consequences for lax educator performance.

LINK TO CASE STUDY 7

In Case Study 7 you are introduced to "My Way Ray," the new superintendent of the Metropolitan Independent School District. The three pillars of the superintendent's vision for the district are planning (specifying expectations), procedures (determining the methods to achieve the expectations), and performance (how to measure progress). How reliably do you think your contributions to student and school performance can be measured? In your context, what are the key benefits and challenges to heightened accountability demands for teaches and school principals?

PERFORMANCE MEASUREMENTS: ISSUES REGARDING EXTERNAL INFLUENCES

At the heart of accountability resides the issue of how performance outcomes can be reliably measured—both for students and schools. These same measurement challenges squarely confront states, districts, and individual schools. *If measurement of student performance is inaccurate, then accountability is thwarted.*

In an ideal world, performance measures for a classroom teacher, a group of classroom teachers, or an entire school or school district would accurately account for and reliably reflect instructional efforts of all professionals involved. However, there presently is no ideal world, and there is much technical, social, and personal complexity that confounds efforts accurately to determine the effectiveness of individual and groups of teachers and other groups of educators.

Assessing what a student knows and can do is a daunting endeavor, as humans vary greatly for a great many reasons. There are many explanations for test scores, including a host of test taker individual differences and the validity of the assessment instrument (test) itself. The key idea is statistically to isolate school and teacher contributions to student achievement from all other sources of possible influence on achievement—in particular, student, family, and neighborhood characteristics.

This isolation of schooling effects on academic performance from other-than-school influences is crucial. Failure to account for differences across schools in student, family, and community characteristics can result in highly contaminated indicators of school performance, over- and underestimates of school effects.

What is crucial for principals and other school leaders to realize is that performance measurements are imperfect and, thus, should be taken in conjunction with other information, for example, other measures of student performance and performance measures stretching over time.

However, even if the world of tests and testing is imperfect, a degree of accurate performance measurement is possible and can be used reliably to determine the effectiveness of an educator or a collection of educators.

APPROACHES TO MEASURING STUDENT AND EDUCATOR EFFECTIVENESS

Across the nation, there are many nuanced approaches taken to measuring student and educator effectiveness. Three primary categories of measurement approaches will be discussed in this chapter. These include "attainment," "gain," and "value added." Each approach is described here, and a comparison of specific features of each approach is provided in Figure 7.1 on p. 214.

Attainment

To measure student and school performance, education agencies from the federal to local level have historically relied on attainment measures such as average achievement levels or proficiency rates. Attainment scores reflect student performance on a particular assessment at a single point in time. These measures are easy to compute and widely used by school systems to determine performance related to benchmarks such as required by the No Child Left Behind Act's provision of Adequate Yearly Progress (AYP).

Individual or Average Attainment Levels

Achievement tests can be used to specify attainment. Assume a student attained a score of 84 on her mathematics achievement test. This does not tell much about the student or her performance. Many questions could be asked, such as is 84 a good score or a low score? Does it mean she has learned a lot or a little? Is she more or less knowledgeable than other students in her class, at her grade level, in her school, or across the nation or the world? Did she learn more this year or in previous years?

Proficiency Rates

Often test scores are converted to some kind of proficiency scale. If our student's score is equated to a proficiency scale, it might be that, judging by her test score of 84, she is "below basic," "basic," "proficient," or "highly proficient." Essentially, experts pass judgment on the degree to which a particular test score or attainment level corresponds to logically defined levels of content mastery and proficiency as determined by testing and content experts.

However expressed (such as a raw score or proficiency rating), and regardless of comparisons to other students (such as "norm-referenced tests" to be described later), or an absolute achievement scale (such as in "criterion-referenced tests"), attainment provides information for only one point in time. It does not provide information regarding how much a student might have learned during the course of a particular class, semester, or school year.

A concern exists that attainment metrics are biased as measures of teacher or school productivity, even if they are derived from highly valid[2] assessments. From a statistical perspective, attainment indicators are biased because these measures reflect out-of-date productivity effects from prior grades and years (back to preschool and early grades) and the effects of education provided by other schools for mobile students. They also reflect prior achievement as well as family and student factors associated with achievement growth. This is particularly important in light of the fact that differences in student and family characteristics, and prior achievement levels, account for more of the variation in student achievement than school-related factors.[3] As such, virtually any measure that takes into account prior student achievement and demographic characteristics is likely to be strongly preferred to attainment.

From a philosophical or behavioral perspective, another problem with attainment measures is that they provide institutions with the incentive to "cream," that is, to raise measured performance by educating only those students who tend to have high test scores or by focusing instructional efforts on those students just below a cut point.[4] Creaming mechanisms include selective admissions; the creation of an environment (not necessarily intentionally) that is unsupportive to potential dropouts, academically disadvantaged students, and special education students; aggressive retention of students; or the migration of high-quality teachers and principals to schools with academically advantaged students.

Gain

Whereas attainment scores focus on student performance at one point in time, and are thus cross-sectional measures of performance, gain measures take a longitudinal approach. Gain in student test scores is the difference between average student performance on an achievement test in one year minus average performance on the test by the same students in the previous year. Calculating gain requires matching individual students from one year to the next so that improvement on the assessment is measured over the same group of students (a matched sample).

Gain is similar to value-added measurement in its emphasis on growth in student achievement from one year to the next for the same group of students. However, there are several important distinctions. Gain is different from a value-added indicator because it is much simpler and lacks statistical rigor due to reliance on controlling for previous student performance as determined not by statistical evidence but rather by using an *a priori* assumption that gain is a well-defined and appropriate measure of school performance. One important consideration is that gain can only be computed if post and prior achievement are measured on the same test scale.

In addition to looking at gain related to actual attainment scores, school systems also consider gains related to proficiency categories. A specific challenge associated with this indicator is that increases in student achievement only "count" if they are large enough to enable a student to cross a proficiency threshold. Here, the same "creaming" concern exists related to the potential negative consequences associated with focusing resources on students just below proficiency cut points.

As gain models take a longitudinal approach, they can produce results similar to value-added indicators of performance when the following conditions are present:

- Students are tested at the beginning or end of the school year so that growth in student achievement does not cut across two school years.
- Students do not change schools during the school year.
- No students are retained in grade or skip a grade from one school year to the next.
- The coefficient on prior achievement is close to one.[5]
- Differences in student characteristics across schools account for little of the variation in average achievement growth.

Practical experience suggests, however, that these conditions are often violated in school settings. If violations are substantively large, then the gain indicator may fail accurately to measure school performance and instead be confounded by factors that are not controlled for in relatively simplistic gain model approaches.

Value Added

There is a growing consensus that value-added models of student achievement provide better measures of school and classroom productivity than the more commonly used attainment measures such as percentage of students proficient or cohort-to-cohort gain scores. A value-added measure refers to an indicator that is derived from a statistical model designed to capture the contribution of a school, classroom/teacher, or other educational unit to growth in student achievement and "filter out" the nonschool factors that contribute to student achievement, including differences in prior student achievement and the types of students served by different schools.

A value-added model is a quasi-experimental statistical algorithm that yields estimates of schools' contribution (or other educational units) to growth in student achievement (or other student outcomes), controlling for other sources of student achievement change, including prior student achievement and student and family characteristics. The model produces estimates of school performance—value-added indicators—under the counterfactual assumption that all schools serve the same group of students. The objective is to facilitate valid and fair comparisons of student outcomes across schools given that the schools may serve very different student populations.

A primary benefit of value-added over gain models is the ability of the former statistically to isolate school and program contributions to growth in student achievement at a given point in time from other sources of student achievement change, including prior student achievement and student and family characteristics. This is important because the goal of accountability or a performance-based compensation system is to measure and reward contributions of a particular teacher or set of educators rather than the cumulative impact of all school and nonschool factors.

Value-added models are highly attractive from a technical perspective. As indicated in Figure 7.1, a value-added model, particularly one that is enhanced and customized to local conditions, is capable of absorbing numerous real-world problems that might otherwise threaten the validity of a simpler model

Figure 7.1   Comparison of Measurement Approaches

Model Feature	Value Added	Gain	Attainment
Measures average attainment gaps by student group	✓	✓	✓
Measures growth gaps by student group	✓	✓	
Decomposes districtwide differences in growth gaps by student group into distinct growth gap factors	✓		
Measures performance in terms of achievement growth	✓	✓	
Responsive to changes in achievement at all points along the scale	✓	✓	
Measures value-added growth gaps by student group	✓		
Allows for decay in achievement over time or resource allocation correlated with prior achievement	✓		
Robust to transformation of test score (linear approximation)	✓		
Controls for test measurement error, if needed	✓	N/A	N/A
Controls for differences across schools in school composition	✓		
Accommodates local conditions (e.g., dose, midyear testing)	✓		
Statistically rigorous	✓		
Easy to compute and explain		✓	✓

Source: Meyer, R. H., & Christian, M. S. (2008). *Value-added and other methods for measuring school performance: An analysis of performance measurement strategies in teacher incentive fund proposals.* Prepared for the conference Performance Incentives: Their Growing Impact on American K–12 Education, National Center on Performance Incentives, Vanderbilt University, February 28–29, 2008

or indicator. Value-added indicators are derived from a statistical model that includes, to the extent possible, all nonschool factors that contribute to growth in student achievement—in particular, prior student achievement and student, family, and neighborhood characteristics.

ALIGNING PERFORMANCE MEASUREMENT WITH PERSONNEL INCENTIVES

Previous Chapters 4 and 5 make mention of the dysfunctional character of most public school remuneration systems. This chapter section suggests alternatives, alternatives that involve incentives and that draw, in part, upon value-added measurement. Incentives can be both material and psychic. The focus here is on material incentives, particularly financial incentives.

Financial incentives, at least in the private sector, appear to have two kinds of consequences. They steer individuals into labor market positions where demand is high and supply is low. They also appear to motivate individuals to strive to meet organizational goals.

Figure 7.2 offers a comparison of conventional public school remuneration practices relative to alternatives that involve financial incentives.

Figure 7.2 Comparison of Across-the-Board Salary Raises and Performance Pay	
Across-the-Board Raises	*Performance Pay Raises*
Are *not* linked to the most important outcomes of schooling, such as increased levels of student performance	*Are* directly linked to the most important outcomes of schooling
Do *not* provide motivation or rewards for elevated levels of school or teacher effectiveness	*Do* provide motivation or rewards for elevated levels of school or teacher effectiveness
Do *not* encourage the continued professional development of teachers and principals	*Do* encourage the continued professional development of teachers and principals
Do *not* provide impetus for schools and districts to align their resources with their core goals	*Do* provide impetus for schools and districts to align their resources with their core goals
Endorse the status quo	*Challenge* the status quo
Do *not* help schools and districts attract and retain highly effective teachers and administrators	*Do* help schools and districts attract and retain highly effective teachers and administrators
Do *not* encourage schools to consider how effectively to assess student learning across multiple grades and subject areas	*Do* encourage schools to consider how to effectively assess student learning across multiple grades and subject areas

Source: Compiled by the authors

There are many ways in which financial incentives can be woven into a school district's and school's remuneration practices. Figure 7.3 illustrates several such means. Here one can see a collection of collective and individual rewards, and, of course, these can be combined.

Figure 7.3   Optional Educator Pay-for-Performance Strategies

Alternative Educator Remuneration Strategies	Target: Individual or Group	Illustrative Performance Measure(s)	Possible Form of Reward	Strengths	Weaknesses
Whole-school reward (inclusion of classified employees optional)	Group	Student test scores Student attendance Teacher attendance Other?	Annual bonus	Reinforces collaborative effort	Free-rider problem
Specialists/ Teaching team reward (e.g., all math teachers in a school, district, region, or state)	Group	Student test scores Student attendance Teacher attendance Other?	Annual bonus	Reinforces collaborative effort Reduces free-rider problem	The larger the collective, the more likely there is a free-rider issue
Teacher value-added reward	Individual	Student test scores	Annual bonus	Possibly enhances instructor motivation	Limited empirical measures could result in narrowing of curriculum Could foster dysfunctional competition
Teacher knowledge and skills reward	Individual	Acquisition of attributes specified as abetting district or school pursuit of higher student achievement	Bonus/Base salary addition or pay scale acceleration	Diminishes dysfunctional consequences of exclusive test score reliance	Lacks uniformity across school districts Not easily linked to empirically verified attributes

Alternative Educator Remuneration Strategies	Target: Individual or Group	Illustrative Performance Measure(s)	Possible Form of Reward	Strengths	Weaknesses
Teacher appraisal-based reward	Individual	Peer or peer and superior appraisals of teacher performance and (possibly) knowledge and skills	Bonus	Diminishes dysfunctional consequences of exclusive test score reliance	Few empirically validated appraisal dimensions Risk/Fear of favoritism and cronyism
Hard-to-staff/Hard-to-serve schools	Individual	Market factors applied to specified teacher shortage definitions	Bonus/Base salary addition/pay scale acceleration	Applies market incentives to solve shortages	Some teachers may oppose
Teacher career ladder	Individual	Peer and superior appraisals of teacher performance Student test scores Student attendance Teacher attendance Other?	Bonus/Base salary addition/pay scale acceleration	Rewards instruction Retains teacher talent	Never has lasted long in past experiments

Source: Compiled by the authors

WHAT TO DO WHEN PERFORMANCE LAGS EXPECTATIONS?

Accountability depends upon specification of goals and accurate appraisals of individual or group progress. It also necessitates consequences, ill or good, for performance. In the absence of sanctions—positive or negative—accountability has no teeth and loses its force of being answerable or responsible for results.

But what should the sanctions be? The preceding section of this chapter illustrates a mix of purposes, performance, and labor market needs that can serve as a basis for positive sanctions—individual or group rewards. A school or district can link financial rewards to the outcomes specified in Figure 7.3. Here, however, the focus is on negative sanctions; what to do when performance is poor or below expectations.

Individual Sanctions

Sanctioning an ineffective teacher is unpleasant, and weak leaders attempt to avoid the responsibility. However, if the objective is constructing a productive school culture, one must face the fact that ineffective instructors undermine the goal in two ways. First, they harm the students for whom they have direct responsibility. Second, they also undermine the efforts of all teachers in the school by setting bad examples and lowering group morale. "Why do I have to work hard and continually strive to improve if Mr. X loafs and gets away with it?"

The purpose of negative sanctions aimed at individuals is not to punish a teacher but, rather, to protect students and maintain high group morale. Poor instruction has consequences, even if not immediately or dramatically visible. When subjected to poor instruction, particularly to a sequence of poor instructors, students fail to learn, and sometimes they never catch up to their well-instructed counterparts.

Sanctions for poor performance should assuredly begin with efforts to remediate the deficiency.[6] Here a school principal can resort to improvement plans involving specified remedial activities of varying length and intensity. What is important is to ensure that the remedial actions are logically linked to whatever is thought to be deficient in the teacher and have some chance of actually enabling the individual being sanctioned to improve.

Remediation should extend for as long as improvement is needed and progress is evident. If no progress is evident, then stronger action is in order. This may involve searching for another post in which the sanctioned individual might have a high chance of success (a transfer).

A transfer, however, should not involve the conventional ruse of the "Dance of the Lemons," wherein principals within a district simply trade incompetent instructors among themselves because they do not want to undertake the enormous efforts, usually involving huge financial, emotional, time, and transaction costs, surrounding an incompetent teacher's dismissal.[7] (Dismissing a teacher for a morals charge usually involves a criminal action and, assuming the charge is accurate and the evidence is sufficient, is much easier.)

Group Sanctions

What can be done if an entire school or a significant part of a school is found incapable of effective instruction? There is a gradient of remedial action that is possible. This can begin with requiring that the school collectively develop and pursue an improvement plan, perhaps involving coaching for the principal and teachers, possibly even involving the provision of additional resources to the school.

However, after a reasonable attempt at self-improvement, or the provision of outside advice and resources, it may be necessary to move to more drastic actions involving permitting parents to opt out of the school, replacing the principal, replacing the principal and all or selected teachers, or closing the school and starting all over again with a new principal and an entirely new staff.

CONCLUSION

Goals—accurate measures of progress—and sanctions—good and bad—will not in and of themselves have a desired effect in contributing to a productive school culture. Accountability, measurement, performance incentives, and consequences must be woven together into a tapestry of high performance. Each of these items is fine, but by itself it will not have much of an effect. It is the sum of the parts that matters. There is no one way in which to weave them together. That is the challenge of a leader. It is the leader's vision of the school that brings these components to productive fruition. The purpose of this chapter is to explain modern school accountability ideas and to illustrate the manner in which a successful principal can use accountability to assist in constructing a productive and cohesive school culture.

QUESTIONS FOR DISCUSSION

1. How have increased accountability demands impacted your current school? What impact have they had upon faculty? Upon students? How has accountability influenced the culture in your district or school?

2. Measuring student, teacher, and leadership performance is a challenging endeavor. Does your school currently use attainment, growth, or value-added measures of performance? In what way would you suggest changing the way student, teacher, and leadership performance is assessed in your school and district?

3. If you have experience with performance pay programs, would you encourage other schools to consider such a program? What are the major benefits of the program? What are the major challenges?

4. Do the potential negative consequences of performance pay outweigh the potential benefits?

5. How do you think school leaders can establish measurement and compensation systems that will positively contribute to student and teacher performance?

6. Which row of Figure 7.2 do you believe provides the most compelling argument for considering performance pay?

7. From your personal experience, what have been the most effective strategies for district and school leaders to employ in response to performance that lagged expectations?

REFERENCES AND SUGGESTED READINGS

Ballou, D., Sanders, W., & Wright, P. (2004). Controlling for student background in value-added assessment of teachers. *Journal of Educational and Behavioral Statistics, 29*(1), 37–66.

Barth, P. (2004). The real value of teachers: Using new information about teacher effectiveness to close the achievement gap. *Thinking K–16, 8*(1), 2–40.

Boardman, A. E., & Murnane, R. J. (1979). Using panel data to improve estimates of the determinants of educational achievement. *Sociology of Education, 52,* 113–121.

Fuller, W. A. (1987). *Measurement error models.* New York: John Wiley & Sons.

Goe, L. (2008, May). *Key issue: Using value-added models to identify and support highly effective teachers.* Princeton, NJ: Educational Testing Service and National Comprehensive Center on Teaching Quality (Washington, DC).

Gordon, R., Kane, T., & Staiger, D. (2006, April). *Identifying effective teachers using performance on the job.* Washington, DC: The Brookings Institution.

Guthrie, J. W. (2006). Modern education finance: How it differs from the 'old' and the analytic and data collection changes it implies. *Education Finance & Policy, 1*(1), MIT Press.

Guthrie, J. W., & Hart, C. C. (2008). *Modern school business administration: A planning approach.* New York: Pearson.

Hanushek, E. A. (2005). *The market for teacher quality.* Cambridge, MA: National Bureau of Economic Research.

Koretz, D. (2008, Fall). A measured approach: Value-added models are a promising improvement, but no one measure can evaluate teacher performance. *American Educator.*

McCaffrey, D. F., Lockwood, J. R., Koretz, D., Louis, T. A., & Hamilton, L. (2004). Models for value-added modeling of teacher effects. *Journal of Educational and Behavioral Statistics, 29*(1), 67–101.

Meyer, R. H. (1996). Value-added indicators of school performance. In E. A. Hanushek & D. W. Jorgenson (Eds.), *Improving the performance of America's schools* (pp. 197–223). Washington, DC: National Academy Press.

Meyer, R. H. (1997). Value-added indicators of school performance: A primer. *Economics of Education Review, 16*(3), 283–301.

Meyer, R. H. (2006). *Student and school performance targets: A framework for unifying the objectives of NCLB and the logic of value-added.* Report prepared for conference with the Institute for Research on Poverty. Madison: University of Wisconsin-Madison, Wisconsin Center for Education Research.

Meyer, R. H. (2007). *Building value-added and longitudinal data systems.* Los Angeles: The Broad Foundation's Pay for Performance Summit.

Meyer, R. H., & Christian, M. S. (2008). *Value-added and other methods for measuring school performance: An analysis of performance measurement strategies in teacher incentive fund proposals.* Prepared for the conference Performance Incentives: Their Growing Impact on American K–12 Education, National Center on Performance Incentives, Vanderbilt University, February 28–29, 2008.

National Commission on Excellence in Education. (1983). *A nation at risk: The imperative for educational reform.* Washington, DC: U.S. Government Printing Office.

Sanders, W. L., & Horn, S. P. (1994). The Tennessee value-added assessment system (TVAAS): Mixed model methodology in educational assessment. *Journal of Personnel Evaluation in Education, 8,* 299–311.

Willms, D. J., & Raudenbush, S. W. (1989). A longitudinal hierarchical linear model for estimating school effects and their stability. *Journal of Educational Measurement, 26*(3), 209–232.

NOTES

1. It had become apparent that mean scores could easily mask consistent low performance by those scoring below the average.

2. "Validity" has multiple meanings when it comes to tests. There is, for example, "content or internal validity," referring to the extent to which test items accurately measure the content being proclaimed. There is also "external validity," a measure of the degree to which test results can be generalized to other activities or populations. "Reliability" is another important test dimension. This concept refers to the extent to which test results from any particular administration of the exam will hold up or be repeated by a subsequent administration.

3. Richard Rothstein, extrapolating from a compilation of research regarding school effects, reports that no reputable researcher has ever found schooling to contribute more than .25 of the variance in student performance measures.

4. Creaming is a widely feared phenomenon because, if it takes place, some youngsters would be disadvantaged unfairly. However, it is not clear that it often takes place. The Research of Mathew G. Springer, involving classrooms in Idaho and using value-added testing, suggests that it is not widely occurring.

5. However, four factors make this restriction implausible: durability/decay in achievement, differential resource allocation, differences in the pretest and posttest scales, and nonlinearity in the test-scaling algorithm.

6. It is usually worth determining if there is a health or personal issue that explains the deficient behavior. Under such scenarios, remediation may assume a vastly different course of action.

7. School districts frequently obfuscate the problem by transferring persistently ineffective teachers to tasks or holding pens distant from students. This is expensive and wastes public resources.

Case Study 8: A Principal Opening at the Grant School

Can a Dysfunctional Culture Be Undone?

Ulysses S. Grant School was constructed in an outer-ring suburb a decade following the conclusion of World War II. When it was built there was not much money for fancy schools. Enrollments were burgeoning, and what was essential was to have sufficient buildings for baby boom children. Architectural ornamentation could come later. Land was still relatively inexpensive. It was easier to build out than up.

Grant School, thus, occupied a sprawling footprint. From the air, Grant appeared as a squat set of flat-roofed bland-colored buildings, much like a round butter carton surrounded on all sides by a series of radiating egg crates. Its administrative offices, auditorium, and cafeteria were in a central hub, with eight classroom wings extending as fingers from the center. Off to one side of the site were a large gymnasium, swimming pool, and a football and track stadium. The building covered several acres, and the extensive playing fields occupied yet more land. From the gym to the central office was a walk of almost a half mile.

Grant had originally been designated as a middle school. During the mid 1980s, however, the district's enrollments had declined precipitously, and the school board consolidated its three middle schools at another site and physically revamped Grant slightly so as to become the site for combining the district's two high schools.

The consolidations had been reasonably well planned operationally and logistically, and high school classes were phased in year by year. The school district planners, however, had paid little attention to organizational and programmatic matters. The functional outcome was that by the mid-1990s Grant was a 1,500-pupil high school characterized by a haphazard organizational amalgam of that which had incrementally preceded it. It had virtually no institutional history of which to be proud, few school traditions, not even been able to settle on a mascot, no student government, no parent-teacher organization, no alumni society, and two merged faculties without a rational apportionment of teachers. There were too many social studies teachers and too few science teachers. However, because of the state's tenure laws, no teachers had been released. Grant had history teachers instructing in chemistry, and the state test results displayed the consequence.

Note: This case study, as with others associated with other chapters, is about an actual school, actual people, and actual conditions. Nothing is fabricated. All cases are about situations school leaders routinely encounter. However, in each instance, names of people, schools, and locations have been altered to ensure confidentiality.

For a while, the newly formed high school had two principals, a compromise condition resulting from the politically fractious consolidation. The principals of the two formerly separate schools had been retained as coprincipals of Grant. This situation contributed to warring factions, one former individual school versus the other.

All of this tumult was happening while the composition of the neighborhood and the student body was changing. What was once solidly white working class was becoming far more of a racial and ethnic mosaic. And while the population was changing, so too were community and parent expectations. Grant now sat in the middle of a regional technology boom, and the engineering and technical households that were being attracted to the neighborhood wanted a rigorous academic curriculum. Grant, as a school, was not in a position to meet these heightened academic expectations. It could hardly field a football team where all members wore the same uniform, let alone offer a unified, consistent, and rigorous set of courses.

After what seemed like an eternity to many of the veteran Grant teachers and some of the parents, the school board pressured the superintendent into doing what everyone knew all along had to be done. The superintendent relieved the two principals of their leadership positions and employed a new principal from outside the district. That is how Ross McLendon, a candidate for the newly advertised principal's position, entered the picture at Grant High School.

McLendon was not from Hollywood's central casting. He did not fit some predetermined stereotype of a charismatic leader. He was not tall. He was not particularly athletic in appearance or gait. He did not carry himself with military bearing. He did not have a booming voice. His initial impression, while certainly that of a poised and confident professional, was not overwhelming and bombastic.

Rather, McLendon looked a little owlish. He had a large, bulging Scottish forehead with receding hair. He wore dark-rim glasses. His somewhat ill-fitting suits and ties were more from the Men's Warehouse than from an Italian designer. He drove a Detroit-made automobile. He walked at a comfortable but not frantic pace. He could easily have been mistaken for a government auditor, traveling salesman, or mid-level manager from virtually any number of manufacturing or service companies. He was married and had two elementary-school-age children.

When one examined McLendon's resume, however, one could see his distinguishing features. He was a disciplined and scholarly professional. He had an impressive track record as a science teacher and assistant principal of a middle school and had operated a medium-sized high school in an East Coast city. At his present high school position, he had a stellar record of elevating student achievement and building a solid instructional team. Parents, students, employees, and district upperlings sang his praises as an engaging leader, a coalition builder, and an able manager.

While being interviewed at the district office for the principalship at Grant, McLendon decided to take advantage of a two-hour break in the otherwise fully booked schedule to visit the school. No one knew him at Grant, and no one knew he was coming. He obtained directions and drove his cash-for-clunker car to the site. It was a windy day, and newspapers and other debris were swirling around the school's entry doors. Even from the curb where he was parking his car, he was taken back by the scruffy nature of the landscaping. While serviceable, the entire complex was hardly inviting. It was more institutional than inspirational.

McLendon entered the lobby of the administration building and approached a reception counter. There were several clerical-seeming individuals at nearby desks, all on the telephone. Their conversations seemed, as best McLendon could overhear them, to be personal in nature. He stood at the counter for a few minutes, but no one ever approached him. Sensing that he was not about to be greeted formally, he decided to take himself for a tour of the school. He was surprised at the absence of any overt security procedures. At all the schools with which he was familiar, an unexpected and unknown visitor would have been confronted, politely but quickly, and certainly would not have had easy access to the remainder of the school buildings and grounds. However, unimpeded, McLendon exited through a door on which signs pointed to the cafeteria and began his informal self-guided tour.

As McLendon walked throughout the array of one-story buildings that comprised the campus, he noted that many physical repairs were in order. He looked through glass windows into many classrooms. Often he saw teachers lecturing to students. Just as often, he saw students ignoring or blankly staring back at teachers. There were a far larger number of shop and vocational classes, located in a far wing, than McLendon had anticipated. There, the behavior of students seemed to be mixed. Some were engaged in sheet metal and other body repairs to automobiles. In other classes, students seemed simply to be standing about in groups. They were not misbehaving, but they appeared to be doing nothing more than talking among themselves.

Several teachers, shop teachers judging from the work smocks and coveralls they were wearing, were clustered in a supply room, off one of the woodshops. They appeared to be drinking coffee and talking informally. The outside basketball courts were filled with boys playing pickup games. He could see no formal PE instruction, either inside or outside. There was an apparent informal soccer match taking place on a playing field near the gym. All the youngsters were in their street clothes. No uniforms or gym outfits were evident.

While on his tour, a passing bell rang, classroom doors opened quickly, and large numbers of students immediately filled the informal asphalt spaces between wings of the academic buildings. There they clustered in small groups. McLendon was struck with the racial composition of these informal groups. White youngsters talked to white youngsters, Asian youngsters to Asians, and so on. While there was no apparent violence or enmity, neither was there much fraternization. Upon reflection, McLendon remembered that even the informal games on the various playing fields were also racially separated.

When the next passing bell rang, McLendon noticed that students exhibited no hurry to return to class. Most drifted off into a building, but many did not enter a class and were not in a desk when the passing period presumably was over. Even teachers did not seem in a hurry to return to their classrooms.

After a total of about 40 minutes touring the school, McLendon headed back through the main offices and asked of a clerk if he might meet the principal. He was informed that the principal was at a meeting "downtown." He asked if there was someone in charge of the school with whom he might speak. He was informed that insofar as she knew, there was no one else authorized to be in charge of the school.

McLendon thanked her, walked out the front door, went purposively toward his car, and drove off. As he headed back to the district office to pick up his bags and say his good-byes to those who had been interviewing him, his mind was racing with thoughts regarding what he had just seen at Grant School. He wondered about the history of the school. He wondered about the role of the central office in the district. He wondered about the school board. He wondered about the teachers and staff at Grant School. He wondered about his own impressions. He wondered about what he should say if anyone asked him questions.

FOR DISCUSSION

1. What do you think Ross McLendon was really thinking about as he drove away from Grant School?
2. What are the clues regarding the culture at Grant School?
3. If you were the district superintendent, what characteristics would you be seeking in a new principal for Grant School?
4. Have you ever known a school with physical and organizational characteristics such as those evident at Grant?
5. How would you speculate that Grant School got into its current organizational and operational condition?
6. Do you think physical facilities can influence a school's culture? If so, how?
7. Do you think McLendon will choose to leave his name in the running to be the principal of Grant?
8. Would you be willing to be the principal at Grant? If so, under what conditions?
9. If McLendon were offered and accepted the Grant principalship, what advice would you give him?
10. What are some of the conditions under which you yourself or perhaps McLendon might accept this Grant principal assignment?
11. Can Grant be rescued? If so, how? What steps will be necessary for McLendon, or anyone else wanting the school to be successful, to take?
12. What about McLendon, as best you can discern, leads you to believe he could be successful at Grant? Is there anything about McLendon that suggests to you he could not be successful as principal at Grant?

CHAPTER 8

Contextual Challenges Confronting the Formation of a Learning Culture

In this chapter a reader will learn about the following:

- External forces and contextual conditions possessing the potential to impede the formation of a high-performing school culture
- The historic evolution of structural elements shaping the United States' system of decentralized school governance and management
- Functional forces contributing to the opposition to school change and reform inertia

ELCC STANDARDS

ELCC standards addressed in this chapter include the following:

- 1.3—Implement a vision
- 2.1—Promote a positive school culture
- 3.1—Manage the organization
- 3.2—Manage operations
- 6.1—Understand the larger context
- 6.2—Respond to the larger context

INTRODUCTION

This chapter concentrates upon structural and functional contextual conditions that shape individual schools. These conditions can be major impediments to creating a productive school culture and dramatically can get in a change agent's way. These may be conditions around which a leader will have to work, strive to circumvent, or somehow finesse. These conditions may necessitate conscious and strategic effort to overcome and often will challenge a change agent's commitment and idealism.

"Structural" in this setting refers to other-than-personal contextual conditions; it refers to matters of government, law, or organizational design. It excludes other equally powerful potential impediments to change such as organizational inertia, historic precedent, political protectionism, or just plain selfishness or stupidity.

Here is an example of a structural impediment: imagine that you as a change agent are eager to recruit only the very best teachers to instruct in your school. You would like widely to advertise all teacher vacancies in your school and select from among the best individuals interested in applying or whom you can persuade to apply.

This is a reasonable position for you to take. However, imagine further that your district's school board has acquiesced to teacher union collective-bargaining demands and has agreed that posted teacher position vacancies are open first to individuals who are already employed teachers in the district, particularly advantaging those with the greatest employment seniority. Under this contractual agreement, a more senior teacher has priority in being placed at your school over a more junior colleague or a new hire. Under such conditions, you have had a substantial amount of your decision-making discretion eroded or at least complicated by a structural condition, a school district collective-bargaining contract.

This is not an immutable condition. It is not God given or specified by Hammurabi. However, it can be a substantial impediment to which a great deal of effort would have to be given to change, and, even then, success is not assured. Here is a concrete example of a functional condition that might challenge the creation of an effective school culture. There is no law dictating the following, simply a set of mental perceptions.

Some superintendents are suspicious regarding the effectiveness of their principals and are reluctant to unbridle them fully, to empower principals as school leaders. Conversely, in the absence of an ability fully to act as a leader, many able individuals eschew becoming a principal. It is a chicken-or-egg problem involving confounding issues of reciprocal trust and empowerment.

Envisioning and implementing details of a high-performing school culture involves ideas and actions that a principal or another school leader can undertake individually. Success in such a venture depends heavily upon individual leaders' actions and cooperation with those in the school building and those in the district central office. If not sufficiently empowered to take important actions, creating an effective school culture may be impossible.

There is a broad spectrum of activities that a well-meaning change agent might want to take that can be deterred by obstacles to change. This chapter describes education's remarkably complicated and frequently influential context, both structural and functional, with the hope in mind that awareness of potential obstacles may better arm a change agent.

AN EXTENSIVE AND SOMETIMES CONFLICTING DISTRIBUTION OF AUTHORITY

Successful leaders must grasp both the big picture and the nuances of the larger external environment in which they routinely operate. Knowing these things is no easy task. Few endeavors are as complicated as is America's system of public education. U.S. school organization is like an onion; there is always another layer to be peeled away before you reach the core. Indeed the manner in which the United States structures and organizes its schools is different from virtually every other industrialized nation, and the description of how public school management fits into the jigsaw puzzle of U.S. governmental operation is often baffling to those from overseas, as it also is to many who actually reside in this nation.

Unlike most nations, the United States does not operate a national system of schooling. Hence, there is no uniform prototype for the selection of and preparation of education leaders or teachers. There is no West Point for public school superintendents and principals. Rather, because of constitutional specifications and the dynamics of federalism, America's schools are the plenary legal responsibilities of each of the 50 individual states, rather than of the federal government.

This decentralization leads to great fragmentation. This is a condition that can be viewed as both a strength and a disadvantage. For example, there are a staggering 1,400 graduate-level education schools empowered by executive branch agencies in each of the 50 states to license public school leaders and teachers. Not only do preparation standards and credential requirements have the potential to vary across states, there is enormous variation from institution to institution within a single state.

From Where Did Such Decentralization Come?

At the time of the 1781 Constitutional Convention in Philadelphia, many colonies were already on a path to statehood and had constructed their own individual constitutions.[1] These governance charters assumed state responsibility for education. Philadelphia Convention delegates, ever sensitive to the complicated negotiations needed to consummate the formation of a new nation, were reluctant to undo and renegotiate existing covenants. Oversight of education was not a pressing issue.[2] Hence, they omitted education and schooling from the federal Constitution altogether. There is no mention of either word in the actual document.

The absence of explicit constitutional authority, acceptance by states of plenary responsibility for schooling, and the social contract language of the Tenth Amendment combine to shape and reinforce the long-standing decentralized structure of U.S. education governance and operation.[3] Education's organization complexity rolls on. The nature of communication and transportation during the colonial period, through to industrialization beginning in the nineteenth century, encouraged states to rely on local school districts to provide schooling. These districts are often, but not universally, municipally based. There are almost 14,000 of them, each with a school board, usually elected but sometimes appointed.[4]

Stemming historically from the 1647 Massachusetts Commonwealth enactment of "Ye Olde Deluder Satan Act," public schooling in the United States historically has been lay controlled. This landmark colonial-era legislation specified that every township would have a free public school, that it would be governed by elected laypersons—not educators or religious leaders—and that schooling would be the preserve of special governments, not falling directly under the aegis of municipal or county councils.

Massachusetts' organizational provisions were modeled in other New England states and spread westward through the early republic's Land Survey Ordinances' participant requirements. Mid-Atlantic and southern states evolved in a slightly different fashion with Anglican Church reliance upon parish borders translated to greater dependence upon county boundaries for local government and school organizational purposes. Still, even if having fewer of them, southern states rely upon local school districts for the primary provision of school services. Hawaii is a dramatic outlier. It was a kingdom prior to becoming a territory and a state.[5] It has a statewide school governance system with no formal reliance upon individual local school districts.

The just-described vertical decentralization involving distribution of authority across federal, state, and local governments is amplified or stretched even further by a number of horizontal decentralization provisions within states and localities. States reflect the federal government, relying upon executive, legislative, and judicial branches of government. Each of these has educational responsibilities involving rule making, rule implementation, and rule adjudication.

However, states vary widely in the manner in which they organize and oversee their education responsibilities. All states have chief state school officers, executive branch officials with responsibility for overseeing public schools. Sometimes, however, these are elected positions, and incumbents have their own political base. Sometimes they are appointed by the governor or a state board of education and are therein administratively subordinate. State boards of education are themselves mixed, with some being appointed and others being elected. Their membership is remarkably diverse in terms of size and individual qualifications.

Similarly, local school districts display organizational diversity, with about 80 percent of local boards locally elected and others being the appointees of mayors or county councils. Some school boards, about 80 percent, have taxing authority. Others must submit annual budget requests to another, and elected, body such as a city council or county board of supervisors.

This conglomeration of organizational arrangements and historical developments results in a contemporary management picture of remarkable diversity. In some ways, American education is centralized beyond what one could expect from such a diverse set of governmental arrangements. For example, 25 percent of the nation's public school students, more than 13 million of them, are enrolled in only 1 percent of the nation's school districts. These are unusually large organizations such as those found in New York City, Chicago, Los Angeles, Houston, and Miami. If the numeric net is expanded, 5 percent of the nation's school districts enroll 50 percent of all U.S. public school students— 25 million of them.

At the opposite end of the scale are thousands of small local school districts, many but not all of which are rural and remote. There exist small school districts with more school board members than students. There are even a few remaining districts, so-called "nonoperating" districts, that enroll no students but serve as political shields protecting landowners from the imposition of higher local property taxes. This behemoth organizational conglomerate employs more than 4 million teachers, approximately 1.5 million classified personnel, and 400,000 administrators and supervisors. *There are more teachers in America than farmers and more school administrators than autoworkers.*

> ### LINK TO CASE STUDY 8
>
> Case Study 8 introduces Grant High School—an amalgam of several schools thrown together onto one sprawling campus. Where once there were multiple schools now there is one—but it has a far-from-unified faculty and leadership team. Have you worked in a context where multiple groups had to come together under one roof? What particular leadership qualities are necessary to bridge two individual organizational contexts into one coherent, productive culture?

A PERVASIVE POLITICAL OVERLAY[6]

Overseeing and directing such organizational and governmental complexity renders school leadership daunting and fragile. Leadership is rendered yet more challenging by education's substantial interaction with the larger political system. Many, if not most, education leaders have technical functions connected with the instruction and management expected of them. In the process of their daily duties, they also must keep political considerations well in mind.

An endeavor of the societal significance, personal consequence, and financial magnitude of public education is assured of attracting political system attention.

Financial support of schools and colleges usually occupies half the budget of states. Thus, elected officials, governors, mayors, other statewide and citywide officials, and legislative members pay close attention to education. In exchange for public financial support and other resource accommodations, elected officials occasionally expect to exert influence on the system and, in selected instances, even seek personal favors.

What is taught, who teaches, who goes to school and to which schools, where schools are constructed, how much employees are paid, and who pays taxes in support of schools are all political decisions that routinely influence schools and those in them.

Progressive Era reform efforts of the 1920s were directed at depoliticizing education. This objective was undertaken for good reason. Progressive Era "Muckrakers" and good government idealists had uncovered a wide spectrum of corruption stemming from unbridled and unscrupulous political machines and powerful ward bosses. However, when it came to education, Progressive Era political reforms also resulted in unanticipated negative consequences, consequences that continue today to restrict the capacity of school leaders to be effective.

For example, reformers advocated the seemingly sensible switching of school board elections to off years and off times. Distancing school board elections from general elections was intended to discourage machine politicians from getting involved in schools and reaping the political spoils associated with corrupt construction and vendor contracts and employment positions. However, this action, while successfully discouraging widespread general public participation, did so at the cost of sacrificing the systemic accountability that results from widespread public engagement in elections. Instead, efforts to separate education and politics privileged education employees and other special interests willing to pay the high transaction costs associated with electoral campaigning because of the resulting benefits (e.g., positively influencing school board election outcomes and gaining school board majorities more sympathetic to union demands during employee contract bargaining).

Political engagement is not restricted to executive and legislative branch activities. Since the 1950s, courts have exercised far greater authority over schools than in the previous century. School racial desegregation, curriculum issues, athletics, student discipline and free speech, financing, collective bargaining, control over afterschool activities, and personnel practices have all been shaped by influential Supreme Court and state court decisions.[7]

Education's heavy entanglement with politics is a mixed blessing. On one hand, the sustained attention of the political system ensures that public schools are sensitive to the preferences of the public, the ultimate stakeholder. On the other hand, when elected officials behave badly (e.g., using state or local board or administrative appointments as political favors or election campaign payoffs or school board members selecting teachers or administrators for other than reasons of competence), the education system's ability to perform to a high standard is blunted, and accountability for results is badly blurred.

MITIGATING CENTRIPETAL FORCES

Education governance and management is complicated. However, this picture is not quite as decentralized, haphazard, and dysfunctional as one might deduce from the foregoing descriptions. After all, the spectrum of America's public schools includes some outstanding school districts and individual schools, education institutions that can proudly compete with any in the world. These successes did not occur as a consequence of a series of random acts. Thus, however cumbersome the governing apparatus and attendant political arrangements, the system does permit islands of greatness. There are forces that inject a degree of commonality into the operation of our schools.

Originally conceived constitutional arrangements regarding education operate like a political centrifuge propelling decisions and authority to the periphery of governance structures. However, there has evolved a countervailing set of centripetal forces that can contribute to a more productive balance between centralization and decentralization.

Among the centralizing conditions in American education are extragovernmental influences such as college admission tests and standards; private-sector-published textbooks sold widely to school district markets across state boundaries; professional associations of administrators, teachers, and others; professional certification such as that provided by the National Board of Professional Teaching Standards; and nationwide publications and convening networks such as the National Governors Association.

If shaped to productive ends, appropriately orchestrated, and strategically employed by education leaders and school reform advocates, these nationalizing forces can mitigate some of the policy fractionation facilitated by a federated and decentralized set of decision arrangements.

CHARACTERIZING THE CONTEXTS OF PUBLIC SCHOOL LEADERSHIP

America's principals and superintendents often feel compelled to operate within a managerial and organizational context that virtually precludes their being successful as leaders. For a present-day school leader to succeed, he or she almost invariably has to swim upstream against innumerable contextual obstacles. Education's organizational theorists have a term for this leadership strategy of responsible rebellion; they label it "creative insubordination."

The fundamental management procedures, personnel strategies, and operating conditions of most American school districts were framed in a prior era, at the beginning of the twentieth century.[8] It is a rare public school district central office that has kept pace with modern private-sector management theory or practice. This condemnation applies to virtually every phase of public school management: human resources, budgeting and accounting, information technology, decision authority, accountability procedures, and even business practices as mundane as payroll procedures and processing of purchase orders.

Whereas modern private-sector businesses have long ago put into place personnel training and evaluation, quality control, performance management, and accountability procedures, most school districts have yet to adopt simple cost control concepts such as benchmarking or the determination of per-unit operating costs. A manufacturing CEO can routinely ascertain the costs of virtually every component of production, marketing, and product distribution. Conversely, most school superintendents have no idea of the costs to their districts of offering ninth-grade algebra or twelfth-grade advanced-placement physics. It makes you wonder if Jack Welch would have become a modern management icon had he ever been assigned as a CEO in a school or school district, rather than at General Electric.

In the private sector, personnel costs are taken as variable. In public education, they are seen as fixed. In the private sector, high-level human talent is a valued component, carefully and competitively recruited, thoughtfully nurtured, heavily incented, and seen as crucial to the present success and future well-being of the firm.

In school districts, teachers are often seen as commodities, as individually interchangeable and personally indistinguishable widgets. Their selection is frequently slipshod, their induction into the organization is usually casual, their performance routines rote and possibly mindless, and their annual costs are seen as a function of time on the payroll, not of their capacity to further the institution's mission.

SOURCES OF LEADERS' CONTEXTUAL CONSTRAINTS

What follows in this section is an illustration of education management's outmoded managerial imperatives and limited mind-sets. However, first a reader should understand that these widespread impediments often stem from two principal sources. Many of these restrictions are a result of state laws and local district collective-bargaining contract provisions brought into existence by and for the protection of powerful special interests. They can be changed.

Additionally, a good proportion of these impediments and dysfunctional precepts are informal, outside the law, and not defined by state or federal policy or brought about by judicial decisions. They are a self-imposed result of organizational inertia, political convenience, and a limited leader mind-set.[9]

The conditions of limited leader imagination and organizational inertia are not all bad news. When it comes to reform, a healthy portion of contextual impediments may lend themselves to change through effective use of information, explanation, modeling, and exhortation from the bully pulpit. Time and energy consuming legislative changes may be needed in selected, but not all, instances.

School Districts Are Frequently Characterized by Primitive Management Precepts

The fundamental management paradigm that has evolved in the information age and characterizes the industrialized world's private sector, military, and many not-for-profit activities strikes a reasoned balance in the distribution of authority between the center and the periphery of an organization. In abstract terms, the modern management paradigm operates as follows.

Mission, money, major strategies, and measurement of progress toward goals are factors determined, organizationally, at the top or centrally. Conversely, detailed managerial operational tactics and day-to-day resource deployment, motivation, and backward mapping of strategies to tactical field conditions are activities undertaken on the periphery, close to the organization's clients and customers or by those routinely engaging with the enemy.[10]

There is a decision rule that assists in determining at which organizational level authority should be affixed. It is known as the "principle of subsidiarity." Under this governance and management axiom, the assumption is that unless there is a compelling reason to the contrary, decision authority is presumed to reside with the lowest-level organizational component. Only if there are persuasive arguments should a decision be elevated up the hierarchical scale.

This balanced decision-making paradigm is not routinely practiced in public education management. Instead, a centralizing decision-making hierarchy generally characterizes education management.

Hierarchical Decision Authority

What follows is a ditty used by school principals to capture their frustration and the way in which they perceive their management situation.

"I am not the engineer; I do not even ring the bell.

However, if the train jumps the tracks, guess who catches hell?"

In contract determinations, New York City principals initially resisted being classified as "management." They claimed that their lack of decision authority rendered them more like airline pilots, responsible for the safe conveyance of a plane and its passengers from geographic point to point, not organizational decision makers.

The tradition of a steep decision hierarchy in school districts places a great deal of operational authority at the central office and with the superintendent. The larger the school district, in terms of enrollment size, the more likely that there are several bureaucratic reporting layers between principals and the superintendent.[11]

This layered decision-making arrangement has its roots in the early twentieth century "scientific management" movement initiated in the private sector by industrial engineering celebrity Frederick Taylor. Taylor was famous for his time and motion efficiency studies and the belief that much of management could be reduced to specific principles and mechanical rules, leaving little room for subordinate discretion and, presumably, leaving little room for subordinate error. For a while, Taylorism was a management fad in the private sector. Taylorism was grafted onto education to capture the high status mantle of private-sector effectiveness and the appearance of modern management. It was rapidly translated into education settings and widely aped by status-deprived school district managers.

Scientific management was a quickly passing fancy in the private sector. The idea that central authorities always knew best and that management of complicated human endeavors was amenable to a few finite rules was rapidly seen as insufficient by business executives. However, scientific management's legacy lives in school district precepts and practices into the present.

Hierarchical management dominates schools out of inertia and mindlessness; however, it also persists because it fills a functional purpose. Superintendents hold the most accountable positions in all of schooldom. They are contracted to school boards. Contracts, typically, run for three to four years. Renewal, or even fulfillment, of the contract is contingent upon approval by a school board majority. Failure to satisfy school board members results in dismissal or nonrenewal. Hence, superintendents are reluctant to delegate decision making, particularly in arenas of substantial technical uncertainty, to principals. If they are to be fired, superintendents would prefer it be for their own actions and not what they perceive as the mistakes of subordinates. Thus, they frequently strive to retain decision making within their more immediate domain. It is this district condition that prompted the illustration of functional impediments provided near the beginning of this chapter.

Insufficient Principal Empowerment

School superintendents, as stated earlier, are among those in education who are most intensely held accountable. School boards may not always concentrate on the most productive dimensions in their annual evaluations, but, nevertheless, superintendents know well that they will be subjected to routine and high-stakes evaluations by their school boards.

Conversely, principal performance is not routinely subjected to the same level of evaluative scrutiny. Moreover, given conventional levels of authority allocated to principals, it is only fair that they are not as intensely held accountable. Of course, local variations exist, and in some instances this general trend of principals not being held to the highest levels of evaluative scrutiny is not supported.

Empowerment and accountability are opposite sides of the same leadership coin. To empower without accountability is to risk an out-of-control or rogue employee. Conversely, to evaluate an individual's leadership performance without granting sufficient authority to act is patently unfair. Principals, presently, are often hamstrung in the operation of their schools. The just-described hierarchical management model holds decisions at the center that are crucial to the success of principals as they seek to operate an organization and shape a school culture.

The Big Ten Missing Authorities

Among the important decisions that a successful public school leader needs authority to make in order to create a productive culture are the following:

(1) Selection of a school's personnel, including teachers and classified staff

(2) Replacing ineffective teachers, where such is in order

(3) Blend of teachers and classified staff in a school

(4) Assignment of teachers to individual classes within a school

(5) Number of pupils in individual classes

(6) Length of the school day and hours of operation

(7) Teacher salaries, performance premiums, and corrective actions

(8) Purchase of equipment

(9) School maintenance

(10) School building appearance and workplace safety

All of these authorities are actions routinely within the power of a plant manager or regional or local office manager in the private sector. Similarly, they are generally within the purview of a charter school principal or a private or independent school headmaster or headmistress. Are they within the authorized decision-making categories of your current principal?

Dysfunctional Resource Dynamics[12]

A principal of a 1,000-enrollee high school, in a district that spends the national-average amount per pupil each year, $10,000, operates a $10 million-a-year endeavor. This often places schools among the largest and highest-spending employers in a community. However, when queried as to the discretion they have over this budget, many principals reply with a figure in the $100,000 range.

Such an understating principal is not being coy or unresponsive. What he or she is referring to is the dollar amount over which there is any principal control. The principal is probably also reflecting ignorance. He or she is unlikely to know with any precision what is spent annually to operate the school. It is not the principal's fault. The district superintendent is also unlikely to know how much is spent in any particular school. Indeed, the district business manager may not know either.

However, resource allocation deficiencies run far deeper. Not only do school principals routinely not know the full magnitude of the resources potentially under their discretion, they also are routinely required by outmoded processes to allocate school resources in ways that are known to be ineffective.

School Budgeting Obfuscation

School districts do not budget in a manner that transparently discloses for what purposes funds are spent or to what individual schools they are allocated. This is one reason why principals do not perceive themselves as masters of their domain.

School district budgets are models of obfuscation. It is virtually impossible to read a school district budget and gain an idea of the mission of the organization or the means by which it is pursuing its mission. A visitor from Mars upon obtaining a conventional school district budget could conclude only that the organization was an employment agency. Why else would a budget list teaching positions by school for page after page? However, what one seldom sees is how much the teacher is actually paid, or what the total is for the actual pay of all teachers and other employees, in a school. Moreover, the function of the budgeted position is usually stated in such generic terms that a reader cannot determine the nature of the assignment.

One can deduce from school district budgets the total amount being proposed to spend districtwide for a particular fiscal year. Careful scrutiny may also reveal how much more this amount is than what was spent in the aggregate in the prior school year. However, it is almost never possible to determine how much is spent per pupil in a particular school, how much is intended for the instruction of particular courses and subjects, or how much is spent for particular services such as counseling.

The Inefficiency of It All

Under present budgetary and accounting procedures it is not possible accurately to discern activities and strategies that are cost effective in enhancing pupil academic achievement gains and which activities are possibly effective but overly expensive.

Food service, transportation, athletics, and possibly maintenance are often budgeting and accounting exceptions. In these categories school districts know what they spend. It is even possible sometimes to grasp a few benchmarks across similar-sized school districts to determine if one's expenses are widely out of line.[13]

However, principals do not have and do not expect to have much discretion over these peripheral activities. These activities are not part of the technical core of schooling. It is instruction that counts, it is instruction that does or should matter to principals, and it is instruction that is the black hole of principals' budgetary and cost-effective knowledge.

School budgets focus upon objects of expenditure, for example, personnel salaries, fringe benefits, supplies and materials, and a select few services such as vendors and consultants. When operational functions are taken into account they are so abstract as to have little meaning. Typical budget functional categories are "instruction," "administration," and "pupil support." These categories are insufficiently granular to permit productive analysis.

This obfuscation results partially from outmoded practices and partially out of conscious design. Detailed financial ignorance serves important political purposes. It is a rare school district that allocates its financial and human resources equitably or productively among all of its schools. Teacher assignment dynamics routinely assist teachers with greater seniority to apply for and have priority access to open teaching positions as they become available throughout a district. More-senior teachers are more highly paid teachers.

The Inequity of It All

As teachers sift themselves through self-selection to the schools in a district, in keeping with whatever they perceive as being the most advantageous working conditions, they take their individual salaries with them. It is through this dynamic that frequently selected, usually high-social-status, schools have higher per-pupil spending, and less desirable schools routinely find themselves with less-experienced and lower-paid teachers.

This teacher salary differential, when aggregated across an entire school, can result in selected schools spending substantially more per pupil, 20 to 40 percent more, than other schools in a district. Initial Elementary and Secondary Education

Act (ESEA) Title I regulations attempted to address this disparate condition, but federal officials eventually acquiesced to special interests and required only that districts impute mean teacher salaries to instructional positions at each school. This accounting ruse continues to disguise intradistrict resource inequalities.

Current object code budgeting, aggregated to the district level, disguises school-by-school per-pupil spending differences. However, even if not widely known, these resource differences between schools are unfair to pupils and disadvantageous to shortchanged principals.[14]

Outmoded Reward Systems

Not only are the resource distribution mechanisms in school districts lacking in transparency, they are also absent productive rationality.

The overall perverse nature of education's reward system, allocating more money and status to those who eschew classroom teaching for administrative duties, was discussed in Chapter 5 of this book. Suffice it here to reinforce for a reader the general ineffectiveness of such and the chilling effect it has upon trying to elevate the sanctity of teaching. Here, however, the focus is on more technical features of educator reward systems.

More than 90 percent of America's public school teachers are paid as a function of college units beyond their bachelor's degree and their years of service as a teacher.[15] This arrangement, resulting from a series of Progressive Era good-government reforms in the early twentieth century, corrected corrupt and inefficient practices of another era. However, as sometimes happens, yesterday's reforms contribute to today's problems. The single-salary schedule is one such problem. Researchers cannot identify a positive relationship between multiple years of teaching experience and advanced college course credits with elevated student achievement.

Management Information Deficiencies

It is difficult to imagine any realm of leadership or management, in any part of the spectrum of societal endeavors, that operates in a data vacuum equal to school principals or superintendents.

At the close of a business day, a Wal-Mart manager has an almost instantaneous account of what items in what quantities were sold, total sales revenues, employee attendance and personnel costs, customer counts, items of greatest sales preference, utility usage and costs, maintenance requests, vendor delivery performance, ratio of direct to indirect costs, and restocking needs for the next day. Similarly, a Wal-Mart regional manager can tell the same for all stores under his or her geographic aegis.

Airline executives have access to a similar report regarding performance matters such as number of flights, passenger miles, revenue per passenger mile, future sales revenue estimates, future passenger bookings, plane maintenance needs and schedules, employee absence or availability, fuel consumption, fuel prices present and future, and on-time performance.

Military field commanders now have GPS data, satellite imaging, drone photographs, and electronic intelligence that routinely enable them to make informed decisions regarding the location and force size of their enemy and potential battle engagements.

At the end of a school day, a principal is fortunate to know the student attendance for that day. The principal, if the school is sufficiently small, might know what teachers were absent, how many substitutes were employed, and how many parents visited the school. In a large school, no principal would easily know anything regarding these dimensions. Virtually no principal has day-to-day knowledge of instructional effectiveness.

Cost figures, be they for personnel, utilities, or supplies for operating a school are almost never part of a principal's data portfolio and certainly are not present on a daily basis. The ability to link student achievement with the instructor of record is seldom present. The ability to use test data to analyze the instructional strengths and deficiencies of teachers in the school is almost never present. What parents think of their child's teacher, other than by anecdote, is almost never systematically recorded.

When it comes to planning, superintendents and principals operate in the dark. They seldom know a sufficient amount regarding unit costs of instructional activities to make informed decisions. Even if they estimate, as one can do knowing that a 30-year teacher costs twice as much as a beginner, that advanced Italian is expensive relative to beginning algebra, they are not always empowered to make decisions relevant to the information. Under present data arrangements it is virtually impossible to apply modern management strategies and skills to schools.

Insufficient Core Knowledge Regarding Instruction and Schooling

Education reform is replete with ideas that seemed fine at the time of their inception and later proved useless or, worse, harmful. Here is a partial list of fads through history: scientific management, phrenology, school consolidation, team teaching, flexible schedules, open classrooms, "new math," whole-language reading, community control, British infant schools, career ladders, education enterprise zones, individually prescribed instruction, zero-based budgeting, teacher scripting, self-esteem curriculum, and on and on goes the list of once fashionable but now faded education innovations.

Schools were once closed because they were too small. Now they are being closed because they are too large. Progressive Era reformers took schools out of partisan politics to preserve professionalism and instructional effectiveness. Now elected mayors are overseeing schools to enhance effectiveness. Back and forth the pendulum swings.

So much of American education reform is like a tempting summer breeze. There is a short pleasant whiff of a budding idea that is extensively touted by a phalanx of politicos and advocates as a silver bullet for schools, and the program rapidly goes to scale as a result. The reality, however, is that this innovative reform once championed to revolutionize schooling inevitably fades for lack of a scientific underpinning or a plausible research base. The absence of an empirically driven technical core and a sense of continuously needing to improve are principal causes of education's addiction to fads.

Badly Needed Empirical Research Regarding Instruction

What follows is an illustrative list of hugely consequential education policy issues and questions regarding practice for which better empirical answers would reduce faddishness and enhance school effectiveness.

- What is the nature of effective early childhood education, what long-term effect on academic achievement and other performance dimensions can it have, what are its relative costs and long-term benefits, and how much should be invested in its operation relative to other alternative reforms?
- What is an effective teacher, what training is necessary to prepare an effective teacher, and what should state credentialing expectations be to promote effective teacher training and recruitment?
- With what sustained professional-development activities should teachers be supplied or mandated to obtain? Who should pay for such activities?
- What is an effective class size, for what grade levels, and for what kinds of students, and what is the relative benefit of investing in this treatment compared to other possible investments regarding instruction?

- What is the optimum size of a school? What are the tradeoffs between operational economies of scale and individual student engagement? To what degree does school size influence student academic achievement? Does the school configuration or the size and condition of the physical facility itself matter?
- What specific leadership skills are essential to the success of valid education reform initiatives, and what are the conditions under which reform initiatives are successfully implemented, brought to scale, and sustained over time?
- What is the role, if any, for instructional supplies and materials? Can technology be deployed to enhance instruction or to augment the labor-intensive nature of American public schooling?
- What are appropriate performance incentive systems? Should incentives be applied to individuals or to teams? Should incentives encompass administrators? By what means should student achievement or performance be gauged when designing incentive systems?

Answers to these, and similar, issues will not eventuate soon. Consequently, school leaders will also need to prepare themselves for acting in a milieu of sustained uncertainty.

The following are specific steps that have evolved in other organizational settings that leaders can take when an organization faces technical uncertainty in pursuing its core functions.

- Specify desired goals but be comprehensive so as to avoid goal displacement
- Place production resources (revenue) close to providers of service
- Encourage diverse and innovative efforts to achieve specified goals
- Construct "internal markets" so that the system has self-correcting tendencies
- Collect unending amounts of data relevant to determining the effectiveness of the diverse efforts to achieve goals
- Engage in "fast failure": weeding out unproductive practices and quickly replacing them with new experimental methods
- Induce competition among providers to see who can be the most successful
- Reward success as lavishly as might be appropriate
- Avoid rewarding failure
- Construct and appropriately reward a culture of continuous improvement

Continuous-Learning Orientation Not a Present-Day Part of School Culture

Leadership matters in the face of uncertainty. Well-prepared leaders know or can sense the difference between fads and fundamentals. They eschew the former and embrace the latter.

What might be most needed is the kind of pragmatic experimentation advocated in *Innovate or Die* by Jack V. Matson (1996), who calls for "intelligent fast failure."

According to Matson, intelligent fast failure is not a goal but an outcome from risking effort. Each experiment undertaken needs to be carefully considered, with determining the conditions for success being the ultimate goal. Experiments must be crafted to minimize downside risks. They must also be designed to minimize the time and resources spent and to accelerate learning from the outcomes. While ordinarily one would test ideas sequentially, starting with the best one, with intelligent fast failure, an institution experiments with multiple ideas simultaneously. As a result, it is possible to accelerate the learning process, compress failure time, and progress more rapidly toward resolution.

Lessons learned by practitioners and researchers represent assets of tremendous value to states and districts interested in designing and implementing performance pay plans. Similarly, empirically based assessments of the short- and long-term consequences of education reforms will allow the policy and practitioner communities to move forward with greater certainty. By harvesting research-based and contextually rich insights, and harnessing the potential of intelligent fast failure, the reform movement moves further away from being a passing fad and closer to being a sound and lasting policy or practice.

CONCLUSION

The authors hope that, while pointing out the challenges involved in impacting a school culture, this chapter encourages a would-be change agent, or an energetic and intelligent individual eager to create, or undertake the transformation of, a conventional school into a productive learning community, to do so with gusto. The intent in describing possible structural and functional elements comprising contextual complexity is to provide a change agent with a road map of possible impediments to change. These impediments can be overcome. While doing so will require remarkably refined and carefully calculated strategies on the part of energetic and creative change agents, truly everything worth achieving involves strategic responses to resistance. To succeed in the face of opposition and iner-tia, one must carefully define one's route, construct coalitions of willing partners, and pick one's battles carefully.

Intensified instructional emphases, elevated expectations for teachers and administrators, concerns for school organization, the reexamination of educa-tion management, and constant revisions to education policy and governance intensely reflect the significant transformation through which American schooling is now evolving. The 2001 No Child Left Behind Act and the Obama administration's proposed alterations symbolize this transformation.

America's policy system is seeking the means for aligning education's mas-sive material resources with the vastly elevated and expanded societal expecta-tions for student achievement. The standards and accountability movement, market and competition strategies, and policy system admonitions for added productivity and heightened student achievement frequently place finance, resource allocation, legal, and accountability issues at the heart of education leadership, policy, and school management considerations.

However, after more than a quarter century of attempting to enhance American education through policy changes, a condition that began as a response to the publication of *A Nation at Risk* in 1983, a parallel set of ideas regarding the significance of school culture is also strongly emerging. Assuredly, having state and district learning standards, adequate resources, well-trained teachers, and appropriate accountability measures matters.

However, even in their totality, these policy levers do not by themselves magi-cally transform a failing or once-mediocre school into a thriving and performance-oriented organization capable of enabling all children to achieve academically at higher levels. A body of knowledge is evolving that suggests means by which schools more effectively can meet many of these heightened expectations for stu-dent performance and added organizational and economic efficiency. This knowl-edge comprises a *strategic* education organizational culture and practice paradigm, and this book embodies a *strategic* outlook and has discussed the sig-nificant role that school culture plays within it and how school leaders can har-ness these ideas in order to create and sustain a successful school culture.

QUESTIONS FOR DISCUSSION

1. How does the vertical and horizontal distribution of organizational authority in American education impede or assist efforts to construct or transform a school into a culture of continuous and high-level human learning?

2. Why is education more given to centralized and hierarchical decision making than many private and nonprofit organizations?

3. Can a strong school district central office, one sure of its mission and filled with talented individuals, be consistent with the idea of productive learning cultures at individual schools within the district?

4. What logistical, organizational, and emotional support should a change agent principal expect of a district central office and superintendent?

REFERENCES AND SUGGESTED READINGS

Casserly, M. (2010, January). *Managing for results in America's great cities.* Paper presented at the American Enterprise Institute Penny Saved Conference, Mayflower Hotel, Washington, DC.

Matson, J. V. (1996). *Innovate or die: A personal perspective on the art of innovation.* Royal Oak, MI: Paradigm Press.

Podgursky, M., & Springer, M. G. (2007). Teacher performance pay: A review. *Journal of Policy Analysis and Management, 26*(4), 909–949.

Rivkin, S. G., Hanushek, E. A., & Kain, J. F. (2005). Teachers, schools, and academic achievement. *Econometrica, 73*(2), 417–458.

Roza, M. (2010, January). *Now is a great time to consider the per-unit cost of everything in education.* Paper presented at the American Enterprise Institute Penny Saved Conference, Mayflower Hotel, Washington, DC.

Wong, K. K., & Nicotera, A. (2007). *Successful schools and educational accountability.* Boston: Pearson.

NOTES

1. An irony related to the constitutional lack of explicit concern for education is that few nations at their founding have had a brain trust of such well-educated and worldly delegates as did the United States.

2. James Madison's diary of the Constitutional Convention's deliberations makes no mention of education, save a short debate over whether or not to authorize a national university.

3. "The powers not delegated to the United States by the Constitution, nor prohibited by it to the States, are reserved to the States respectively, or to the people."

4. A century ago, there were 127,000 local school districts. Reforms initiated in the Progressive Era, beginning in the 1920s, triggered consolidation of literally thousands of local districts into larger governing and operational units. Consolidation proponents, an unusual coalition of business, higher-education officials, and government advocates, promised greater financial efficiency and educational effectiveness. Neither occurred to the degree proclaimed by advocates.

5. In 1810, King Kamehameha I consolidated Hawaiian tribes and islands under his unified rule.

6. Comprehensive scholarly coverage of this topic is provided in *The Political Dynamics of American Education* (4th ed., 2009) by Michael W. Kirst and Frederick M. Wirt.

7. See *School Law: Cases and Concepts* (7th ed., 2001) by Michael W. LaMort and *Schoolhouses, Courthouses, and Statehouses: Solving the Funding-Achievement Puzzle in America's Public Schools* (2009) by Eric A. Hanushek and Alfred A. Lindseth.

8. Two excellent histories chronicle the formative developmental years of education management. See *The One Best System* (1970) and *Managers of Virtue* (1982) by David B. Tyack.

9. This latter point is argued persuasively by Frederick M. Hess in *Cages of Their Own Design: Five Strategies to Help Education Leaders Break Free* (2009).

10. These conditions are explained by William G. Ouchi in his book with Lydia G. Segal, *Making Schools Work* (2003).

11. Ironically, the more hierarchically organized a school district, the less sure a high-ranking education executive can be of subordinate adherence to fidelity of centralized directives. See Weick, K. (1976). Educational organizations as loosely coupled systems. *Administrative Science Quarterly, 21*(1), 1–19.

12. For added detail regarding conditions and processes described in this section on resources see Guthrie, J. W., & Hart, C. C. (2008). *Modern school business administration.* Boston: Pearson.

13. For example, the Council of the Great City Schools is undertaking a significant benchmarking process for operational activities such as transportation, administration, food service, and utilities.

14. The premier analyses of these disparate financial distributions and the interaction with teacher salary and transfer privileges has been undertaken by Marguerite Roza and can be found in the publications of the Center for Reinventing Education at the University of Washington, Seattle, Washington. See, for example, Roza, M., & Hill, P. (2005, August 21). *Equalizing education dollars.* Seattle: University of Washington, Center for Reinventing Education.

Index

About the Authors

James W. Guthrie holds three degrees from Stanford University, has undertaken postdoctoral study in economics and education at Harvard and Oxford universities, and was Professor of Education at the University of California Berkeley from 1967 until 1994. He has been a classroom teacher, high school principal, and state and federal government education executive. He has undertaken education studies in numerous foreign nations, contributed to the design of school finance arrangements in more than 40 states, and testified as an expert witness in three dozen education-related equal protection court cases. He is the founder and presently serves as chairman of the Board of Management Analysis and Planning (MAP), one of the nation's premier education management consulting companies. He is the founder and presently serves as chairman of the Board of Class Act Publishing (CAP). He was a vice president of the American Education Research Association, distinguished senior fellow for the Education Commission of the States, and past president of the American Education Finance Association. Until 2010, he was the Patricia and Rodes Hart Chair of Education Policy and Leadership at Peabody College, Vanderbilt University, where he was professor of public policy and education at Peabody College, chair of the Leadership, Policy, and Organizations Department, director of the Peabody Center for Education Policy, director of the National Center on Performance Incentives, and policy director for the Center on Educator Compensation Reform. He now is a fellow of the American Education Research Association and a senior fellow at the George W. Bush Institute at Southern Methodist University.

Patrick J. Schuermann is a research assistant professor of educational leadership and public policy at Peabody College of Vanderbilt University. He serves as the policy director and director of technical assistance for the Center for Educator Compensation Reform (CECR), the comprehensive assistance center for the federally funded Teacher Incentive Fund (TIF) grant. He is also chair of the Independent School Leadership Institute, a joint venture between the National Research and Development Center on School Choice and the Peabody Professional Institutes. Peabody's Department of Leadership, Policy, and Organizations is among the most highly rated academic units in the nation concerned with the preparation of education leaders and offers advanced degree programs for both researchers and professional practitioners. Patrick is a member of the team of experts providing professional development seminars and online materials for school leaders participating in the District Award for Teacher Excellence (DATE) program in Texas. He developed and serves as the faculty chair for the Leadership Institutes at Peabody College. For several years, Patrick operated, in conjunction with the Leadership Development Center at Vanderbilt University, several professional development initiatives for local and state education leaders. Patrick has authored numerous articles, commissioned reports, policy briefs, and books on topics pertinent to education leadership and teacher development. Previously a teacher, tutor, and leader at the elementary, middle, and high school levels, Patrick holds BS and MA degrees from Furman University and an EdD from Vanderbilt University.

SAGE Research Methods Online

The essential tool for researchers

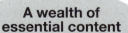
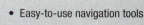